A HALF CENTURY OF
RELIGIOUS DIALOGUE
1939-1989

Making the Circles Larger

D1416152

A HALF CENTURY OF
RELIGIOUS DIALOGUE
1939-1989

Making the Circles Larger

Edited by

Franklin H. Littell

with the assistance of George Estreich

Toronto Studies in Theology
Volume 46

The Edwin Mellen Press
Lewiston/Queenston/Lampeter

Library of Congress Cataloging-in-Publication Data

This book has been registered with the Library of Congress.

This is volume 46 in the continuing series
Toronto Studies in Theology
Volume 46 ISBN 0-88946-926-1
TST Series ISBN 0-88946-975-X

A CIP catalog record for this book
is available from the British Library.

The Edwin Mellen Press   The Edwin Mellen Press
Box 450   Box 67
Lewiston, N.Y.   Queenston, Ontario
USA 14092   CANADA, L0S 1L0

Edwin Mellen Press, Ltd
Lampeter, Dyfed, Wales
UNITED KINGDOM SA48 7DY

Printed in the United States of America

This volume is dedicated to the memory of

Willem Adolph Visser 't Hooft

1900 - 1985

TABLE OF CONTENTS

IV.   Confrontations Issues and Lessons

V.   Intensive Local Ecumenism

Afterword

FOREWORD

The idea for a 50th Anniversary volume to commemorate the First World Conference of Christian Youth came naturally: ten years ago we published a 40th Anniversary volume, a special edition of <u>Journal of Ecumenical Studies</u>. This time we are publishing the volume at the Edwin Mellen Press, another wellspring of lively interreligious dialogue. I want to thank my old friend and colleague, Professor Herbert Richardson, for facilitating the practical arrangements, and my assistant, George Estreich, for handling so much of the day to day work of getting the articles in shape for publication. I would also like to thank my colleague, Leonard Swidler, for giving permission to use again the important piece by W.A. Visser 't Hooft.

Edwin Espy, who worked so closely with Willem Visser 't Hooft at the Amsterdam: 1939 Conference, edited the 40th Anniversary volume and pushed this volume along. He has been a mentor and friend to many of us for more than half a century, and I am glad for this chance to express gratitude to him in print. It was his plea that we include again Visser 't Hooft's fine essay of reflections on the meaning of Amsterdam, and that we dedicate this volume to him - the man who for so many decades, at the center of the World's Student Christian Federation, the World Council of Churches in Formation (during World War II) and the World Council of Churches, so uniquely expressed the brains and soul of the ecumenical movement.

Amsterdam 1939 in the Perspective of 1979:

An Introduction

W.A. Visser 't Hooft

Why do we commemorate the First World Conference of Christian Youth held in Amsterdam in 1939? That meeting did not make any far-reaching decisions. It did not even adopt resolutions on the great issues of the life of the world and of the church. In those aspects it had less historical weight than the ecumenical world conferences of 1937 at Oxford and Edinburgh. Why then do the participants of the Amsterdam Conference feel that this particular meeting was unique and that it played a decisive role in their spiritual history? Or, to put it in another way: Why did that conference become for a large part of the generation of Christians who were then between eighteen and thirty years of age the occasion of a definite commitment to the ecumenical cause?

The answer to that question is not simple. Those of us who have attended many ecumenical meetings know that the work of the Holy Spirit remains largely mysterious. We can, nevertheless, point to a number of factors which created a situation in which the Spirit could operate, especially the nine following.

1.   It was an adventure in close cooperation among the various Christian youth movements.   There had been of course a certain amount of cooperation among the Christian youth movements. There had been a good deal of overlapping in leadership between the Y.M.C.A., the Y.W.C.A., and the World's Student Christian Federation.   Later, when the ecumenical church organizations appeared, there was the Ecumenical Youth Commission in which they were all represented. But the World Conference of 1939 was the first occasion when all those bodies accepted common responsibility for a large-scale enterprise. That meant that we had in Amsterdam both men and women, both university students and young people engaged in commerce or industry, representatives of both the tradition of independent movements and the tradition of church-related bodies. We could share our special gifts and our leaders. And the realization that this was really the first occasion when Christian youth from so many different backgrounds were called together made us glad to witness to and participate in this great event.

2.   The Conference reflected the geographical extension of the world Christian community and the cultural variety within it more clearly than any of the large ecumenical meetings had done so far. In its early days the ecumenical movement was a very "Western" affair. Some outstanding Asian and African leaders had made important contributions at the early meetings. The Y.M.C.A. had had considerable delegations from Asia at its world conferences. The International Missionary Council had brought a number of Asian and African leaders to its meeting in Jerusalem. But Amsterdam 1939 with its 108 Asian and forty-seven African delegates was the first large ecumenical conference in which the representatives of the younger churches

were sufficiently represented to ensure that every conference participant would have not only an international but also an intercontinental experience. Compared with the developments of the 1960's and 1970's it was of course still a modest advance, and Latin America with twenty-three delegates was tragically underrepresented.

And there were other open places. At that time representation from the U.S.S.R. was out of the question, but we had seventeen Russians from the church-in-exile. As to Germany there had been long and complicated negotiations to ensure that different sections of the church should be represented, but the national socialist authorities considered the ecumenical movement to be a dangerous enemy, and participation in the Amsterdam Conference was strictly forbidden. Some courageous young Germans, however, succeeded to reach Amsterdam on their own initiative. It was decided that I as chairperson would talk with each of them individually to make sure that they were there for the right reasons. I could thus give entrance tickets to ten of them, but of course had to keep their names secret. One of these, Herbert Jehle, is today a well-known scientist and expert in nuclear problems. But though the Germans were not physically present, they were very much present in the spirit, for who could forget that so very near the place of our meeting a confessing church was facing tremendous temptations and tremendous opportunities for witness to the CHRISTUS VICTOR who had called us together? As to the interconfessional composition, we had very few Roman Catholics, but the Orthodox from Eastern Europe were well represented.

3.   <u>Amsterdam 1939 was a well-prepared meeting</u>. It has been said that the quality of large conferences depends on the thinking and study which has preceded the meeting. That observation was confirmed by the Amsterdam Conference. The conference committee had spent a great deal of time and

energy thinking out the program. At an early stage preparatory study materials were distributed. In this connection the name of Walter Gethman should be mentioned. He had been General Secretary of the World's Alliance of Y.M.C.A.'s, but had suffered a heart attack. He turned his handicap into a blessing, for he concentrated his remaining energy on thorough study of the issues which the youth movements should face. And so he wrote with Denzil G.M. Patrick (of Scotland) the first study outline for the conference, which was used by groups all over the world. Much help was also given by Suzanne de Dietrich, who played a decisive role in the revival of Bible study in the 1930's.

The international secretariat was in the capable hands of Edwin Espy, who was just thirty years of age, in the age range of the participants. Local preparations in Holland were made by Dr. Jo Eykman, a man full of imagination and energy, who could mobilize everybody in Amsterdam whose help was needed.

4.   Amsterdam 1939 became the encounter between the ecumenism of the Christian youth movements and the ecumenism which had more recently arisen among the churches. This was reflected in the purpose of the conference as defined by the preparatory committee:

> "It aims at confronting youth with the results of the world gatherings of the Christian Churches and the Christian youth movements in the years 1937 and 1938. Its purpose is to mobilise youth to witness to the reality of the Christian Community as the God-given supranational body to which has been entrusted the message of the victory of Jesus Christ over the world's spiritual, political and social confusion."

The Y.M.C.A., Y.W.C.A., and W.S.C.F. had been the pioneers of a spontaneous ecumenism before the churches and the mission bodies became ecumenically active, but that early ecumenism could only become effective on a larger scale if the churches would respond to the call to unity. On the other hand, the churches asked questions about ecumenism which the youth movements had to face.

Fortunately the youth movements and the churches did not represent two sharply separated worlds. On the contrary, the ecumenical movement of the churches was largely started by men and women who had had their first ecumenical awakening in the youth movements. And several of those were among the speakers and leaders of Amsterdam 1939. I think especially of John R. Mott-- world leader of the Y.M.C.A., founder of the W.S.C.F. as well as the International Missionary Council, and one of the outstanding figures in the ecumenical church conferences of Oxford and Edinburgh-- and William Temple, at that time Archbishop of York, who had since his student days maintained close contact with the Student Christian Movement and was now the recognized father of the ecumenical movement.

As the two streams of ecumenism became one stream it seemed that the idea of one worldwide Christian community was becoming at last a reality. It was a privilege to be allowed to belong to that community.

5.　　The Conference took place at a crucial moment in the life of the world. The first part of the year 1939 was a period of great uncertainty. Many did not believe or, rather, did not want to believe that the world was drifting toward war, but there were those who read the signs of the times correctly. One of those was Dietrich Bonhoeffer. I met him in London in March. His strong conviction that within a few months Hitler would go to war and that we should immediately prepare ourselves to make a truly Christian response to that calamity made a deep impression on me. There was no question of giving up the World Conference or postponing it indefinitely. For the bringing together of young Christians from all over the world was one of the best ways to demonstrate that we believed in deepening international understanding. But would the war begin before the dates set for the conference? I told Edwin Espy, the secretary of the conference, that I would give him a present, if we managed to hold the meeting before the fatal moment would arrive.

The Dutch government was at that time nervous about the repercussions which the conference might have. So I was informed that Reinhold Niebuhr, who was to give one of the main addresses, would not be allowed to speak, since he was considered too leftist I went to see the Dutch Minister of Foreign Affairs, who said that he was in favor of socialism, not communism. Rather surprisingly the minister said that there was no great difference between the two, but he gave the needed permission.

In the light of this situation the words of the statement drawn up by the daily chairperson and read to the conference on the last day take their full meaning:

> "Characteristic of this time in which we meet is not only the
> fact of the international tension and social unrest, but also the
> fact of a rising ecumenical consciousness. The nations and
> peoples of the world are drifting apart, the churches are
> coming together...In war, conflict or persecution, we must
> strengthen one another and preserve our Christian unity
> unbroken."

At the time of the conference we could of course not know that within one month the Second World War would begin. But when we sang together for the last time "A toi la gloire," we prayed for each other that whatever trials might come we would be found faithful.

6.   The Conference took place at a crucial moment in the life of the
churches. For the generation which the Amsterdam delegates represented
the church had taken on new meaning. This was mainly due to the fact that
in a number of countries the churches had to meet the challenge of
totalitarian ideologies and that in many cases they had shown far more
spiritual vitality than its opponents or even its sympathizers had expected.
The resistance of the Confessing Church in Germany to national socialist
infiltration had made a deep impression in other countries. At the same
time in biblical and systematic theology the nineteenth-century individualism
was being overcome, and it was again understood that one church is part of
the gift of God's revelation. Moreover the fact that the churches were now
coming together and that in the two years before the Amsterdam
Conference the plan for the formation of a World Council of Churches was
drawn up and presented to the churches also underlined the relevance of the
church in the present situation.

These convictions were clearly expressed in an address at the
beginning of the conference by Frans Kooyman, the General Secretary of the
Student Christian Movement in the Netherlands. He said:

> "We are once again believing in the Church as the Body of
> Christ and the communion of the faithful; and we are once
> again learning to believe in it in such a way that we take our
> place in one of the churches into which Christ's Church is
> divided. We acknowledge ourselves to be guilty for the division
> and the human arrogance in the churches and for the lack of
> love in them; but we have to take our place in one of these
> shamed churches because we must take upon us our share in
> its guilt and its calling, and may not stand outside and criticize."

7.   Bible study had a central place in the Conference. It was a somewhat
risky undertaking to consecrate each day a considerable period of time to

Bible study in small groups. This had not been tried out in any of the ecumenical world meetings. But the risk was taken because there had arisen a strong conviction that only a faith nurtured by the Bible could have substance enough to meet the challenge of the hour and also that the Bible was not-- as had been said so often-- the book that divided Christians, but rather the book that was the deep bond between them.

The groups did not have an easy time. It was a baffling experience to come up against so many different approaches and ways of interpreting the Bible. But in most of the reports which delegates gave after the conference the Bible study is mentioned as one of the most truly worthwhile parts of the program. The statement of the daily chairpersons puts it this way:

> "We believe that those who planned this Conference were guided by God when they placed Bible Study in such a central place. Many of us have discovered the Bible afresh and in so far as we have allowed God to speak to us, He has become a living God, declaring a living message for our own lives and our generation."

8.   Worship was based on the principle of maximum ecumenism. In the lengthy discussions which took place during the preparation of the conference a distinction was made between minimum ecumenism and maximum ecumenism. The first was used to indicate common worship on a common-denominator basis that is a simple service without confessional coloring. The second was used to describe worship according to other traditions than they knew in their own church life. Here again Amsterdam 1939 pioneered for the whole ecumenical movement. For the first time in the history of world conferences, services were held according to the tradition of the main confessions represented in the conference. The

question was raised whether a meeting for young people was the right place
to make so great a venture. I think it was, for only in this way was it
possible to expose the delegates to a more-than-superficial understanding of
the ecumenical reality with its richness and its perplexing aspects. There
were, therefore, also a number of communion services. The largest one was
the Netherlands Reformed Service in the Nieuwe Kerk where, according to
the custom of the Netherlands Reformed Church, the delegates sat down at
long tables. But, since it was not possible to have one common communion
service in which all delegates could take part, there was a service of
preparation for the Holy Communion at which Robert Mackie preached and
Benjamin Mays said the prayers of penitence. In this way our disunity,
though real, became overshadowed by our unity in Christ.

9.   The Conference had a strong central message. The danger of the
conference theme, "CHRISTUS VICTOR," was of course that it could be
understood in a triumphalist spirit: here are the young Christians who are
going to solve the problems of the world. But the situation in which we met
made such an interpretation clearly impossible. It was very obvious that to
say "CHRISTUS VICTOR" would mean for most of the participants that
they would have to say it as a confession of faith in spite of the evidence
with which the world presented them.

And that was the true reason why Amsterdam 1939 was so vitally
important to those who had the privilege to be there. They felt it a grace
of God that just before entering into the years of darkness and temptation
they had been allowed to hear in such a clear way, confirmed by a cloud of
witnesses from the whole Oikoumene, that Christ had overcome the world.

Nine years later in that same Nieuwe Kerk and in the same
Concertgebouw the first Assembly of the World Council of Churches took
place. It was typical that at the opening service the two speakers were John

R. Mott, who had given an inspiring address in 1939, and D.T. Niles, who had been one of the daily chairpersons in 1939. And there were many others who proved by their presence that the Amsterdam Conference of 1939 had produced a new generation of leaders who were ready to take over from the first generation.

The Amsterdam Youth Conference:
Recollections and Reflections
R.H. Edwin Espy

Orientation

What follows is not a theological assessment but a personal/historical account. It is recollections from before, during and after the First World Conference of Christian Youth in Amsterdam 1939. My purpose is to try to bring that pioneering event alive to people today.

If there is a theological and spiritual assumption behind this statement it is one that I feel is basic but often over-simplified: the prayer of Christ "that they all may be one." The historical pursuit of this dictum has led to division as well as unity, but the imperative is always there.

The World Council of Churches has made clear that we can be ecumenical wherever we are, in our particular local situations--"all in each place one." That must be the base of ecumenism, not a unity imposed from the top or from a global entity that may have little local foundation. We do not need to establish a completely inclusive ecumenism to be one in Christ wherever we are, though to be totally ecumenical we obviously have to be one at every level.

In this respect the Amsterdam Youth Conference was rooted not only in world movements and churches but more strikingly in a developing local experience. Of course the world bodies made the event possible, but the real miracle is that it was an event bursting to happen in some form before the conference ever convened. It was a gathering of people from over the world, in many nations and localities in becoming "all in each place one." The conference supported and furthered this urge under the inspiration of its theme: CHRISTUS VICTOR.

The other articles in this compilation are intentionally different from this one. They fall into two categories. All except three of them deal with ecumenical and related developments in the fifty years since Amsterdam '39 without necessary reference to that experience at all. But they are written by people who were there.

In contrast, the leading piece by W.A. Visser 't Hooft, the chairman of the conference, is an appraisal of the long-range impact of the conference itself on subsequent ecumenical issues and events, written in 1979. That clear statement is just as valid and important now as it was ten years ago.

The other exceptions are the article by Oliver Tomkins, which focuses on the contribution of the Youth Conference in Amsterdam '39 to the founding assembly of the World Council of Churches in Amsterdam '48; and the one by Francis S. House on its particular contribution to the concept and practice of ecumenical worship.

One more item of orientation. I was asked to set down some "personal recollections" of Amsterdam, which I assume includes reflections both then and now. Therefore this will be a largely anecdotal account.

It will also be personal in another sense. To give it life, I shall focus on people--people who in connection with the conference made a real difference either in the youth/student movement or in the ecumenical movement as a whole, or both. Amsterdam '39 was an unprecedented blending of the two. Persons are cited for their illustration of significant events or issues.

My recollections will be subject to fallible memory. Through a misadventure when I left Europe hastily by ship from Italy--in mid-October of 1939--because of the outbreak of World War II, most of my papers were lost. Even the many letters I wrote home are now beyond recall. So this is a free-wheeling reconstruction. Because it is relevant to the way some things were being done ecumenically fifty years ago, I shall start with a report on how this run-of-the-mill graduate student became involved. It came out of the blue.

An Unscheduled Turn

It was late winter or early spring of 1936. The smooth Swiss express was speeding me from Basel to Geneva. I was aware that the scenery was beautiful, for I had traveled the route twice before. But I was lost in reverie and speculation: what was I getting myself into?

A student at Heidelberg University, I had received an invitation from world Christian organizations ehadquartered in Geneva. They wanted to talk with me about having a part in an international youth conference--a conference that sounded like a far-out dream.

I was completing my studies and had not yet decided on where I was headed--for academia or the ministry. I had not seriously considered anything else. Yet I sensed that, depending on the nature and outcome of this proposed enterprise might well determine the course of the rest of my life. In the end it did.

As I recall now, I had three major reactions in that Geneva interview. On the one hand I was both overwhelmed and strangely attracted by the inter-organizational complexity of this new venture.

At the same time I was deeply impressed with the vision and experience of this group of world Christian leaders who had conceived the idea. They would largely determine the broad policies of the enterprise and would stand behind and work closely with whomever they chose to be its coordinator. I reflected that I might be their third or fourth choise (I never enquired), but if that was not important to them it was not to me.

Thirdly, what about my own principal drives and experience? Was it really what I had been preparing for and was I ready for it?

It certainly was in line with my own values, and in a sense with the course of my life up to then. I remember reflecting: from my boyhood in Oysterville, Washington, a remote village of about a hundred people, my horizons had been expanding: High school in Ilwaco, small town seventeen miles away; summer jobs in the forestry, fishing, dairy and construction industries of the Pacific coast; college at the University of Redlands in California; study at Union Theological Seminary in New York with attendant field-work assignments in Baptist, Congregational-Chritian and Presbyterian churches; graduate work at Tuebingen and Heidelberg; many planned exposures to alarming aspects of developments in Germany; participation in six international student conferences in four countries of Europe. By 1936 I was predisposed, probably more than I had articulated in my own mind, to world-wide ecumenism.

I doubtless was strongly influenced by my earlier associations with the World Student Christian Federation's general secretary, Willem Visser 't

Hooft. He was familiar with my international conference background and was the only person in the Geneva interview whom I knew. It was also he who had written inviting me to consider the position. I was quite sure that the whole approach to me was at his initiative.

There seemed to be a congruence between the dream of a world conference of Christian youth and my own ecumenical commitment. At least that was the case that Visser 't Hooft was making to the others in the interview--and to me! I didn't have to try to sell myself because he was doing it for me. I recall reflecting that I was being considered not because of special merit but because of circumstance. I had the good fortune to have been "in the right places at the right times and to have known the right person."

Early Seminal Forces

For those who today do not know the ecumenical configurations in Geneva fifty years ago, some facts and impressions may be in order. The initiating bodies of the World Youth Conference were:

> The World Alliance for International Friendship through the
> Churches
> The Universal Christian Council for Life and Work
> The World's Alliance of YMCA's
> The World's YWCA
> The World's Student Christian Federation

These were to be joined later in the sending of delegates to the conference and in the planning of it by representatives of the Faith and Order Movement. Also involved in planning and helping to recruit delegates from around the world was the International Missionary Council. International Christian Endeavor participated in preparation in some countries and sent delegates. The World Sunday School Association gave friendly cooperation and James Kelley, its general secretary, was added to the Preparatory Committee.

The basic seminal forces that drew all these bodies together were two-fold: a commitment to ecumenism and a common concern for the future of their young people. It may be surprising to some to have the Geneva-based youth movements referred to as ecumenical. This is a matter of context and definition, but there can be no question that in broad terms they had been ecumenically oriented from the beginning and had produced much of the leadership for the ecumenical movement of the churches themselves--from the late nineteenth century on.

To divide the Geneva-based bodies into "youth organizations" and "church organizations" is itself an over-simplification. In the first place they all were not primarily organizations but spiritual movements. Secondly, in many countries these "lay" movements were not strictly lay or independent of the churches in their governance but were related to or even controlled by the churches. Great stress was placed upon active church participation not only by their leaders but by the membership.

By the 1930s many historical forces were drawing world Christian leaders into a clearer sense of their common mission. The menace of fascist, communist, and other ideological movements, with their challenge to all Christian thought and piety; the widespread opening of theological dialogue on a world scale, particularly in relation to Christian unity, social issues and international affairs; the growing threat of a world conflagration that would further divide the nations and test the developing sense of solidarity of the world Christian community--these were among the forces that were drawing these movements into a deeper common commitment. This all reflected an essentially ecumenical commitment.

One way to express and foster this perspective would be for all of the interested world bodies to bring together young people from all their constituencies in a world gathering--an unprecedented venture.

In my own case, adding to the complexity of the conference assignment, I was being asked to take another one. I was also to be the secretary of the Ecumenical Youth Commission of the World Alliance for International Friendship through churches and the Universal Christian Council for Life and Work. These church-related bodies were in fact my two joint employers, and my official reporting relationship was to their joint general secretary in Geneva.

The Youth Commission had been in operation for several years with a half-time executive and a varied program devoted to promoting world peace through the young people of the churches. Its work was not originally related directly to the preparations for the youth conference at Amsterdam, but it organized mini-conferences on peace, world-wide essay contests and other programs which were consonant with the purposes of the conference and the Youth Commission was increasingly caught up in preparations for it.

An ecumenical symbiosis was truly in the making. These differing but similarly motivated world Christian movements were embarking on a common witness, on a scale never before attempted by so many world bodies. But all this did not arise from depersonalized organizations and institutions. It was a spiritual movement that had spiritual leaders.

Some representative persons

As I have said, in my interview I was deeply impressed by the leaders of the Geneva-based world movements. As I now recall, with apologies to those who may have been there, the following persons were present:

H.L. Henriod, general secretary of both the World Alliance for International Friendship through the Churches and the Universal Christian Council for Life and Work.

Tracy Strong, general secretary of the World's Alliance of YMCA's.

D.A. Davis, fraternal representative of the International Committees of the YMCA (U.S.A.) in southeast Europe and the Near East.

M. Marianne Mills, secretary for youth work of the World's YMCA (the general secretary, Ruth Woodsmall, traveled almost constantly to member movements and was away at the time; but she was to become an indispensable supporter of preparations for the conference, including the recruiting of delegates from distant countries.)

W.A. Visser 't Hooft, general secretary of the World's Student Christian Federation.

Before I left Geneva on that trip in 1936 I was also to meet others, including Walter Gethman, who had recently retired for health reasons as general secretary of the World Alliance of YMCA's. He and Denzil G.M. Patrick, its editorial and study secretary, were later to write the basic preparatory study book for the conference: "The Christian Community in the Modern World."

These and many other leaders of the world bodies gave further evidence of the interpenetration between the youth organizations and the church organizations. The former (except for the YWCA at that time, when there were few ordained women) had a number of ordained persons in top staff and volunteer positions; and the latter had a number of lay persons similarly placed. This mix of personnel obtained in varying degrees in many of their member national movements as well.

While not alluding to it each time, I shall be referring in these recollections to other persons at all levels who illustrate this interesting phenomenon of ecumenism. This subject would merit a definitive examination by itself.

Though the nature of my two relationships meant that I conferred with many persons in many countries, my direct reporting line was to Henriod for the Youth Commission and Visser 't Hooft for the conference. The conference preparations rapidly began to absorb most of my time.

But the work of the Youth Commission led me into many relationships critical for the conference. In the United States, two of the persons with whom I worked closely were Henry A. Atkinson and Henry Smith Leiper, executive secretaries respectively of the World Alliance for International Friendship through the churches and the Universal Christian Council for Life and Work in the U.S.A.

These leaders of the U.S.-based units of the two world bodies employing me, as well as Samuel McCrae Cavert, general secretary of the then Federal Council of Churches, gave me the needed access to their respective church constituencies. Similarly, Roy G. Ross, general secretary of the International Council of Religious Education, opened the way to the leaders of the church-related youth organizations, most importantly the United Christian Youth Movement. This organization also had the participation of the high-school age youth movements of the YMCA and YWCA, especially in relation to Amsterdam.

The executive of the United Christian Youth Movement was Ivan M. Gould, a young Methodist minister who had been a classmate of mine at Union Seminary. Ivan and his wife Helen were instrumental in motivating, preparing and bringing together the many elements of the U.C.Y.M. that were to be represented at the conference.

I of course related directly and through correspondence to the fine company of student movement leaders in the United States too numerous to mention here. At that time the movements were the Student YMCA--YWCA-SCM and the national student organizations of the churches.

There had been little national relationship before Amsterdam between the UCYM, which worked primarily with young people still oriented to their home churches, and the "student work" field, directed to students in college. In the college field itself there had been little national coordination between the Y-related and the church-related student movements.

Nor were the church-related movements in the United States members yet of the World Student Christian Federation. Their coming together around the Amsterdam experience--before, during and after--contributed to their urge to work more closely together and to join the W.S.C.F. It was to be my privilege in the United States with the Student Volunteer Movement and the National Student YMCA, from 1940 to 1955, to have a part in helping to draw them all closer together.

In Geneva I of course worked closely with four successive chairmen while I was there of the Ecumenical Youth Commission, to which I have referred. They were Canon Leslie Hunter of Great Britain, Pasteur Andre Bouvier of France, Pastor Sparring-Peterson of Denmark and the Very Rev. (later Bishop) Thomas Craske of Britain.

Speaking of Britain and anticipating reflections I shall recount later, I must mention two successive general secretaries of the International Missionary Council, with headquarters in London, who were of great help in preparation for the Amsterdam Conference, J.H. Oldham and William Paton. Dr. Oldham was a member of a small group of (very) senior advisors, including also Professors Robert Calhoun of Yale and John Oman of Cambridge, with whom I met very early to start laying out basic ecumenical and organizational principles that were to govern the holding of the conference.

Dr. Oldham, of course, already was deeply engrossed as the principal intellectual architect and editor of the study books in preparation for the Oxford Conference on Church, Community and State to take place in 1937. As I recall now, I did not know then that I was to head the youth delegation to that conference but in reflection I should not be surprised if he and Visser 't Hooft had in mind trying to help prepare me for both Oxford and Edinburgh '37!

Dr. Oldham also helped us later in developing appropriate approaches to missionary and ecumenical issues in our dealing with the younger churches on behalf of the Amsterdam Youth Conference. Beyond that he and Dr. Paton opened many doors for us in the recruiting of delegates from those areas. Of course the world youth and student organizations, with their long global experience, played a central role in recruiting and preparing their delegations from far-flung parts of the world.

The leader of the corresponding youth delegation to the world Faith and Order Conference in Edinburgh right after Oxford was the Rev. (later Bishop) Oliver S. Tomkins of the Student Christian Movement in Great Britain. He too was a tower of strength in preparations for Amsterdam '39 and in leadership at the conference. He was later to be for many years the chairman of the Faith and Order Commission of the World Council, a key member of the Joint Working Group between the WCC and the Vatican and a strategic participant in the historic study on Baptism, Eucharist, Ministry--among many other ecumenical responsibilities. In the Vatican relationship I was to be privileged to join him from 1965 to 1975 as the WCC representative from the churches of North America.

In Geneva itself, in addition to the persons I have mentioned in this connection, I referred earlier to H.L. Henriod, a former Swiss pastor, who had preceded Visser 't Hooft as general secretary of the World Student

Chritian Federation. And Visser 't Hooft was to move from the WSCF to become general secretary of the World Council of Churches.

We must mention one more prime example of this in-and-out movement of pastors into the youth student movements and vice versa. Robert C. Mackie, a Presbyterian minister from Scotland, had been general secretary of the Student Christian Movement of Great Britain before succeeding Visser 't Hooft as general secretary of the WSF when Visser 't Hooft became secretary of the Provisional Committee for the World Council of Churches in Process of Formation. After the establishment of the World Council of Churches Mackie became its associate general secretary.

Dr. Mackie was a fine addition to the planning for the Amsterdam Youth Conference and at the conference he led the critical preparatory worship service preceding the separate communion services, which many of the delegates thought should not be separate. More about this later.

The best known example of what we are illustrating was of course Visser 't Hooft, who had taken his doctorate in theology in the Netherlands, was called as a very young man by Dr. Mott to be the Boy's Work Secretary of the world's YMCA, became general secretary of the World Student Christian Federation and later general secretary for nearly twenty years of the World Council of Churches. Along the way he was ordained in the Reformed Church in Geneva.

Wim (as his friends and close colleagues came to call him) was much like an elder brother to me, eight years my senior. Because he was chairman of the planning committee for the Amsterdam Youth Conference and I was its executive we worked together very closely. He was a tough, creative and fair leader, and he taught me a great deal.

He was the one person in Geneva whom I knew before, during and after Amsterdam '39. He had proposed me to the search committee and was largely responsible for my decision to accept the position. I had official contacts with him from 1933 until he retired in 1965, and we continued to keep in touch until shortly before his death in 1985. The fact that he knew my background and stood behind me all the way did not mean that we always agreed. But there was mutual respect.

The second person whom I came to know especially well was Tracy Strong, general secretary of the World Alliance of YMCA's, and hence another member of the conference planning committee. A man of wide experience and deep understanding, his counsel was always of help, and his world-wide contacts were an invaluable resource to us all. He and his wife Edith were to become to me like parents-away-from-home. It was they who in a Paris restaurant were the first persons to persuade me to eat escargot, which I did not then consider the greatest favor they ever did for me!

The more I worked with the leaders in Geneva and especially in the national movements and churches,the more I realized that the preparations for Amsterdam were both manifesting and precipitating a remarkable development in ecumenism. Youth and their leaders from the various bodies in country after country, having scarcely known or even heard of one another before, were coming together in support of a common endeavor across long-held barriers of separation. Under the exhilaration in anticipation of the conference, they were having profound ecumenical experiences before the event ever took place. Some of the most lasting results of the Amsterdam experience have been in national and local situations that developed both before and after the conference itself.

An ecumenical symbiosis, or in many cases synergism, was developing around the world and paralleled what was happening in Geneva. To use again the later language of the World Council of Churches, they were becoming "in each place one." It was an awakening of the hearts and minds of leaders and members of the participating bodies to a new and larger vision.

Conference Preparations

It was under this inner persuasion that we prepared for the Amsterdam '39 Conference. We felt that we had been called to bring Christian young people together in an intensive experience of unity across all the "dividing walls of partition" and in so doing to bear witness to the world of this unity and its consequences in Christian living.

The plans for the conference developed over a period of more than three years. We were blessed with the participation of the most experienced ecumenical leadership of the time, regardless of age, drawn from all the cooperating organizations, their national units, the seminary world and other sources.

The determination of basic objectives, conference methodologies and leadership was a demanding task. Visualize the multinational, inter-organizational, interconfessional, intercultural, multilingual, transpolitical and various theological differences that had to be synchronized. The undertaking clearly needed a clear focus if it was to succeed.

In due course the theme chosen was CHRISTUS VICTOR. This proved to be an inspired decision. With this determined, the planning had a clear direction that was bringing a ringing challenge and kept the conference itself from straying off course. The theme was incisive, yet inclusive. Its impact has endured to the present day.

To sense after fifty years the substantive thrust of the conference, it is important to note the contents of the official preparatory study book "The Christian Community in the Modern World." This was presented in two volumes, appearing about a year apart. They were edited and largely written by Walter Gethman and Denzil Patrick.

The preface to the first volume put the study material in the perspective of the basic objective of the conference. "The conference will gather representative young members and leaders of the youth work of the Churches and of all national and international Christian youth movements. It aims at confronting Youth with the results of the world gatherings of the Christian Churches and the Christian youth Movements in the years 1937-38. Its purpose is to mobilize youth to witness to the reality of the Christian Community as the God-given supra-national body to which has been entrusted the message of the victory of Jesus Christ over the world's spiritual, political, and social confusion."

The extent to which the conference was drawing upon Oxford, Edinburgh, Madras (International Missionary Council), Mysore (the World's YMCA) and other major world Christian gatherings in the years just before the Youth Conference is indicated by the tables of contents of the two volumes and the suggested supplementary reading in the first.

The first volume:

Section I	A Creed to Live By
Section II	The Church of Christ as a Community
Section III	The Christian Community and the Secular Sovereignties
Section IV	The Christian Community and the Social Order
Section V	The Christian Community in the World of Nations

Supplementary Reading:

That They Go Forward--Eric Fenn, published in London, Edinburgh 1936--Hugh Martin, London.
Christianity in the Eastern Conflicts--William Paton, London.
The Churches Survey Their Task (The Oxford Conference Official Reports)--J.H. Oldham, London, New York and Chicago.

Flaming Milestones (Report of the 1937 World's Conference of the Y.M.C.A., Mysore, India)--Basil Mathews, Geneva.

The Church and its Function in Society--W.A. Visser 't Hooft and J.H. Oldham, London, New York and Chicago.

Christian Faith and the Modern State--Nils Ehrenstrom, London, New York and Chicago.

Our Faith--Emil Brunner, London and New York.

Evangelism--D.T. Niles--Mysore, India (later by the S.C.M. Press, London).

Christian Faith and Life--William Temple, London.

The Church of Christ and the Problems of the Day--Karl Hernon, London.

An Interpretation of Christian Ethics--Reinhold Niebuhr, London and New York.

Christianity and Our World--John C. Bennett, London and New York.

The End of Our Time--Nicholas Berdyaev, London and New York.

A Christian Sociology for Today, Maurice Reckitt, London and New York.

None Other Gods--W.A. Visser 't Hooft, London and New York.

What is a Living Church?--J.S. Whale, London.

The second volume, "Further Studies on the Christian Community in the Modern World," was a series of six self-contained study outlines to correspond to the six days of the conference when discussion groups would be held, but they were designed primarily for preparatory study before the conference took place. As the Preface stated, these studies were "on the subjects for which the earlier volume has set forth in a more systematic manner the basic issues...Their general form and subject matter will be the basis of the agendas of the groups in Amsterdam itself."

The seven discussion subjects were:

> Christian Youth in the Nation and the State
> Christian Youth in a World of Nations
> Christian Youth in the Economic Order
> Christian Youth and Race

Christian Youth and Education
Christian Marriage and Family Life
The Church: Its Nature and Mission

In each case the format consisted of an introduction, discussion questions, biblical references and a bibliography. The bibliographies included books in English, German and French and in some cases writings by Roman Catholic authors.

For the conference itself a little booklet entitled "CHRISTUS VICTOR--Worship at the Conference" was prepared. It interpreted in terms accessible to lay persons the basic meaning and significance of Holy Communion.

Then there was a brief introduction to each of the four forms of celebration to be observed at the conference--the Holy Supper of Jesus Christ (Dutch Reformed), the Anglican Eucharist, the Lutheran Communion Service and the Orthodox Liturgy.

There was also an explanation of the six non-eucharistic services held each morning in the Concert Hall, the site of the main daily sessions. These were a Free Church service, led by a British woman, the French Reformed Liturgy, a service in the Hungarian Lutheran tradition, an African service of worship, an Indian service of worship (Asian Indian) and an American service of worship.

There were also of course the printed conference program and the various detailed materials that any such conference requires. All of this required a gigantic and pioneering effort.

There obviously was endless work organizationally as we dealt with all the minutiae of interrelationships. But this is not the aspect of the preparations in which the readers of this account are primarily interested.

The vision of assembling for the first time a world gathering of Christian young people as widely representative as this under the challenge of "CHRISTUS VICTOR" began to take hold. The conference was aiming to engage the delegates with some of the most basic issues confronting the churches and the world.

As the momentum for the conference built, the problem in many countries became not one of recruitment but of keeping to their quotas. The Amsterdam experience was not to be a mass convention for everybody who wanted to come. Its intent and format were too fine-tuned for that and a gathering any larger would be unwieldy.

The theme, as we have said, was both incisive and inclusive.

In country after country it was bringing people together across organizational and church lines who had not even known one another. Some very deep human impulses were being tapped but more basically the Holy Spirit seemed truly to be at work--in some cases a kind of Pentecost.

This congruence with the ecumenical symbiosis that was taking place in Geneva was a major reason why the Amsterdam Conference was so solid and lasting in its uniting impact, particularly striking during and after World War II.

The process in the countries was of course closely coordinated with preparations in Geneva. We were listening to the ground-swell and preparing and disseminating material internationally that took national realities seriously. The Gethman-Patrick study book was the chief example.

The input from the countries was invaluable. There were bible studies from France by Suzanne de Dietrich, worship materials, hymns and other offerings from various sources. "Ten Authorities Other Than God," the little U.S.A. study book by Edward F. Ouellette, had a particular background. He had been a special assistant to J.H. Oldham in preparation for the Oxford Conference on Church, Community and State in 1937 and communicated much of its thinking.

A significant think-tank that made a difference in the conference planning was one in Great Britain and Geneva coordinated by Francis S. House of England. With the participation of Orthodox, Protestant and Anglican representatives they developed a pattern for ecumenical worship built around the use of the pure forms of the major historical worship traditions instead of services that were a melange of this and that.

The adoption of this confessional approach and its observance at Amsterdam had had a rich and soul-stretching background of study, debate, prayer and experimentation over many years. Francis House, in his accompanying article, has vividly recounted the remarkable story--the early years of which were also unknowing preparation for Amsterdam '39!

The (now) Very Rev. Francis House also had a major part in the direct planning and organizing of these services at the conference and was later to become a staff member of the World Council of Churches. As Visser 't Hooft reports in his article herein, this approach to the observance of the Holy Communion was to be one of the important contributions of Amsterdam '39 to ecumenical practice in the future.

To lighten all this a bit, since this is "personal reflection," let me report two incidents. They reflect the varying ways in which my involvements in preparing for the conference were received. The first one, humorous in retrospect, suggests the sense of effrontery with which some veterans must have regarded the selection of an untried stripling to organize the conference!

Shortly after I took the position, Tracy Strong, I suspect with mischievous malice aforethought, asked me to be sure to call on Z.F. Willis, general secretary of the British YMCA, on a trip I was making to England.

He didn't say in particular why, and I assumed it was to be another of my routine visits to the heads of various national movements.

Mr. Willis--Zed F., as I learned later all of his colleagues called him-- received me with appropriate courtesy. But we had not proceeded very far in our conversation before he exploded.

"What does Tracy think he is doing?" he said. "You seem to be a nice enough young man. But they are sending a boy to do a man's work! We are embarking on an important world enterprise, we are entering uncharted waters. The organizations in Geneva should have seconded one of their most experienced people for this." (I was twenty-seven years old at the time).

I do not have a clear recollection of the doubtless hasty, but I am sure courteous, conclusion of the interview! I began to have a hunch that Tracy had set me up on this one. I quickly learned from others in England that Zed F. was highly regarded as a brilliant man but also known for his forthright and sometimes devastating expressions of opinion.

As I recall, I did not have any further contacts with him for a long time. But I was to learn of his unstinting support for the Amsterdam Youth Conference. He released one of his top associates in the British YMCA, Edwin Barber, both to assist in the conference preparations and to participate in the conference as one of the group leaders. I also found that he and I shared another common concern, the nurturing of closer relations with the Roman Catholics. This mutual interest led to our being in touch many years later.

I of course reported to Tracy on my return to Geneva. My suspicions were confirmed when his principal response was a knowing chuckle. But we had more important things to discuss!

Later on in the period of conference preparation the second episode was far more significant. On one of my trips to the States I was asked to speak at a special convocation at Union Seminary. It must have been a command performance, because there was a standing-room only crowd of students and faculty in the auditorium. I could not have attracted that audience without some compulsion, which had been rare in my seminary days.

I was asked to speak primarily about Germany. There was widespread disbelief in the United States that the situation there was as bad as reported. There was particular controversy at Union, with powerful persons on both sides.

In two and a half years as a student in Germany I had had intimate experiences of the satanic force of National Socialism and of its long-range objectives, including complete domestic subjugation and world domination. I had made it a part of my responsibility to learn as much as possible about what was happening in its many dimensions and in various parts of the country. I travelled by bicycle about 9,000 kilometers in Germany. I began to feel that I was more a student of National Socialism than of theology!

In my talk at the seminary I told it as I thought it was. When I had finished my talk and responded to some questions I felt the response was mostly positive but with an intermixture of incredulity that it could be as bad as I said it was. Then Paul Tillich, a guest professor as a refugee German intellectual, approached me with a glow on his face.

"Ich kann jedes Wort das Sie gesprochen haben herzlich unterstreichen," he said. "I can heartily underscore every word you have spoken."

An experience like this, showing Dr. Tillich's passionate viewpoint on the German situation, so different from that of some in the same audience, corresponded to the similar divisions but growing anxieties in the general public. In view of this widespread concern, I was sometimes asked why a prospective world conference to be held on the very border of Germany was being contemplated at all.

This leads us to examine the climate of apprehension that prevailed in Geneva and in Europe generally, especially in the last few months before the conference was to convene. There was more and more uncertainty as to whether the conference could take place before the outbreak of war.

A Race Against the Unknown

The members of the organizing committee were divided on the probable timing of overt hostilities and eventually it was decided that Geneva had no right to make this decision alone. We would do so only after conferring with the local committee in Amsterdam. It was they and their country that would stand in the immediate path of the Germans whenever they decided to invade to the west. And they and we of course felt a special responsibility for the fate of people from many lands who could be trapped, or worse.

Someone from the Geneva committee, it was agreed, should go in person to Amsterdam, convey the concern of Geneva and try to get the response of the local hosts. We were to make it clear that we would cancel the conference if they felt it would be too risky to proceed. Edwin Espy was made the messenger to convey our dilemma to the Amsterdam committee and get their response.

I recall reflecting on why I was chosen for this assignment. It seemed to me that Visser 't Hooft especially wanted me to be the one to go. I asked Tracy Strong if this was true. The following is approximately what he said. "Yes," he replied. "Wim feels he is too emotionally involved to be the messenger. On the one hand no one is more eager than he to have the conference take place. On the other hand he is convinced that we can't make it. The war will start, he believes, either before or during the conference. Also, he is so close to all the people there that he feels we might question his objectivity and possible influence on the committee's decision."

I knew also that Visser 't Hooft and I were in basic agreement about the German situation which both of us knew at first hand. We had discussed it many times. I felt that he and the committee as a whole thought that the Amsterdam group would recognize my full awareness of the risks and that I could fairly represent the anxieties of the committee.

On the other hand, Wim and I were not in full agreement as to when the war was likely to start. Our data were essentially the same but no one could know for sure and our hunches were slightly different. He even made a wager with me that the conference would not be held.

So again, more than three years after my trip from Germany to Geneva to be interviewed, I was on a train in Basel, down the Rhine through Germany toward Amsterdam. It was another fateful journey, this time not so much for me personally as for the whole World Conference of Christian Youth.

While on the previous departure from Basel I was not interested in the scenery, on the present trip I was finding myself strangely fascinated by it. I knew the Rhineland quite well but this time I seemed almost mystically identified with the impressive panorama of the mile after mile of flourishing crops. It began to come to me that this might have a bearing on my mission. Would Hitler decide to invade, at least on the western front, before these great crops, a significant part of the food supply of Germany for the winter months, were harvested? And what would would the timing be?

My growing premonition, albeit without solid evidence, became a conviction: Hitler would play it safe on the harvest and the conference would be held! But I reminded myself that my trip to Amsterdam was not to share a personal hunch; it was to share the ambivalence of the Geneva committee and its insistence that the prospective hosts in Holland should make the decision for us. So I bottled up my premonition when I met with the Amsterdam committee.

I was cordially welcomed by the Amsterdam hosts. I stated briefly my purpose in coming, of which they had been apprised in advance by Visser 't Hooft by telephone. I was then a listener for most of the rest of the meeting.

Understandably, some of the discussion sounded almost apocalyptic. They were facing an awesome decision not only with their homeland but with hundreds of lives of guests from all over the world possibly at stake. Yet it was a sober, objective discussion, as Geneva's had been. Dr. Joseph Eijkman, the distinguished general secretary of the Amsterdam YMCA and chairman of the host committee, presided at the meeting.

Quite a number of persons, including at least one government representative (I could not be sure how many) were present. Various persons excused themselves from time to time, probably to touch base with others whom they were representing.

It was hard for me to tell which way the discussion was trending. They naturally were considering essentially the same issues and unanswerable questions that we had discussed in Geneva.

In due course I was pressed for anything I had to say personally. I repeated what I had said at the beginning about the purpose of my visit but they insisted, perhaps as a matter of courtesy, and I felt I had to respond. So with hesitation I told them that all I could report, beyond the many issues they had discussed, was what had come to me on my trip down the Rhine. There was some polite nodding of heads but I recall no overt response to my inconsequential comment. If they had any reaction at all they probably preferred to discuss it by themselves.

It was suggested that they had covered the subject and that it was time to vote. I asked to be excused, as I did not want anyone's decision to be affected one way or the other by my presence.

There apparently was further discussion because it was some time before I was called back. They decided to go forward. I never asked the tally but from the tone of the discussion I doubt very much that it was unanimous.

This obviously was an historic decision. The Geneva committee of course honored its compact to abide by that decision. It immediately notified all national movements and resumed all-out preparations for the conference, on which there had been a period of hesitation and slow-down.

Just three post-scripts to this. First, the conference was held from July 24 to August 2. Less than a month later, on September 1, Germany invaded Poland, and two days after that war was declared by Britain and France. Just a month after the conference adjourned!

Second, on a very different note, something that could be told at the end but fits better here. After the conference I was invited by the Visser 't Hoofts to their home for dinner. At my place at the table was a handsome volume of religious paintings by Rembrandt. I protested that the giving should have been the other way around, which was how I felt because of what Wim had meant to me. "You won the wager about Amsterdam," he said. I had completely forgotten it.

I need to interpolate here what some of the readers of this piece may already know. Visser 't Hooft was not only a connoisseur of Rembrandt, but had written a widely acclaimed book on "Rembrandt and the Gospel." This was but one of his many books, reflecting the amazing range of his creative mind. As evidence of his remarkable world-wide standing, doubtless few persons have received as many honorary degrees from as many ranking institutions in as many countries as Visser 't Hooft.

Third, something again that belongs here rather than later. Tragically, it is an epitaph for Dr. Eijkman. His influence in the Netherlands extended far beyond the YMCA and the World Youth Conference to many sectors of Dutch society. He was a confidant of government and the royal family. His heart was with all the people of his homeland, regardless of station or condition of life. Doubtless he was a marked man even before the Nazis occupied the country.

It was this standing, his profound convictions and his courage to act on them that were to lead to his death. I do not know that the circumstances have ever been fully disclosed. But, during the Nazi occupation of Holland, he was active, among other things, in the shielding of the Jews (remember Anne Frank!). For this and other acts he was executed. This Christian martyrdom, tragedy that it was, helped to make even more real in the hearts of Amsterdamers and others the ultimate claims of CHRISTUS VICTOR.

The Conference Itself

Gathered at the conference were nearly two thousand persons, most of them young people between the ages of eighteen and thirty. With them were their leaders, conference speakers, seminar and other group chairmen, worship leaders, various co-opted personnel and others. They came from some seventy countries.

It was reported in the press that more countries were represented than at any previous international conference of any kind. If that was true then it of course would be not true at a similar conference now, when there would be far more countries represented. The number of independent nations in the world has greatly increased since decolonization following World War II and international networking of all kinds has grown.

We must note the absence of representation from three particular countries and a church. There was nobody directly from the U.S.S.R., though there was a strong delegation from the Russian Student Christian Movement in Exile and the Russian Church in Exile. There was good representation from other Orthodox churches and Student Christian Movements, with one important exception.

No one was permitted to come from Greece. The then dictator Metaxas, doubtless fearful of exposure to "communist" influences, imposed a complete ban on attendance from his country. There doubtless would otherwise have been good Greek representation because the world youth and student movements as well as the world church bodies had strong relationships and constituencies there.

This ecumenical partnership was symbolized after the World Council of Churches was established by some important appointments. The Ecumenical Patriarch Athanegoras of Constantinople (Istanbul) appointed the Very Rev. James Iakovas, now since many years primate of the Greek Orthodox Church of North and South America, to be his representative in Geneva to the W.C.C. In this post he was very active and made a signal contribution to the ecumenical movement as a whole. The World Council, from its side, named the young Greek theologian Nikolas Nissiotis to the strategic post of Director of the Ecumenical Institute at Bossey, Switzerland, a position he was to hold for many years with great distinction.

Persons likewise were prohibited from coming from Germany. But through clandestine planning in advance, with the collusion of Dietrich Bonhoeffer and others, a number of student "tourists" just "happened" to be in France, Belgium and elsewhere at the time of the conference. I had little to do with this but I suspect that the Dutch authorities at the borders had been instructed to let them into the country without the usual papers.

Their presence was never made public and most of the delegates and others never learned that they were there; they managed unobtrusively to attend most of the sessions and other events. Of course after the war Germany, like Greece and eventually the Soviet Union, embraced participation in the ecumenical movement. The fate that awaited those who returned to Germany I do not know. Others never returned home or returned only after the war. I kept in touch, until his death, with one who did not return, to whom I shall refer later.

The other notable absence, not of a country but of a church, was in representation from the Roman Catholic Church. The Church authorities specifically forbade attendance by any of their people. But Visser 't Hooft and others who had unpublicized contacts with some of their people, especially from the Church Orders, made sure that they were there incognito.

It was even reported that some of the top people in the national cabinet of the Netherlands, under pressure from the Church, were the ones who most opposed the entertaining of the conference at all, and that Queen Wilhemina herself had had to take the rare step of intervening to break the deadlock.

I have referred to Dr. Eijkman--his ability, influence and courage. He was in full command of everything one could expect of a conference host. He put Visser 't Hooft, already well known in his native Holland, in touch with key government people and even with the royal family, preceding and during the conference.

He had also secured the commitment of Princess Juliana to visit the conference and perhaps to extend a welcome. But her daughter Beatrice, now the Queen, was born just a few days before the conference and no public appearances were possible. Dr. Eijkman arranged for Prince Bernhard, her consort, to attend some sessions instead; and for a very small group from the conference to make a courtesy call on Princess Juliana when she was able to receive them.

Years later, when Queen Wilhemina had abdicated the throne in favor of Princess Juliana, the ecumenical movement became one of her most ardent and active concerns.

A few top government officials looked in on the conference and the Minister of Education, Science and Art hosted a gala reception under government auspices at the Reijksmuseum.

We must pay tribute to some of the people related to the conference, both before and during. On the conference Preparations Committee we need not mention again the original Geneva members except to say that in due course H.L. Henriod succeeded Visser 't Hooft as chairman.

Members who were added included the following to whom we have referred: F.W.T. Craske, Suzanne de Dietrich, Francis H. House, William Paton and Oliver Tomkins. Others were Etienne Bach of Switzerland, Charles Guillon of France (World's YMCA, also mayor of Chambon-sur-Lignon, later famed as a valiant haven for Jews during the German occupation), P.C. Toureille of France (Ecumenical Youth Commission), Leo Zander of France (Russian Student Christian Movement in Exile) and Nikolas Zernov of England (Russian Orthodox Church).

At the conference itself the Steering Committee also included the Geneva members of the Preparatory Committee. In addition to these, some of whom we have mentioned in other capacities and carrying special responsibilities at the conference were Suzanne de Dietrich, Joseph Eijkman, Henri Johannot (YMCA, Geneva), Ivan M. Gould, Denzil G.M. Patrick, Oliver S. Tomkins and Nikolas Zernov. Not previously referred to were Shizue Hihari (Japan) and C.C. Liang (China).

Also on the Steering Committee were the young people serving as the daily chairpersons of the conference:

Madeleine Borot of France
Jean Fraser of Britain
Martin Harvey of the United States
D.T. Niles of Ceylon (now Sri Lanka)
Wilfred C. Lockhart of Canada
Bengt Redel of Sweden

The speakers at plenary sessions were Archbishop William Temple of England, Mrs. Liliana Miron of Roumania, Frans J. Kooijman of the Netherlands, Paul J. Braisted of the United States, Archimandrite Cassian of the Russian Orthodox Theological Academy in Paris, Reinhold Niebuhr of the United States, George F. MacLeod of Scotland, Elie Laurial of France, T.Z. Koo of China, Manfred Bjorquist of Sweden and John R. Mott of the U.S.A.

The daily worship leaders were Moira Neill (now Mrs. Symons) of Britain and YWCA Geneva, Jacques Courvoisier of Switzerland, Brun Foltin of Hungary, Mina Soga of South Africa, Robert C. Mackie of Britain (and Geneva), Benjamin E. Mays of the United States, Oliver S. Tomkins of Britain, Hendrik Kramer of the Netherlands, G. Sparring-Petersen of Denmark, Einar Molland of Norway, E. Sambayya of India, Ivan M. Gould of the U.S.A. and W.A. Visser 't Hooft.

There were of course many group leaders and other key people whom I have not mentioned. In addition to such persons as these and others whose names did not appear in the conference material, we should be grateful to Hanna Schokking and her many associates who worked valiantly on the host committee and all local arrangements.

Similarly I want to express personal thanks to a person without whose participation the arrangements for the conference, especially the liaison between Geneva and Amsterdam on practical preparations, could have been a shambles. He was Robbins Strong, son of Tracy Strong, who took a year out from the seminary before the conference to perform this role. Without his help I could not have performed my function as the over-all executive. As further evidence of his ecumenical commitment he spent about half of his career of Christian service on the staff of the World's YMCA and half on that of the World Council of Churches.

My own role at the conference, once it had assembled, could have been assumed by others if necessary. I of course had to relate to all the leaders and committees and keep all the aspects tied together. But with Visser 't Hooft at the helm and so many other involved veterans present there would have been no problem. Most of my work had been done in the previous three-plus years.

But the fact that I had to be conspicuous on the platform, making the announcements, giving directions and keeping the machinery running, made me appear more important than I really was. This led to a rather poignant incident reflecting the inexorable turn-over of leadership that comes in every movement and organization. This one I think should be told because it relates to a unique and long-time leader in the world-wide youth and ecumenical movements.

John R. Mott was at the conference to deliver a major address and of course to be present throughout. He and his protege/assistant for thirty-five years up to then, Paul B. Anderson, would sit together in the balcony--an unaccustomed location for Dr. Mott! One of Anderson's functions was to interpret for him whatever was taking place, including the proceedings on the platform, in English, French, German and occasionally Russian, in all of which Paul was fluent.

Finally Dr. Mott whispered to Anderson, "Who is that young American giving the directions in three languages?" Dr. Mott was not a linguist and he doubtless did not recognize the execrableness of my performance in French!

"His name is Edwin Espy," Paul replied, "and he is the organizing secretary of the conference." The Amsterdam Youth Conference was rather a sad step in the decline of John R. Mott's central leadership role in his fifty years of organizing and leading international assemblies. This was one of the first times he had not been the commanding figure and master of every detail. Dr. Mott was experiencing the arrival of a new era, though there were still to be a number of world meetings at which he was at least nominally at the helm. He of course was to continue for another fifteen years in various positions and was to become the first Honorary President of the World Council of Churches. But never after World War II was he to be the principal organizer, inspirer and the real person in charge.

Another incident with Dr. Mott may seem trivial and even impertinent but it reflects another fact--that many of the younger people of the conference, in contrast to the students of my generation a dozen years earlier, scarcely knew about Dr. Mott and did not hold the venerable Doctor in great awe. Opportunity was given for those who were interested and free to do so to meet with him. They had a session with him. I was not present but was told that a young lady later was asked what she thought of him.

"I was fascinated by his eye-brows," she replied! This probably was not intended as disrespect but if this was all that impressed her, it spoke more eloquently than many words.

However, Dr. Mott's remarkable address on "Ambassadors of Christ" was widely hailed as one of the great utterances of the conference, of which there were many. He spoke with his customary vigor and charisma and again he gripped the oncoming generation. But the "Eminence Gris" was receding from the other pinnacles of the past.

Of course there were numerous greats, more nearly of Mott's era, in the youth and ecumenical movements. We have already mentioned some of them and there were others at the Amsterdam Youth Conference. But we shall let the case of Dr. Mott speak with gratitude for them all.

A quite different episode about another major speaker needs to be recounted because it reflects the highly-charged political/international atmosphere in which the Conference was held. We have noted the understandable apprehension among the Dutch, especially within the government, about the holding of the conference at all.

The incident referred to was a bizarre melodrama, but to the people playing in it, including the planners of the Youth Conference, it was very real. Another of the main speakers was to be Reinhold Niebuhr. Apparently the secret service in the Netherlands had received word that he had written an article betraying a leaning toward communism!

He was widely known, as Tillich was, for his abhorrence and dread of fascism as represented especially by the National Socialism of Germany. It is very possible that he may have implied somewhere that if he had to make a choice he would take communism before German National Socialism.

Thus the concern of the Dutch authorities was not only that he might be pro-communist. It was that the use of him as a speaker at a major international gathering in the Netherlands might not play well in Germany! The Dutch wanted nothing to be done that would incite the Germans against them if and when they occupied their country.

The security people were adamant that the invitation to Niebuhr should be revoked--and that in any case they would not let him enter the country. But fortunately he had left the United States considerably ahead of time to spend some time in England speaking and otherwise. An agreement was finally struck that he could come to Holland and to the conference on two conditions.

One was that people from the Dutch secret service should go incognito to England and sit in on some of his speeches and seminars, making their own assessment of his political leanings. The second was that he should submit to the Dutch authorities in advance the text of the address he was to deliver at the conference. On the basis of these advance precautions, he was allowed to come.

Beyond this, the secret police accompanied representatives of the conference to meet the controversial man at the Hoek van Holland and escort him to Amsterdam.

There was a somewhat amusing if highly risky development when Niebuhr spoke. Some of us, in good faith, had been given a copy of his speech. The security people also had it and were present to monitor it. But Reiny, a master virtuoso at verbal improvisation, departed at many points from the text. Those of us who had the responsibility became apprehensive lest the security people would remove him from the podium or cut off the microphone.

But he sometimes spoke in a manner, both in verbiage and circumlocution of thought, that often had not been easy for even his own students to follow. Add the fact of his physical histrionics, twisting about the lectern with little regard for the microphone. Pity the security guards whose English at best was only a second or third language. Niebuhr had them baffled!

The power of Niebuhr's oratory and thought broke through to most who heard him, and he was heartily acclaimed. As to substance, somewhat garbled tapes gave proof that there was nothing in it that should give the authorities concern. Another crisis was behind us.

Quite a different incident at the conference mirrored international tension in another part of the world. It took place at the memorable communion service in the Nieuwe Kerk which the great majority of the delegates attended. This raised for two delegations, the Chinese and the Japanese, whose countries were at war, an excruciating issue.

How could they reconcile their loyalty to their respective countries with the taking of communion together from the same cup? There had been efforts at the conference to get the members of the two delegations together in small numbers or as participants in the same discussion groups and also as full delegations. These had met with only mixed success. The emotions ran very deep.

At the service, because of where the communicants happened to find themselves at the table before the altar, a Japanese and Chinese were side by side. An observer noted the painful pause as the person who first received the plate with the chalice and bread was hesitant to pass it on, and the other one showed no sign of accepting it. They both seemed to freeze.

Then there came a palpable relaxation and they both communed. They did what they knew their presence together at Holy Communion required of them. I have no knowledge of their subsequent relationship but I am sure their memory of the sacred bond that united them in that moment must have remained with them the rest of their lives. At least in that experience the reality of CHRISTUS VICTOR had prevailed.

The other incident was not around tension between two national delegations but between one delegation, or at least a large and vocal part of one, and the basic plan that had been developed for the communion services. I have referred to this format before as an ecumenical break-through. Basically it was a departure from the somewhat homogenized service in most ecumenical meetings in the past in favor of several services, not simultaneous but successive, in which each of the major traditions would hold a separate service with all participants in the conference invited to attend.

In the planning process itself the adoption of this plan had not been an easy decision, but the persuasive case made for it by Francis House, Leo Zander, Nikolas Zernov and others had prevailed. Many in the American delegation were the ones that were most vociferous in objection. They seemed shocked and bewildered, and some of them angered.

The issue for the Americans seemed basic. Especially those from the student movements not related to the churches and from the United Christian Youth Movement, a coalition of the youth movements of most of the "main-line" churches in the United States, were not prepared for this.

To oversimplify what seemed to be the prevailing American view, ecumenism means sublimating our differences and uniting around what we have in common, sacrificing if necessary many of our long-held traditions and practices. Those "hangovers from the past" had to take second place in the setting of ecumenical gatherings.

There were many less formal worship experiences at the conference, but this was one of the first times in a major world meeting that the new mode prevailed. Every one was encouraged to attend all the services in the major traditions and to a remarkable degree the concept of "maximum ecumenism" was welcomed, at least as a promising innovation.

In due course, however, I was informed that the Americans were having a meeting and that they wanted me there. I went promptly but did not stay long. I explained that I had duties for the conference as a whole. But I informed them that I would send some one who could deal with the issue far more helpfully than I. It was William Adams Brown from Union Theological Seminary.

We had invited a number of seasoned people, some well beyond the age of the delegates, to serve as consultants on various subjects. On the age criterion, Professor Brown fully qualified. He could have been the grandfather of the oldest delegate! He was a reassuring but not overbearing man exuding an aura of wisdom and obviously the master of his subject. He had long been a consultant and conceptualizer for the ecumenical movement. He must have been persuasive, for most of the opponents were impressed, and respectfully withdrew their overt opposition.

But the convictions and emotions ran deep, and I learned that there were still was disappointment, not only among the Americans but in some other delegations as well. Fortunately, here again there came a spiritual if not wholly intellectual and emotionally supported reconciliation.

Knowing that the pattern set for the communion services would present problems for many at the conference, the planning committee built into the schedule a service of preparation. Beautifully conducted by Robert Mackie, it could not but have calmed the feelings of all and evoked a climate of inner readiness throughout all the delegations.

A moving prayer by Benjamin E. Mays, later president of Morehouse College in Atlanta, Georgia, was said by some to have been for them the most gripping single moment of the conference.

I should share with the readers, most of whom will be Americans, a fact about our delegation that is relevant to the communion issue. The American delegates on the whole were inclined to be unschooled in matters of worship, theology and tradition. I have reflected earlier that Americans in general were also tardy in grasping the realities in issues of world affairs. The majority seemed to be innocently optimistic in both areas. Most of their leaders, of course, were better informed.

It may be symptomatic that the refrain of the theme hymn of the largest American group, the United Christian Youth Movement, should be "We would be building temples still undone" to the stirring tune of Finlandia. Its text and upbeat melody both reflected and fostered a laudable idealism, grounded in faithfulness to Christ, that cannot but be applauded.

This enthusiasm played an important part in inspiring young people, drawing them together in a spiritual movement of which we could wish that we had a comparable counterpart today. It was a strong and good impulse but one that needed to be matured by experience. This was part of the impact of Amsterdam '39, deepening but not dampening the ardor.

Perhaps these random reminiscences will suggest some of the atmosphere of the First World Conference of Christian Youth.

Some Outcomes

So what was the enduring deposit of the Amsterdam Youth Conference?

At the minimum it has been widely remembered, reported and celebrated by those who were there. An official report was of course produced in Geneva but the war delayed its publication and especially its distribution. Some countries did not receive it until after the war was over. Meanwhile, war-induced preoccupations intervened and the report never received the attention that had been given to the preparatory materials.

Across the years there have been countless articles, speeches, "mini-Amsterdams," study outlines and other follow-up observances. Many of these took place in a number of countries even during the war and have continued, with decreasing frequency, up to the present time. The half-century Festschrift of which this article is a part is one example.

We have noted previously the 1979 symposium in the United States. It was led off by the definitive and succinct evaluation by Visser 't Hooft which is reproduced in this volume because of its clear appraisal by the principal architect of the conference.

That collection brought together forty articles by forty persons from the United States, Canada and Latin America in commemoration of the fortieth anniversary of the conference. Also included were excerpts from twenty-six unsolicited letters by delegates who had learned of the prospective publication and wanted to affirm their indebtedness to Amsterdam '39. It was published as a special edition of the Journal of Ecumenical Studies.

In the same year Visser 't Hooft invited and circulated widely thirty-five substantive letters from persons in fourteen countries who had been key people at the conference. One of them was Prince Bernhard of the Netherlands.

There also were numerous commemorative gatherings in 1979, bringing together many delegates after forty years. I shall mention those of which I know in just three areas.

In Switzerland Visser 't Hooft convened a number of alumni/ae from Europe and other countries. In the United States and Canada there were at least seven such gatherings, from coast to coast.

The most striking observance was held at Coventry Cathedral in England on the weekend of the fortieth anniversary of the declaration of war by Britain and France against Germany. Some fifty Amsterdamers were present, including a number from countries on the Continent and several from the United States.

Among the principal leaders of this Coventry conference were Robert Mackie, Oliver Tomkins, Francis House, Jean Fraser, Edwin Barker and Moira Neill Symons, all of whom we have mentioned as leaders at Amsterdam. My wife Cleo and I were invited to attend. I had been asked to preach at the morning service. Hence in keeping with the "personal reflections" of this account I shall say a world about that experience.

As in many other countries, but with very special memories of the war, the people of Britain were thinking back with both grief and thanksgiving. Coventry of course was a place of pilgrimage for millions, not only from Britain but from around the world. On this particular Sunday the Cathedral was packed with worshippers and pilgrims.

Adjoining the rebuilt Cathedral is a small chapel, a gift of people from the churches of Germany who wanted to express contrition and continued unity in Christ and the Church. Doubtless many people in the congregation that morning had already visited the chapel.

Most of those at the service had of course come expecting an emphasis on the fortieth anniversary of the war. Probably very few of them had heard of the Amsterdam Youth Conference! So I had an unenviable task.

Invited at the behest of the Amsterdamers, my subject was expected by them to be ecumenical. Moreover I was not a Britisher and could never be a spokesman for their emotions as a people in remembering the war. But the chapel gift of the Germans came to my rescue. With this and some other connectives that I was able to bring to bear I was able to preach at the same time on the meaning of ecumenism and on peace between the peoples. Christ had prayed "that they might be one" in Him. Obviously if there is not a mutually sustaining relationship between ecumenism and peace there is something wrong with them both. Probably some in the congregation who had come for the rousements of a patriotic address went away disappointed. But I had tried to preach the Gospel.

During the years that such commemorations of Amsterdam '39 were taking place, what was happening at the world level and nationally in the relationships between the bodies that had convened the conference? The story of that half century presents a mixed picture, particularly in the coordination between the youth and student movements and the churches which I have gloriously called an ecumenical symbiosis.

In 1948 the World Council of Churches was born in Amsterdam after a long period of gestation. In due course all of the world church bodies, with the partial exception of one, that were related to Amsterdam '39 became integral parts of it, headquartered in Geneva. This development has been called osmosis! The partial exception was the World Alliance for International Friendship through the Churches. Under a different name it continued to conduct a study, seminar and publishing program in New York, still funded by the Church Peace Union located there. The international work of the World Alliance was largely absorbed into the World Council.

The three Geneva-based world youth and student organizations-- YMCA, YWCA and World Student Christian Federation--are still of course independent and located in Geneva. International Christian Endeavor, so far as I know, no longer is in operation as a world body, though it has units in some countries.

All the principal world church bodies participating in Amsterdam '39, integrated in the World Council of Churches, are now situated in Geneva--quite a change.

However, the relative headquarters strengths of the two groups of organizations--church and youth/student--are the reverse of what they were in 1939. At that time the two church bodies located there--Life and Work, and Friendship through the Churches--were meagerly staffed and funded compared to the youth and student organizations.

Now the World Council of Churches has an impressive headquarters establishment with a large staff and its own imposing building, the Ecumenical Center. Located there also are the offices of other important world church bodies such as the Lutheran World Federation.

The present staffs and organizational strenghts of the World's YMCA and YWCA are probably substantially what they were in 1939, but the World Student Christian Federation has undergone a long period of readjustment to the new day and still is struggling but carrying on.

The two types of world bodies that united for the Amsterdam '39 Conference held conferences on the same general pattern in Oslo in 1947, Kottayam, India in 1952 and Strasbourg in 1957. Since then there has been none with the same level of interorganizational participation.

In the United States, there has been a decline of interorganizational collaboration in recent decades. The United Christian Youth Movement, after a period of good health into the sixties, lost its momentum and eventually disappeared as such. Some of its programs were picked up by local and state councils of churches and other agencies, but the identity and vibrancy of the U.C.Y.M. has not been replaced.

In the student field the YMCA, YWCA, Student Volunteer Movement and national student organizations of the churches prospered and cooperated closely for two decades or so after the war. Some of the factors leading to this were the increasingly open dialogue on theological and social issues within their own memberships and also among their parent bodies; the achievement of membership by all of them in the World Student Christian Federation; their experience together in the Amsterdam Youth Conference; increasing ecumenical cooperation and movement toward unity among their own churches; the creation of the World and National Councils of Churches; in many state and city councils of churches a network of support for cooperation in the student field; and the increasing overall awareness that the witness of all the ecumenically oriented bodies in the colleges and universities was and had to be basically the same witness.

Over time and a series of stages these common impulses brought into being for extensive cooperation a united National Student Christian Federation, organizationally administered by the National Council of Churches. In due course this too foundered like the older United Christian Youth Movement. There is now only a shadow of the former collaboration nationally between the church-related and Y-related student movements but there still is considerable cooperation among the church-related movements and in staffed situations between the YM-YW and church programs.

Such cooperation is important, partly because all the "traditional" student movements are confronted with the growing competition of the conservative and often fundamentalist student movements. It must also be recognized that in many ways the prevailing tone of campus life has changed, as we shall see in another paper in this series.

These developments in the student field in the United States merit serious study and vigorous and united action. If the importance of this be questioned, there are two reasons why it is fundamental for the future of ecumenism not only here but world-wide in view of the American role in the wider Oikumene.

First, as we said at the beginning, the health of world ecumenism requires a base in ecumenism nationally, "all in each place one." This means not only in a given country but within smaller locations in a country.

Secondly, it is axiomatic that the ecumenical movement needs constantly to regenerate its leadership at all geographical levels of its life. Where is it to find and start moulding such leadership except in the colleges and seminaries? As we have seen, practically all of the leadership for the Amsterdam Youth Conference had had this kind of background and a large number of these in their turn were to become key leaders ecumenically all the way from local churches and campuses to the World Council. This source of leadership for the future must continue to be enlisted and nurtured.

We have cited some gains and losses in ecumenical youth and student work in the United States. In the broader scene of ecumenism in the churches in the United States and world-wide the progress on the whole in the last fifty years has been memorable.

The following is a partial listing: Note the basic change in climate, contact, cooperation and theological/cultural dialogue between the Roman Catholic Church and the other churches of Christendom; the profound expansion of these realities among practically all of the Christian confessions, including the study in recent years on Baptism, Eucharist and Ministry; the entry of the Orthodox, Armenian, Roman Catholic and Baptist/Evangelical churches of the Soviet Union into the ecumenical fellowship through the

World Council of Churches, as well as country-to-country relationships and recent contacts of some of them with the Vatican; the increasing attention of many seminaries to ecumenism as a subject of study; the phenomenal growth of ecumenical participation and impact from the developing countries; the growing attention to the relationship of Christianity to culture world-wide; the increasing firmness of the ecumenical address to critical social and international issues; the growing serious intercourse between the Christian and Jewish communities; the establishment and progress of the World Council of Churches; the proliferation of national, regional and local councils of churches around the world; the number of major church unions achieved and the further ones now in progress.

This has been a great half-century for ecumenism. No claim is made that these developments have flowed from the World Conference of Christian Youth! Our purpose is to put the deposit of that conference in the setting of broader ecumenical developments. But there is ample evidence that the 1939 Amsterdamers have had more than their share of input.

An amazing proportion of the young people and leaders who were there continued to grow in ecumenical understanding and leadership, some through their life vocations and others as ecumenically oriented lay or ordained persons in their churches, Christian organizations and daily life in the world. In most cases they also had become more committed to relating the perspective of ecumenism to the issues of the secular society, including the world of nations.

The names of many of these persons belong in a Who's Who of ecumenism at the local, national or world level, or all three. It would be a flagrant exercise to try to rank these persons in any manner. But I must mention one American leader and two American delegates who reflect the interpenetration of ecumenical leadership among various types of Christian organizations which we have lifted up in this account. They had early exposure to ecumenism. They also served in local, national, and world settings.

Roswell P. Barnes was a group leader at Amsterdam. At the time of the conference he was associate general secretary of the Federal Council of Churches in the United States. He had been a teacher and pastor and for about fifteen years an active representative of the American Student Christian Movement to the World Student Christian Federation. He was to become successively the executive secretary of the Division of Christian Life and Work of the National Council of Churches, associate general secretary of the National Council and associate general secretary of the World Council of Churches in the New York office. Until a number of years after his retirement he continued as unofficial but valued consultant to the W.S.C.F. and the W.C.C.

Robert S. Bilheimer, a student at Yale Divinity School, was a delegate of the World Student Christian Federation at the conference. I single him out because of his subsequent ecumenical vocation, another example of interpenetration between the student movement and the churches. He was to become successively associate general secretary of the Student Volunteer Movement in the United States, executive secretary of the Interseminary Movement, pastor of a predominantly Black congregation in Brooklyn, a major staff associate in several critical positions in the World Council, pastor of a Presbyterian Church in Rochester, New York, secretary of the Department of International Affairs in the National Council of Churches and executive of the National Institute for Ecumenical and Cultural Research in Collegeville, Minnesota. This latter is a pioneering enterprise with especially strong Roman Catholic sponsorship and participation.

Franklin H. Littell, a student at Union Theological Seminary, was a delegate of the National Council of Methodist Youth. He travelled in Germany before the conference and gained an abhorrence of Hitler and a concern for the Jews that stayed with him throughout his life and led to his present national and world leadership in major movements on Christian-Jewish relations, with special emphasis on the Holocaust. He is the Founder and Honorary Chairman of the Anne Frank Institute in Philadelphia and is Adjunct Professor in the Institute of Contemporary Jewry of Hebrew University in Jerusalem. Across the years he has served as pastor of Methodist churches, on the faculties of a number of colleges, universities and seminaries and as president of Iowa Wesleyan College. He continues as Emeritus Professor of Religion at Temple University. Through it all he has maintained a close relationship with the World Student Christian Federation.

At the world level, as we have suggested, Visser 't Hooft came the closest of anybody to inheriting the mantle of John R. Mott. As a very young man he was on his staff in the World's YMCA. He succeeded Mott as general secretary of the World Student Christian Federation. As chairman of the 1939 Amsterdam Conference he performed a role that Dr. Mott had performed in youth and student conferences all over the world.

When Dr. Visser 't Hooft became general secretary of the World Council of Churches and Dr. Mott became its first honorary president, he headed an organization that eventually brought together the Universal Christian Council, which Mott, Archbishop Soderblom and others had founded; the Faith and Order Movement of which Mott had long been a presiding officer; and the International Missionary Council of which Mott had long been the world president. When Visser 't Hooft retired as general secretary of the World Council and became its honorary president, again he succeeded Dr. Mott as well as Dr. Oldham, who had held that position following Mott.

Obviously Visser 't Hooft was not as early a pioneer as Mott, but he entered new territory and broke new ground that Mott had not equally trod, especially theologically; and ecclesiologically as general secretary of the World Council of Churches.

Would that there were space to mention many other striking cases of ecumenical leadership reaching out across various organizations and illustrating the interaction between the youth/student movements and the churches. It would include all of the writers of articles for this symposium.

I shall close by referring again to World War II. We have noted its impact on Amsterdam '39 before, during and after the conference. How can we claim so much for a youth conference when the shattering event that erupted just a month following the conference disrupted normal life almost world-wide and obstructed international communications for six years after the conference?

There are many answers to that question but I shall mention three. Though normal communications between many countries were cut off, Switzerland remained neutral and became a center of improvised world-wide contacts. Within the ecumenical movement there was devised an incredible secret network in Geneva penetrating belligerent nations--a network that would provide material for a good thriller novel. Another device was to decentralize world staff. Robert Mackie, general secretary of the World Student Christian Federation, established his base of operations in Toronto, Canada.

A second response, related again to "all in each place one," is that ecumenical development proceeded, often at an accelerated pace. In many countries this was a preparatory period for the creation of national councils of churches. At the world level preparations for the World Council also went forward apace. World upheaval was actually calling forth Christian unity, drawing the churches together.

Thirdly, and some would say paradoxically, the cloud of apprehension that hung over Amsterdam, and the world-wide trauma of the war itself, fostered a profounder sense of unity in Christ among the participants in the conference across all the lines of division. God was supreme. CHRISTUS VICTOR became a more controlling reality transcending human alienations. Three profound war-time experiences will illustrate this.

Most people returned hastily to their countries, some started soon but by slower routes, others did not arrive until after the war and a few never got back to their homelands at all.

In one case a number of leaders and delegates from the Americas and Asia booked passage on the Athenia for North America. They took advantage of this to overcome barriers and strengthen the ties that had developed at Amsterdam. But en route the ship was torpedoed, which was said to be the first such fate of a passenger vessel in the war. The lives of all the Amsterdamers were saved.

Some of them were from countries that already were belligerents, on opposing sides. Yet they kept in touch afterwards by correspondence, through prayer and in other ways. Can there be any doubt that CHRISTUS VICTOR prevailed?

In another case a young lady from Lithuania, unable to penetrate the battle front to the east, went in the opposite direction. After a tortuous journey through France, Spain and South America, aided by understanding people along the way, contacted primarily through churches, she arrived eventually in the United States and settled in Colorado.

In this country she was assisted by Henry Smith Leiper and many others. She married and I know that for many years she did not return to her homeland, if indeed she ever did. She must have had times of disappointment and even disillusionment along the way. But I was told by Dr. Leiper that the trust and succour she found among Christians of various nations and persuasions had re-inforced her fidelity to CHRISTUS VICTOR and deepened her sense of the trans-national oikumene.

The other instance is that of a brilliant young German scientist and ardent pacifist, Herbert Jehle. He was one of the people who had attended the conference incognito and he decided not to risk returning to Germany. Instead he went to France, where in due course he was incarcerated in a detention camp.

Madeleine Barot of France had been a daily chairperson at Amsterdam and was to spend the rest of her life in ecumenical leadership and works of Christian mercy in her own country and elsewhere, especially through the World Council of Churches. She had a moving "rencontre" during the war. She had been given permission to visit some of the detention camps in France for humanitarian purposes, to conduct worship services and to bring news, comfort and aid to the persons incarcerated. She quite unexpectedly discovered Dr. Jehle, was able to secure his release, and assisted him in getting to the United States.

His qualifications led him to important teaching posts in American colleges. He became a leader in societies of physicists and devoted his non-academic time to the pacifist cause, the Student Christian Movement, and the ecumenical movement, witnessing to his allegiance to the World Christian Community. I was privileged to be in touch with him until shortly before his death.

Such was the stuff that went into--and in more clear and purposeful forms came out of--the Amsterdam Youth Conference. It cannot be claimed that Amsterdam was the only force that had this effect, since obviously in most cases there was a predisposition and in all cases there were other consonant exposures, both before and after. It also is obvious that I don't know all who were there, and the ones I know best are chiefly North Americans and Europeans.

But it was my privilege for forty years after Amsterdam '39 to meet with hundreds of alumni/ae and to be a colleague of scores in the youth-student movements and the Church in the United States and around the world. Even in the past decade, since retirement, I have continued in close touch with a goodly number. There is ample evidence that an unbreakable bond was forged in 1939.

The reality of CHRISTUS VICTOR had fixed its hold on the Amsterdam participants, and the grip has held. The conference deepened for the rest of their lives their transcendent loyalty to God as revealed in Christ and their commitment to unity in Him and his Church--"all in each place one." That experience brought new young strength to the ecumenical movement. It also brought new insights, inclusiveness and approaches to ecumenism that are still being felt after half a century.

The First World Conference of Christian Youth was ecumenical history in the making.

The Lutheran World, The Ecumenical World
and the World at War

Stewart Herman

The common denominator in the title of this piece is the word <u>world</u>. Dictionaries define "world" not only as the whole earth and its inhabitants but also as "a particular part of the earth" or as "a field or sphere of human endeavor" or simply as "a large amount." What follows here is definitely not a full account of any one of the indicated worlds but the circumscribed effort of one person, relying heavily on personal impressions, to describe the way in which the three worlds of the title impinged upon each other in his lifetime.

Prologue

The roots of all three "worlds"--including modern ecumenism--are to be found in the 19th century, so we must begin there. Very sketchily!

In 1868 a number of German church and mission leaders organized an Allgemeine Evangelisch Lutherische Konferenz, largely to provide a basis of support for young Lutheran churches in the United States, little realizing that the flow of help would one day be reversed. First impulses thereto had actually stirred 25 years earlier. The founding of the Lutheran World Federation 104 years later can be traced to this seedling.

Scandinavian Lutherans had launched their own cooperative movement in 1857 and in due course their fraternal visitors were welcomed to the German Conference. By the end of the century said Conference had assumed distinctly international, if not ecumenical overtones, involving not only the Scandinavian countries but also Finland, Russia, Holland, France and the USA. Some of nearly a score of meetings were held in Scandinavia until the First World War disrupted these gatherings. Meanwhile, however, the same conflict brought together most of the American Lutherans in a National Lutheran Council (1918) which became an effective instrument of postwar interchurch aid.

In 1923 at the joint invitation of the Allgemeine Evangelish Lutherische Konferenz (Bishop Ludwig Ihmels) and the National Lutheran Council (Dr. John A. Morehead) 151 delegates from 22 nations assembled in Eisenach to organize the Lutheran World Convention. A doctrinal basis was now adopted:

> The Lutheran World Convention accepts the Holy Scriptures of the Old and New Testaments as the only source and infallible norm of all church doctrine and practice and recognizes the confessions of the Lutheran church, especially the Unaltered Augsburg Confession and Luther's Small Catechism as the pure interpretation of God's Word.

One of the LWC's stated purposes was "to contribute to Christian unity." An executive committee consisting of two Germans, two

Scandinavians and two Americans was set up. What we today call the Third World was still regarded as a "foreign mission" field. Subsequent conventions were held in Copenhagen in 1929 and Paris in 1935. Plans for a meeting in Philadelphia in 1940 were intercepted by World War II, and it was not until 1946, at Lund, Sweden, that the Lutheran World Convention became the Lutheran World Federation.

Meanwhile the evolution of the Protestant ecumenical movement was roughly paralleling--if not preceding--the growing self-awareness of Lutherans and other confessional bodies. This was an outgrowth in the early 19th century of the interconfessional labors of various Bible societies and foreign mission agencies. The most notable fruit of this interdenominational activity, initiated and led by dedicated individuals rather than by their churches, was the World's Evangelical Alliance (1846). A number of other organizations proliferated, such as the World's YMCA (1855), the Student Volunteers for Foreign Missions (1886) and the Ecumenical Missionary Conference at New York City (1900).

Anglo-American denominations responded to the ecumenical challenge by forging world links of their own. The Anglican Lambeth Conference came into existence in 1867, the World Presbyterian Alliance in 1875, the Methodist Ecumenical Conference in 1881, the Baptist World Alliance in 1905. Lutherans, as already noted, did not really come together until 1923.

Among the good reasons for this relatively late blossoming were, on the one hand, the lack of a Lutheran "Canterbury" to serve as a natural focus or center around which to gather and, on the other hand, the restrictive disparity of the state-church relationships prevailing in the territorial divisions of Germany and in Scandinavia. But the trend toward Christian unity was running strong, as exemplified in the World Alliance for

Friendship through the Churches (1914) and above all in the decisive World Mission Conference at Edinburgh in 1910.

Can the World be One?

The tremendous trauma of the First World War generated an equally tremendous resolve to make it the last. As governments strove to establish a League of Nations, churches, with an equivalent burst of reckless or cautious idealism, dreamed of having an international league of churches. By 1920, three major trends were becoming clearly apparent among a plenitude of movements aiming at greater Christian unity and world peace. Each of these trends now found full expression in an important international assembly: the conference on Life and Work at Stockholm in 1925, the conference on Faith and Order at Lausanne in 1927 and the International Missionary Conference at Jerusalem in 1928.

Perhaps the most distinctive new feature of these gatherings, aside from the fact that they embodied a fresh vision of great cooperative goals, was that what had been until then the concern of interested individuals was becoming the concern of churches as churches.

By 1937, when Life and Work and Faith and Order met consecutively, the former at Oxford and the latter at Edinburgh, not only were the participants to a very large extent officially appointed by their churches but they came fully prepared to espouse the idea of a world organization of churches. One year later at Utrecht the designated representatives of both conferences met to establish a provisional council and authorize a small office in Geneva. A constituting world assembly was scheduled for 1941. The outbreak of the Second World War effectively cancelled these plans. Providentially, a World Christian Youth Congress at Amsterdam in 1939 invested the burgeoning ecumenical movement with an enthusiastic momentum which made the nine-year wait for "Amsterdam" (1948) more tolerable.

During this interbellum period--roughly 1918-1938--Lutheran leadership in ecumenical matters was not prominently in evidence. With one notable exception. That exception was Sweden's multi-lingual Archbishop Nathan Soederblom, whose single-minded, warm-hearted vision was responsible for the creation of the Universal Christian Council for Life and Work in 1925. The pragmatism of his concept appealed to both his German and American fellow-Lutherans, if for quite different reasons.

The tendency of Lutheran leaders in general was to be wary not only of the possible theological bogs in the Faith and Order movement but even of the implications for doctrinal purity in the new Lutheran World Convention which they cautionsly approached from a wide variety of theological, church-political and linguistic positions. It must also be kept in mind that of the three major divisions represented in the LWC, the Americans and Germans had been on opposite sides of the recent war while the Scandinavians had remained sternly neutral. Fortunately, postwar relief work under the inspired leadership of Dr. John A. Morehead proved to be a significant reconciling factor.

A totally different Lutheran situation was developing by the time the two major ecumenical conferences met at Oxford and Edinburgh in 1937. Adolf Hitler had come to power in 1933 and his ultimate ideological goals, although incredible at first, were becoming clearly apparent. The "Positive Christianity" he professed was revealed as nothing more nor less than undiluted National Socialism, as the Minister for Church Affairs, Hans Kerrl, bluntly and publicly admitted on Feb. 13, 1937 to a group of church leaders. Many recalcitrant clergy were already under arrest or in concentration camps. A few months later Pastor Martin Niemoller was taken into custody.

Nazi Germany preoccupied everybody arriving at Oxford to discuss "Church, Community and State."

It came as a severe blow to prospective German delegates and to other participants that the only German representatives permitted to attend Oxford and Edinburgh meetings were three of the more complaisant heads of the Methodist, Baptist and Old Catholic communions. Henceforward the important German Lutheran contribution to ecumenical thinking and planning occurred, if at all, only very indirectly or clandestinely.

As pastor of the American Church in Berlin (1936-1941) I was able to go to Oxford, hoping to serve as the source of information regarding the church situation. The following year, for the same reason, I went to Utrecht, where the Committee of 90 was meeting to lay the foundation for the WCC.

In spite of onerous political impediments imposed by Hitler and the angry emotions aroused by him, the sympathetic ties between the Protestant churches, even during the ensuing war, were much closer than they had been during the 1914-1918 conflict. Two factors mainly contributed to this: on the one hand, the Nazis' manifestly anti-Christian attitude coupled with the courageous resistance of the Confessing Church; on the other hand, the existence and effective activity of the small staff of the WCC "in the process of formation." Lines of communication were brilliantly exploited by the General Secretary, Dr. W.A. Visser 't Hooft, with the devoted assistance of Dr. Hans Schoenfeld, Dr. Nils Ehrenstrom and Dr. Adolph Freudenberg at considerable personal risk to many of the people involved. As the war progressed and the Nazi war machine overran most of Western Europe, communication became more tenuous and more hazardous but the lines held.

When World War II neared its end in Europe the WCC Geneva office swung into action. Dr. J. Hutchison Cockburn had come from

Scotland in February 1945 to be the first director of the Department of Reconstruction and Interchurch Aid. In July the first American contingent arrived, including Dr. S.C. Michelfelder from the National Lutheran Council, Dr. Benjamin Bush on behalf of the United Presbyterian Church in the USA and the author of this article as assistant to Dr. Cockburn.

The Michelfelder mandate, using the WCC as his base and point of reference, was to administer American Lutheran relief funds in Europe and to reestablish relations with the members of the Lutheran World Convention. The prevailing American assumption was that church-sponsored relief efforts would be coordinated through the WCC and would be confined to the rebuilding of churches and church life.

It soon became apparent that such a focus was too narrow. Other needs were enormous. Dr. Michelfelder was asked to assume additional responsibility as director of a Material Aid Division within the Department of Reconstruction and Interchurch Aid. Having obtained the consent of his stateside office, the new director immediately began to solicit and/or purchase supplies of food, clothing and blankets wherever they could be found. Another unanticipated challenge which soon made its presence acutely felt was the plight of Displaced Persons who, it was naively assumed, would quickly return to their homes.

It should be noted in connection with the Michelfelder mandate that some circles with the Lutheran "world" felt that if a permanent international headquarters were to be established it should be closer to the center of Europe's Lutheran population. Copenhagen, for example. The matter was subject to some discussion but the obvious advantages of Geneva carried the day.

Not only did John Calvin's old city now contain the office of the new WCC--albeit still "in the process of formation"--but it was the home of the

World's YMCA, the World's YWCA and the World Student Christian Federation. It was also a major hub for a number of important secular organizations, including the International Red Cross and the quondam League of Nations where the International Refugee Organization was opening its United Nations Relief and Rehabilitation Agency (UNRRA).

The Lutheran Urgency

There is an old saw to the effect that every case is unique. Lutherans keenly felt that their church had been hit harder by the war than any other Protestant denomination and that their predicament called for special consideration. At the same time the enormous job to be done required that available resources be dispensed with maximum equity and economy. The churches associated in the National Lutheran Council saw the wisdom of ecumenical cooperation but at the same time kept hoping to bring the strong Lutheran Church-Missouri Synod along. The LC-MS for its part was willing to participate with Lutheran World Relief (an American agency) but was as always wary of any association with even the members of the Lutheran World Convention and of its successor organization, the Lutheran World Federation-- a situation that still pertains.

American and Swedish Lutherans were, in fact, the only ones in a position to be of much help in the postwar situation. The predominantly Lutheran countries of Denmark and Norway had been overrun and occupied by the German army. Finland had suffered grievously at Russia's hands in two small wars. There was not only a great deal of sympathy for these countries in the U.S. (as elsewhere) but a determination on the part of American Lutherans that a substantial portion of the first $10,000,000 raised for postwar purposes should be earmarked for these three nations; in fact, $1,000,000 each, a sum that seemed larger than it does today! Estonia and

Latvia, also largely Lutheran, had been annexed by the USSR and were out of reach; only their refugees could be helped.

Statistically speaking, the Germans of course constituted the major national grouping in the Lutheran world family. Many were in the fourteen distinctively Lutheran provincial churches and today belong the the LWF. Many more were in Union churches, that is, Lutheran-Reformed. Both groups fall under the general heading "Evangelisch," which was the term that Martin Luther preferred. It is usually used along with Lutheran in church titles. Hitler vainly tried to set a Reichsbishop, Ludwig Mueller, over a merged <u>Deutsche Evangelische Kirche</u> after 1933. At war's end the church leaders adopted the name <u>Evangelische Kirche in Deutschland</u> (EKID). Although a federation rather than a church, it was admitted after some discussion into the membership of the WCC.

Condemnation of the Nazi government was universal but attitudes towards the Christians of Germany with respect to their behavior under the Nazis was decidedly varied. The Stuttgart "declaration of guilt" by the EKID leadership in October 1945 did much to alleviate criticism. In any event, a strong tide of sympathy for the prostrate people soon set in, far sooner than was the case following World War I. Here too was evidence of the new ecumenical spirit, a deeper Christian fellowship. It was greatly encouraged by the German determination to help themselves. An <u>Evangelisches Hilfswerk</u> sprang into action under the energetic leadership of Dr. Eugen Gerstenmaier which, by being interdenominational, won the confidence of the whole spectrum of denominational donors.

Additional strain was put upon all available resources when hundreds of thousands of ethnic Germans (<u>Volksdeutsche</u>), including a very large percentage of Lutherans, began flooding in from the USSR, Poland, and other other areas of Eastern Europe. Technically they were not DPs;

UNRRA could provide neither relief nor resettlement assistance for them. It was a German job. The WCC Service to Refugees, being heavily dependent upon UNRRA financial support, was also unable to be of much help, especially in the matter of resettlement. LWF Service to Refugees policy, however, was based on treating Volksdeutsche refugees on the same level as DPs.

The most tragic result of the Second World War and its aftermath, humanly speaking, was the permanent dislocation of millions of victims. It is here that the Lutheran populations--within the new ecumenical fellowship-- suffered the most. It is estimated by those in the best position to appraise the situation that one Lutheran in ten had become a refugee or was rendered homeless. This included not only the 10-12 million Germans, whether of German nationality or Volksdeutsche, but people of many other nationalities from Finland to Yugoslavia.

The case of Poland is particularly poignant and, for purposes of this article, may be cited as a prime example of the fate which had befallen so much of the Lutheran "world." The major displacement of that nation's boundaries was of course the main cause of the violent disruption of all life in Poland. Approximately one-third of the pre-war area was severed and annexed by the USSR, involving the resettlement westward of most of the Polish population. In compensation, Poland "regained" a great section of Germany up to the Oder-Neisse Line as well as Danzig (Gdansk) and some of East Prussia. This involved evacuating practically the whole German population. In the process the Lutheran church of Poland lost more than half of its prewar constituency.

Here again some background material is in order. Back in the 16th century the Lutheran Reformation had captured almost all of Poland but the ensuing Counter-Reformation recaptured most of it. Nevertheless, the

Evangelical Augsburg Church remained historically rooted in the western and northern areas of the country as well as in the major cities. This was a Polish-speaking church. Then, during the 19th century, large numbers of German immigrants moved eastward and became German-speaking Poles. In the years before World War II the Lutheran population numbered some 500,000 souls. But by 1947, thanks to Hitler's machinations, these numbers had been cut in half.

Before the war there had been 210 ordained pastors, but only 125, when polled, affirmed an allegiance to the Polish language and a Polish church. Of these 125 pastors, 57 were arrested and the head of the church, Bishop Bursche, perished there in 1942. After the war the badly crippled church tried its best under the leadership of Prof. Szeruda to minister to the widely-scattered remnants in a badly battered country.

The effort encountered other obstacles. First, it now had to cope with a government which officially had little or no use for religion. Secondly, it had to contend with the tendency of most Poles to equate "Lutheran" with German," reinforcing the idea that to be a real Pole one had to be Catholic. Thirdly, other churches were ready to commandeer Lutheran property as soon as or even before the "Germans" moved out and there was little or nothing that the military or civil authorities would do about it. By 1948, according to official statistics, the Roman Catholic church had taken possession of 2,895 out of 3,020 evangelical churches in the western and northern parts of the country.

In June 1946--one year after the end of the war--I visited Poland and was able to spend three days in Wroclaw (formerly Breslau) with Prof. Niemczik, who had been sent there 13 months earlier for two purposes: to gather and minister to the autochthonous Poles who had been partially "Germanized" and also to serve as a link between the Polish military authorities and what was left of the Evangelical Lutheran Church of Silesia. The Germans were moving out by the trainload every day, including pastors and deaconesses who of necessity had to abandon not only their churches but their hospitals and charitable institutions. Within another year the German city of Breslau, once studded with large flourishing Lutheran congregations, had become Wroclaw, an almost wholly Polish Catholic city.

EPILOGUE

As already intimated, the Lutheran Church of Poland is offered here as only one graphic illustration of the devastation wrought by the Second World War. Within a few years, nevertheless, these Lutherans succeeded in gathering pastors including the remnants of the former German nationals who stayed on in Silesia. The church would continue to be a link in the fellowship of both the WCC and the LWF.

It would be gratifying to think that an end has therewith been put to the uprooting of Lutheran peoples and churches, but it hasn't. It is happening even today, not only in far-off Namibia as a result of more recent conflicts but in Europe, where the aftershocks of World War II are still being felt. Thousands of ethnic Hungarians--Lutheran and Reformed--are being driven from their homes in Rumania and tens of thousands of Volksdeutsche who had been resettled in Siberia nearly 50 years ago are streaming out of the USSR into the Federal Republic of Germany.

If the 19th was the century of emigration, the 20th has been the century of deportation. The world at war, the ecumenical world and the Lutheran world continue to impinge upon each other. The goal of Christian unity still beckons.

The Russian Orthodox and Worship at 'Amsterdam 1939'

Francis House

'At Amsterdam the services of worship dominated the conference to an extent which even the leadership had hardly expected. They were at once the focus of the profound disagreements which have torn the Church of Christ in so many pieces, and the place above all others where the conference found its unity...No attempt was made to produce some colourless form of devotion which none could acknowledge and to which none could take exception...It was the definite purpose of this programme, not only to show the variety of Christian worship, but to place the Church's worship at the very heart of a Christian conference.'[1]

In those forthright terms Denzil Patrick, the chronicler of the conference, described the distinguishing feature of its programme--the centrality of confessional worship. No previous major ecumenical conference had followed this pattern. The services had usually been ad hoc compilations of various liturgical elements. But for the next generation all

---

1. Christus Victor, The Report of the World Conference of Christian Youth, edited by Denzil G.M. Patrick. Geneva 1939. p.9.

major ecumenical assemblies adopted the "Amsterdam" model, and even later the place given to worship at the W.C.C. assemblies at Nairobi and Vancouver owed much to the precedent set at the First World Conference of Christian Youth.

The decision to make what was considered at the time to be a revolutionary measure owed everything, under God, to the experience, convictions and advocacy of a small group of Russian Orthodox refugees in Paris. (This was the first of two Russian contributions to the development of the ecumenical movement before the Moscow Patriarchate was able to join the World Council. The second was the draft for the reformulation of the Basis of the Council which was made in Moscow in 1959 and adopted in New Delhi in 1961).

How did it come about that representatives of Russian Orthodoxy were able to lead the Christian Youth movements along this new and fruitful line in 1939? The story begins much earlier with Dr. John R. Mott's visit to St. Petersburg in 1899. There he spoke with Baron Nicolai, the founder of the Russian Student Christian Movement, about the possibility of associating his pioneer groups with the World's Student Christian Federation. Baron Nicolai was himself a Lutheran but he had gradually been led to welcome Orthodox students into membership and to win the confidence of individual Orthodox priests. As a result of his trans-confessional experience he had become an advocate of inter-confessional relationships which transcended his own Protestant pietistic upbringing.

At the meeting of the General Committee of the W.S.C.F. on the Turkish island of Prinkipo in 1911, Dr. Mott and Baron Nicolai persuaded the leadership to make membership of the Federation effectively inclusive not only of Protestants but also of Orthodox and Catholics. It was agreed that 'no student, to whatever branch of the Christian Church he might

belong, should be excluded from membership of any national movement.'
This ruling greatly facilitated relationships with Orthodox bishops, especially
in South-Eastern Europe. But it was left to the Russian Orthodox refugees
in Paris after the First World War to work out the consequences for worship
at ecumenical gatherings.[2]

The next step was taken at the meeting of the W.S.C.F. General
Committee at Nyborg Strand in 1926. It came through a commission on the
attitude of the Federation to the 'confessional groups' which had been
recognized in principle at Prinkipo. A leading part in the discussions was
taken by the Russian Orthodox from Paris. They said that Orthodox
students could not find full spiritual satisfaction in groups which were only
'inter-denominational' in a minimal sense. They affirmed that Orthodox
students must be able to come into the life of the student Christian
movements as members of their own Church, and be able to make their full
ecumenical contribution through living the liturgical life of their tradition.

In approving the development of such confessional groups the
Federation warned that the aim was 'to encourage ecumenism and not to
foster an exclusive confessionalism', for they believed that by this means 'the
spiritual riches of a particular confession could be brought into the common
life' more effectively than by individual membership.[3]

In 1923 the Russian S.C.M. had been refounded in exile, and one
happy consequence of the Nyborg meeting was the development of a
deepening friendship with the British S.C.M. Nicolas Zernov, then a student
at the Russian Orthodox Academy of St. Sergius in Paris, and Miss Amy

---

2. The World's Student Christian Federation. Ruth Rouse. SCM Press 1948. p.
163.

3. Tissington Tatlow. The Story of the Student Christian Movement. SCM Press
1933. pp. 419-20.

Buller and Miss Zoe Fairfield of the general secretariat of the British movement were encouraged to plan a first Anglo-Orthodox student conference at St. Alban's, England, in January 1927. The leaders were Fr. Sergius Boulgakov, Professor (later Bishop) Cassian Besobrasov, and Bishop Charles Gore, the doyen of the Anglo-Catholic movement in the Church of England. A dozen Russian students came from Paris and twenty-five British students from Oxford and Cambridge and three theological colleges. The absolutely vital decision was taken that each day would begin with the celebration either of the Russian Liturgy or of the Anglican Eucharist, and that <u>all members of the conference should be invited to attend both services</u>. The operation of the novel plan was facilitated by the fact that both the Orthodox and the Anglo-Catholic students were accustomed to the idea of 'non-communicating attendance' at High Mass or the Liturgy. Most of them knew little or nothing of the other tradition before they met, but many testified afterwards that they had experienced a close spiritual fellowship. Canon Tissington Tatlow, the general secretary of the British S.C.M., wrote that they 'entered into as deep, simple and moving a fellowship with one another in their Lord as he had ever known'. And Sonia Zernov, Nicolas's distinguished sister, spoke for other Orthodox participants when she wrote: 'It seemed that the light of Christ's truth shone on our path. We, all of us-- Children of God--were building up a way to our common Father, laying a common track, laying it down in love, in quiet, in prayer.'[4]

Each following year a similar student conference was held and accompanied by a conference of more senior people who were members of the Fellowship of St. Alban and St. Sergius (founded in 1928). Alternate daily celebrations of the Liturgy or Eucharist continued to be at the heart of

---

4. <u>Op. cit.</u> pp. 778-84.

both meetings.   Before long the significance of these developments was recognized by the presence both of Metropolitan Eulogie from Paris and of the Archbishop of Canterbury (Dr. Lang).   During the nineteen-thirties the membership came to include Anglicans who were not Anglo-Catholics, English Free Churchmen and Scottish Presbyterians (who later founded their own Fellowship of St. Andrew and St. Sergius).   Dr. Zernov himself eventually became a member of the staff appointed jointly by the British S.C.M., the W.S.C.F. and the Fellowship.   Thus he was better able to influence the ecumenical policy of the Federation in the period leading up to the Amsterdam conference.

Other small experimental inter-confessional conferences were organised by the French and Russian S.C.M.s in which Protestant, Orthodox and Roman Catholic students took part.   (In principle the latter required special permission from their local church authorities).   At these conferences the Catholic Mass, the Orthodox Liturgy and Reformed Church services with Communion were celebrated.   All present were invited to attend all three services, but they communicated only at services of their own Churches.   The conferences were described as 'having a liturgical basis.'   This did not mean that they only considered liturgical issues but that they shared as far as was permitted in one another's eucharistic worship.

Professor Leo Zander, one of the leaders of the Russian S.C.M., wrote that

> 'the very essence of the ecumenical work is to show to other Churches the image of Christ imprinted in our Church.   The whole richness of doctrine, the whole beauty of ritual, the whole depth of the people's piety, must be revealed to our non-Orthodox brothers and expressed in language which would enable them to penetrate into the treasure-house of Orthodoxy.

This can best be done by actual participation in the Holy Liturgy.'[5]

As the result of such experiences the Federation made significant changes in the pattern of worship for its General Committee in 1938 and the European Theological Students' Conference in January 1939. At a Saturday night service of preparation for communion, representatives of the Churches announced the services, a devotional address was given by a minister of the Reformed Church and traditional prayers of penitence were led by an Anglican priest. Early on the Sunday morning all attended the Communion service in the local Reformed Church where it was announced that 'members of any branch of the Church of Christ would be welcomed at the Table of the Lord.' And most of the Monday morning was reserved for the Orthodox Liturgy, which nearly all attended though only one or two of the Orthodox were communicated.[6]

So the way was prepared for the consideration of the pattern of worship in the programme of the First World Conference of Christian Youth which was being planned by the international Christian youth organisations at Geneva. The crucial discussion took place at an enlarged committee meeting at Bievres in July 1938. The sub-committee on worship, in which Russian Orthodox representatives took an active part, reported that they had 'come slowly to a very strong conviction that opportunity must be provided

---

5. Leo Zander. The Essence of the Ecumenical Movement. WSCF Geneva 1938. p.13.

6. See Venite Adoremus, the prayer-book of the WSCF Geneva. Vol. I 1936. Vol. II 1938.

for all members of the conference to share in the fullest expression of the worshipping life of the main Christian tradition.'[7]

In the debate on this report two main questions were raised: Was it right to encourage attendance at confessional services at an 'ecumenical' meeting? and Was a conference of young people the right place to make so great a venture? Some said that the plan might have educational value but would hinder common worship. Others said that attendance at three services of Holy Communion, at none of which all could receive together, would over-emphasize the disunity of the Church. Some Barthian theologians said that 'acts of spiritual communion' could easily become a substitute for actual reception; that they were an expression of human and sentimental rather than spiritual fellowship, and that to invite young people to attend services of which the doctrinal implications were condemned by their own Churches, was to encourage 'disloyalty' and 'betray true ecumenism.'

On the other hand the Orthodox contended strongly that their Church tradition could only be understood through its liturgy, and they added that they had only come to recognise that Protestants were truly their Christian brothers and sisters when they saw them taking part in the communion services of their Churches. Other participants in the debate told of experiences at smaller conferences at which they had been able to share in confessional services. Others said that they had found that what were described as 'simple undenominational services' did not really unite in worship those who came from different liturgical traditions. Speakers from China, Egypt and Switzerland believed that a youth conference was the right

---

7. The author was secretary of this sub-committee and of the committee on worship at the conference.

place for the adventure to be made. And the objections of the Barthians were answered by the argument that careful explanation and spiritual preparation could meet most of the suggested dangers.[8] (In the event every member of the conference received a pamphlet explaining each of the services, and translations of the liturgical texts were prepared in all three of the conference languages).

So the decision was taken to go ahead. In the end the pattern of services of Holy Communion in the programme became more complex than had been anticipated, but it was still based firmly on the principle of confessional representation. The actual programme[9] came out as follows:--

1.   Saturday evening.   Service of Preparation for communion, conducted by the Rev. Robert Mackie of the Church of Scotland and Dr. Benjamin Mays, the distinguished Black American Baptist from Atlanta U.S.A. The service included psalms and anthems sung by the Orthodox choir, official announcements by the participating Churches, the recommendation that every member of the conference should attend at least one service other than that at which he or she would be able to receive communion, a sermon on the resurrection appearance of Jesus on the road to Emmaus (Luke 24, 28-33), a litany of penitence, silence, and an extempore prayer for unity led by Dean Mays which ended with the heartfelt cry 'Forgive us God.'

---

8. See Francis House in the Student World volume xxxii 1939 pp. 169-179 and in Christus Victor pp. 18-19.

9. Christus Victor pp. 18-34.

2.   The central service on Sunday morning was the celebration of the Lord's Supper according to the tradition of the Dutch Reformed Church. Eleven hundred of the sixteen hundred participants in the conference sat down by a hundred at a time to communicate at the table of the Lord, and five hundred others attended.

3.   Earlier that morning one hundred and eighty conference members communicated and another hundred attended a service of Holy Communion according to the Anglican Book of Common Prayer.

4.   On the Sunday evening two hundred Lutherans and about four hundred others took part in a traditional Lutheran High Mass. (Some non-Lutherans were particularly impressed by the practice of giving absolution individually to intending communicants at the altar rail).

5.   On the Monday morning the Holy Liturgy of the Eastern Orthodox Churches was celebrated in the main conference hall transformed as far as possible into the appearance of an Orthodox cathedral.   The celebrant was Archimandrite Cassian Besobrasov from Paris assisted by Bulgarian and Serbian clergy. (Metaxas, the Greek dictator, had prevented a Greek delegation from attending).   The Russian choir from Paris, led by M. Dennisov of the Opera, sang the anthems and responses.   A small number of the Orthodox communicated.   A number of problems concerning jurisdictions were disregarded.   Nearly all the members of the conference attended.   One Protestant expressed the experience of many: 'The atmosphere of mystic, timeless devotion and adoration gave an insight, otherwise unachievable, into the very soul of the Orthodox Church.'

So deep was the impression made by this pattern of worship that a similar plan was adopted for the Second World Conference of Christian Youth (Oslo 1947), at the Assemblies of the World Council of Churches at Amsterdam 1948, Evanston 1955, New Delhi 1961 and Uppsala 1968, and at other ecumenical meetings. Numerous participants testified to the depth of their own experience of worship in services of other traditions, and to the strengthening of their commitment to seeking the removal of continuing obstacles to the manifestation of the unity of all in Christ.

Thus over the last fifty years Christians of many traditions, Reformed, Lutheran, Methodist, Baptist, Orthodox, Roman Catholic and Anglican, have been spiritually enriched through an initiative by members of the Russian Orthodox Church in exile, and the whole modern ecumenical movement has been enabled to reach deeper levels of common worship through a fuller appreciation of the liturgical riches of other Christian traditions. I believe that this development should be recognised as a singular gift of the Holy Spirit. Leo Zander often used to quote this Whitsunday anthem from the Orthodox Liturgy:--

'When Thou camest down, O Most High, confounding the tongues,
Thou didst divide the nations one from the other; but when
Thou didst bestow the tongues of fire, Thou didst call all
men to unity; and with one accord we glorify the all-Holy
                                        Spirit.'

Ecumenical Missiology Since Amsterdam
1939-1989
Thomas J. Liggett and Virginia Liggett

Introduction

The modern missionary movement, having begun at the end of the 18th century, was already 150 years old when the World Conference of Christian Youth was held in Amsterdam in 1939. As the movement grew in the 19th century, there emerged both practical and theoretical issues which led its leaders to early forms of ecumenical dialogue and cooperation. Regional consultations proved fruitful and led to the holding of world conferences on Mission in New York (1900), Edinburgh (1910), Jerusalem (1928), and Tambaram, outside of Madras (1938). Historians have long recognized the importance of these mission conferences in the rise of twentieth century ecumenism. The developments in ecumenical missiology since Amsterdam have their roots in this long history of Christians who sought unity in the fulfillment of mission. In this article, we identify five dimensions of ecumenical missiology which have had transcendental importance for our understanding of mission in the last half-century, some of which were already visible on the horizon at Amsterdam.

I. The Disappearance of "Christendom"

The modern missionary movement seems to have affirmed without question a division of the world between "Christendom" and "non-Christendom." Mission was understood as transporting the Gospel from the one to the other. Persons and resources were sought within "Christendom" to make possible a Christian witness in the non-Christian world. Terminology, maps, methodology, organizations and institutions all reflect this view of the world. There is no question but that Western colonial and imperial political views were unconsciously absorbed into this understanding of mission.

Prior to the Amsterdam conference, there were a series of crises in the so-called Christian world which clearly challenged the presuppositions about the existence of "Christendom". In Germany, the cradle of the Reformation, National Socialism, with its anti-Jewish component all too prominent, seemed to replace Christian values. In Russia the Marxist revolution had included a repudiation of religion as a part of its ideology. In Italy, the center of Roman Catholicism, Fascism seemed to negate many if not most Christian values. Secularism was everywhere apparent in the West and the economy was in deep crisis in the 1930's. But until the Western crisis reached its peak in World War II, Christians seemed to be prisoners of the assumptions of "Christendom".

The Amsterdam Conference exposed its participants to the magnitude of the crisis in the West and launched a new generation of youth leaders, who would raise fundamental questions about the assumptions of earlier leaders. In ecumenical missiology, this reassessment seems to have reached a new level at the Willigen Conference of 1952. Here, ecumenically oriented missionary leaders affirmed that "no nation can call itself Christian any more, there are Christians in every nation, the whole world is a 'mission field,' every church is a mission church and every Christian is a missionary." The result of this sweeping affirmation was to call for a re-thinking of mission policies and strategies. The process resulted not only in significant changes in operational style by mission agencies and the emergence of new insights about "mission on six continents," but provoked serious soul-searching among Christians in earlier "Christendom" about the relationship of faith to culture and the need to reassess the ways in which the "Christ transforming culture" had to replace the "Christ of culture."

The disappearance of "Christendom" created a new context and new partners for dialogue. Whereas earlier, Christians in "Christendom" could indulge in polemics in which heated debates could take place about relatively minor differences between Christians--now a secular and often hostile environment called for a rediscovery of apologetics in which believers had to respond to the challenges to the very basic assumptions of Christian faith.

Without the reassuring context of a presumed Christian culture, Christians now were forced to engage in a serious reflection together about the mission which God has given to the Church--ecumenism and mission are now more deeply interwoven than was true in Amsterdam in 1939.

II. The Missionary Character of the Whole Church

The modern missionary movement arose as an adjunct to the Church--not as a central reality of church life. Rooted in a pietistic faith, its leaders often had to cope with a church establishment which was at times indifferent and at other times hostile. Missionary societies frequently emerged as semi-independent agencies, supported by individuals who were committed to its goals. Participants in the early mission consultations and conferences tended to be leaders of mission agencies. The agendas dealt with pressing issues facing the mission movement. It became evident as early in Edinburgh in 1910 that issues were arising which dealt with basic elements of Christian faith and order--but when these issues became the central topic of a world conference, it was not as a part of the missionary movement, but rather as the incipient "faith and order" movement. Pressing societal issues seemed to call for yet another type of conference (Life and Work). When, at the close of World War II, the World Council of Churches came into being, it embraced Faith and Order, and Life and Work--but "mission" remained a specialized topic of reflection with its own arena for discussion and its own institutions.

But the 1950's saw a significant development both within the denominations and in the broader ecumenical environment. Increasingly it was realized that the "raison d'etre" of the church was to play a crucial role in God's mission for the whole world. Churches began to define their own existence in terms of their understanding of mission--mission agencies realized that their relative isolation from the official church structures was a weakness which needed correction. Dialogue continued and what had been a lamentable separation in modern history began to be overcome. In 1961, the International Missionary Council became a part of the World Council of Churches. This decision was more than a mere organizational realignment-- it reflected fundamental changes in thinking both within ecclesiastical leadership circles and missionary strategists.

One creative dimension of the bringing together of "church" and "mission" was the study of the "missionary structure of the local congregation" which was launched by the World Council of Churches following the New

Delhi Assembly in 1961. Following a decade when the rapid social changes in the modern world were analyzed and evaluated, leadership turned to an examination of church structures in light of these rapidly changing environments. Traditional patterns of parish life were called into question and structures were tested, not by their fidelity to historic patterns, but by the degree to which they facilitated the mission of the church. The closing years of the 20th century witnessed sustained efforts to overcome the earlier separation of "mission" from the central life of the Church.

III. Proclamation Expanded to Dialogue

The modern missionary movement generally assumed that truth was to be found exclusively in the Gospel. Other religious traditions were viewed as erroneous, humanistic, or at times demonic. The stance of Christians vis-a-vis these religions was a one-way communication-proclamation. On occasion imaginative and valiant exponents of the Gospel did look with tolerance and qualified acceptance at the values in other traditions. But these efforts did not enjoy the endorsement of official policy and usually did not endure.

This posture of equating mission with "proclamation" was reinforced by the rise of neo-orthodoxy, especially in the European tradition. The implications of this rising theological current were most clearly seen in the work of Hendrik Kraemer. As a preparatory volume for the 1938 Tambaram conference, Kraemer wrote THE CHRISTIAN MESSAGE TO THE NON-CHRISTIAN WORLD. There is no clearer statement of mission as proclamation than Kraemer's. Mission involves speaking--it does not require listening. The Amsterdam Youth Conference was held the following year--there was little if any place in its program for the voice of non-Christian religious insights.

While neo-orthodoxy flourished in Europe and North America, its influence among leadership in the "younger churches" was considerably less pervasive. Especially in Asia, Christians lived in daily contact with the great religious heritages of Islam, Buddhism and Hinduism. What seemed to be an entirely warranted posture to Western Churchmen, often seemed to be Western arrogance to Asians. The struggles of young nations to find their place in the family of nations often found Christians and non-Christians sharing common positions and discovering new ways of mutual understanding. Societal crises in what was coming to be called the "Third World" frequently resulted in effective joint efforts by Christians and non-Christians. It was probably a dialogue dictated by circumstances which opened the eyes of Church leaders to some new and wider possibilities than what was envisioned by the one-way proclamation posture.

In recent years, the world ecumenical movement has discovered the excitement and challenge of a dialogical relationship with persons "of other living faiths." The WCC program of formalized dialogue, especially with Marxists, Buddhists, Muslims and Hindus, has resulted in a fertile, disturbing and renovating climate in missiological thinking. The writings of many of the early Fathers have been re-discovered. The New Testament itself was found to provide creative stimulus for restating the Gospel in ways which more adequately expressed the dimensions of universality not only to God's love, but also to God's truth. The risks inherent in an open and honest dialogue have been acknowledged. Such dialogue does not impede a vigorous exposition of one's Christian faith. But it does mean that in the last half-century, proclamation is no longer viewed as a monologue, but rather as a responsible witness to the Gospel within the context of authentic dialogue.

IV. Salvation in Broader Dimensions

In keeping with the orientation of pietism, the initial impulse of the modern missionary movement was the offer of salvation to women and men whose souls were in danger of being "lost". Evangelism, in a traditional sense, was the authentic expression of mission. But Christian agape has never allowed the proclaimers of the Gospel to be indifferent to human suffering. It is interesting to note the efforts which were made to "justify" service projects as valid expressions of mission. But the justifications "won the day" and in the late 19th and early 20th centuries, Christian missionary work normally involved educational, medical and agricultural programs, as well as the original concern for evangelism. There was vigorous debate whether these "service" programs were valid in and of themselves, or only if they contributed to the unchallenged program of evangelism.

In the 50 years since the Amsterdam Conference, "service" (diakonia) has been elevated and affirmed as one of the "marks" of the Church. Initially understood in its most direct and obvious sense, service was understood as an immediate response to human need--it meant feeding the hungry, caring for the sick, alleviating the suffering of the poor and the oppressed. With the passing of the years, "service" has taken on new and broader meanings. Feeding the hungry meant not only distributing food to hungry people, but addressing the root causes of hunger. Curative medicine was followed by preventive medicine and long-term programs of hygiene, nutrition and public health education. With these expanded services, it was not easy to distinguish between enlightened governmental programs and broad-based, long-term programs of Christian service. When it became apparent that the basic problems of human welfare actually resulted from deplorable social structures and oppressive political regimes, Christians began to see "diakonia" as the category in which social action, sometimes radical, was taken.

Following World War II, the ecumenical movement was vigorously involved in the agendas of "faith and order" and "mission". But the "life and work" concern which was one of the fore-runners of the WCC did not receive comparable attention. It was in 1966 that the Geneva Conference on Church and Society restored the agenda of "life and work" to the center of the ecumenical movement. Prominent in the leadership of that conference were distinguished leaders from the "younger churches" who first distinguished themselves in the deliberations of the "missionary conferences." With no vacillation in their commitment to "mission", these leaders warmly embraced the concerns of the Geneva Conference.

In 1973, the Bangkok Conference on World Mission, organized by the Commission on World Mission and Evangelism (continuing the work of the International Missionary Council), dramatically portrayed the ways in which mission, evangelism, salvation and witness had become broader and deeper in the course of the century. Under the theme "Salvation Today", the conference clearly marked new dimensions to the Christian understanding of the Gospel and the salvation which God offers. Unity, mission, evangelism, social action, service and church leadership came together in a creative way. Life and Work and Mission were welded together as never before. Fifty years after the Amsterdam Youth Conference, there was emerging a holistic understanding of the nature of the Church, the scope of the Church's mission and the breadth and depth of the salvation which God offers the world in Jesus Christ.

V.   Theological Education for "Such A Time As This"

The expansion of Christianity around the world in the 19th century was achieved primarily through the work of Western missionaries. As new communities of faith emerged, the need for "national" leadership was acknowledged. Bible training schools and institutes came into being. While there were many locally unique characteristics, they tended to follow a common pattern. The teachers were Western missionaries, the courses of study were patterned on Western seminaries, the libraries were limited and overly stocked with Western-language books. The students were seen as future pastors, evangelists and church leaders. The fact that there were occasional exceptions to this pattern does not invalidate this generalization. Prior to World War II, (and the Amsterdam Youth Conference of 1939), the exceptions were few indeed. In fact, the leadership patterns in the churches were not radically different from those of colonial administrations. After World War II, most of the former colonies became autonomous nation-states. New leadership emerged. The dawn of the new day had come suddenly (as history usually goes) and neither political nor missionary policy had prepared adequately for it. In the 1950's it became clear that a new initiative would be required if the churches of the Third World were to have the quality of leadership which they now clearly needed. The strategic locus of the initiative was clearly the theological seminary. In 1957 at the Ghana meeting of the International Missionary Council, the Theological Education Fund was created. Its initial program was designed to up-grade the libraries of strategic seminaries in the Third World, to publish a substantial number of theological "tools" in the twenty primary teaching languages of the seminaries and to enable promising young scholars to pursue graduate study in preparation for assuming leadership in theological education in Asia, Africa and Latin America.   Few ecumenical initiatives have seemed more providential than the T.E.F. Originally designed to be a short-term, emergency program of five years, it was given new mandates for a second and third period of service and in 1976 was incorporated as a permanent program unit of the World Council of Churches with the title Programme of Theological Education (PTE). The thrust of the TEF-PTE programs has been ecumenical in character, with a strong emphasis on high scholarly endeavor. Now, thirty years after its creation, this program can point to dramatic changes not only in theological seminaries, but also in the quality of church leadership which has emerged from this program. The best of Western scholarship has been made available in non-Western languages, new scholars have emerged who have made major contributions to the theological enterprise, thousands of pastors have entered their ministries with vastly improved preparation, the scholarly production from the Third World has invigorated theological dialogue everywhere and significant progress has been made in forging an arena which is world-wide in scope in which the pressing new challenges to Christian faith and morality can be better understood.

Of the many facets of this development, one is selected for emphasis. It is generally acknowledged that faithful Christian witness involves both universality and local relevance. Historically, Protestant Christianity chose to contextualize the Gospel even at the expense of the unity of the Church. Roman Catholicism held to a universal commitment (based on Latin culture) and found difficulty in being "at home" in the many cultures of the world. In our century, a fragmented Protestantism has sought unity through the ecumenical movement. Roman Catholics have authorized a degree of accommodation to individual cultures through such steps as the vernacular mass. In both traditions, the best minds are at work to discover the most creative ways to affirm both a contextualized church and a universal faith. In Asia and Africa the drive to free Christianity from its identification with

European thought forms and contextualize the Gospel in these traditionally non-Christian cultures is crucial. This enormous task requires the finest of minds and the most effective theological tools. The TEF-PTE came into the ecumenical movement at a providential time and has made an enduring contribution to the preparation of theologically equipped leaders for "such a time as this."

Summary

The ecumenical movement involves a search for unity and for effective fulfillment of mission. In the past 50 years, the demise of "Christendom," the rediscovery of the missionary nature of the church, the broadening and deepening of our understanding of salvation, the practice of proclamation in a dialogical context and the emergence of qualified leadership on a world-wide scale--all are dimensions of 20th century missiology which give promise of a more effective witness to the Gospel.

Fifty Years of Ecumenism in Latin America
Luis E. Odell

In order to understand the way in which the work on behalf of Christian unity developed in Latin America in the fifty years following the Amsterdam Conference of 1939, we must go back seventy-five years earlier, to the well-remembered missionary conference of Edinburgh 1910. It is a well known fact that in the planning of this conference, the Latin American continent was left aside, as it was not considered, strictly speaking, a missionary field, due to the fact that Roman Catholicism was so strongly rooted in the region.

However, it is significant to meditate on the fact that such a negative decision, from a human point of view, turned, by the grace of God and, in His hands, into a positive event. A group of participants, the majority from the USA, who were convinced what the challenge of the evangelization of the Latin American countries meant, decided to constitute themselves into an un-official committee that would study the situation, needs, and possibilities of spreading the Gospel in this part of the world.

As a result of the work of this group, a meeting was held in New York in 1913 with the purpose of preparing a Pan-American Congress, where the Latin American situation and a future strategy might be studied and planned. The different boards of missions that were already working in this field definitely supported this initiative. So the meeting took place in Panama, under the title of Pan-American Congress, in the month of February 1916.

Actually, the Congress was practically a meeting of delegates representing the boards of missions, since in a total of 230 members, only ten percent were Latin Americans. The Assembly served as a means to give to all those participating, as well as to the churches of the Western world in general, a clear vision of the possibilities for Protestant work in this large field. The development that has been reached since then shows that the vision was not exaggerated.

One specific outcome of the meeting was the decision taken to give a permanent status to the committee that had organized the Congress, naming it the Committee on Cooperation in Latin America (CCLA). Therefore, it can be said that this was the true beginning of the ecumenical movement on the Latin American continent.

In a short time, the CCLA obtained the formal support of some forty boards of missions which were already engaged in the task of spreading the kingdom of God on the continent. The organization of this committee has meant an exceptional chapter in the promotion of the Protestant work in general, and of the Christian cooperation on the continent in particular, and for this we will always be grateful.

In closing this introduction, it must be said that, after the beginning we have just described, the Protestant churches on the continent showed a growing and irresistible vocation towards unity. A superficial analysis of the situation might lead to doubt of this affirmation. However, having observed the many international meetings that have taken place during all these years, it is possible to detect with certainty the fact that whenever the Church of Christ has had a chance to come together, that vocation has been fully manifested, affirming the fundamental unity of the Christians and their imperative need to testify and bear witness to the message, in the words of our Lord Jesus Christ, according to John 17:21.

That vocation for unity has covered a long road which, though in a slow manner, has been of constant progress in the interdenominational as well as ecumenical relationships of the continent, as will be seen in the following description of the different periods of development.

Five stages can be pointed out with precision, which in our judgment are the following:

1. The pioneer stage, from 1916 to 1928;

2. The stage from 1929 to 1940, in which the Latin American conscience emerged, followed by the establishment of movements of interdenominational cooperation at the national level;

3. The development of initiatives and practical cooperation at the continental level from 1941 to 1965;

4. The ten years from 1965 to 1975 is the period in which the ecumenical movement defines itself more clearly and expands with the creation of UNELAM--The Commission for the Evangelical Latin American Unity.

5. The following stage gave rise to the present period, in which the ecumenical movement has given an important step forward, starting

with the Conference of Oaxtepec in 1976. At this meeting, called by UNELAM, it was decided to confer a stronger basis to the movement by creating a new body, officially integrated by the churches themselves, which was named "Latin American Council of Churches"-- CLAI.

From now on we will try to describe the main characteristics manifested at each stage:

I.   The Pioneer Stage

Here the main characteristic was the fact that the initiative was in foreign hands. Impressed by the Congress of Panama, and in answer to the challenge received there, the Committee on Cooperation in Latin America decided to call another two regional meetings, one to cover South America and the other for Central America and the Caribbean area. The first one, entitled "Congress of Christian Work," took place in Montevideo, Uruguay, in 1925, and revealed a great progress with regard to the participation of Latin American delegates. It is to be noted that, of the twelve previous reports on which the Congress based its work, only two dealt with specific problems of the mission boards. The offical language was Spanish, and the chairman, Mr. Erasmo Braga, was an eminent Christian leader of the Brazilian Church. Even here the Latin Americans were a minority, but their influence was very strong. At this Congress a serious analysis was made of the existing problems, as well as of the opportunities. Going over the findings it is surprising to appreciate the validity of many of them for our present time. The findings and recommendations were impressive, as can be seen by some of the most important, as follows:

> --creation of several regional offices of the CCLA, which resulted in the formation of an important number of national Christian councils in the following decade;

--the adoption of comity agreements in several countries and regions;
--surveys of unexplored fields for Protestantism, such as Haiti and the Dominican Republic;
--the publication of a magazine intended to reach the intellectuals under the name of "La Nueva Democracia";
--encourage the setting up of interdenominational theological seminaries;
--promotion of training programs for Christian workers, for which the CCLA named a secretary of education;
--the development of a program of Christian literature by means of the publications of books and periodical magazines, as well as the organization of interdenominational evangelical bookstores;
--emphasis on the need to promote the advance of Latin American Protestantism in every field;
--organization of campaigns to obtain funds in order to strengthen the work of institutions of primary, secondary, and professional education, etc.

All this work, as well as the natural growth and development of the churches, caused a remarkable change in the situation. Latin American Protestantism began to gain prestige as well as public recognition. Furthermore, this growth justified the full participation of the continent in the II International Missionary Conference held in Jerusalem in 1928. It can be said that in this way, the cycle started by the Edinburgh 1910 decision was closed. The Latin American Protestant (or Evangelical) Church had thus earned a place in the ecumenical world, and was on its way to coming of age.

II.   The Phase of the Surge of National Awareness

This second stage begins with the celebration of the Latin American Protestant Congress of Havana (Cuba) in June 1929. As a matter of fact, this Congress should, in all justice, belong to stage I, since it was planned by the CCLA at the same time as the one in Montevideo four years earlier. It is interesting to note that, undoubtedly as a consequence of the experience already acquired in Montevideo, the organization of this meeting was almost completely entrusted to the national or "Latin" leaders.   The main responsibility fell on the leaders of the Cuban churches, who also had the collaboration of the brethren of Mexico and Puerto Rico.

The book that contains the history and findings of this Congress is certainly fascinating. It tells about the wide field covered, the qualifications of the participants, and about the sound and mature recommendations adopted.   This meeting marked the beginning of a new era in the development of the Latin American ecumenical conscience, as can be appreciated in the following quotation from the above mentioned book that was entitled "Towards the Religious Renewal in Hispanic America":

> "The certainty that this Congress should be the first experiment in asserting our personality as Latin American churches, was felt in the hearts of the organizers as well as in the observers' and more understanding Christians'...The main object of our effort points out to the need that the Protestant church in Latin America has, of discovering by itself the meaning of its own life, and becoming aware of it in its own environment...In Havana, the key to all methods and approaches will be 'Latinism'."

Aware of Latinism, this new concept of its nature and mission, it is not surprising that this Congress also made some creative contributions. The section of the report that studied the subject "Unity and Cooperation" produced a report that is a really outstanding statement in favor of that vocation of Christian unity that has been mentioned earlier. In fact, all the work of the Congress was carried out in an atmosphere of strong unity in Christ, and in the knowledge and belief that to start working for the "religious renewal" of our countries, accordingly with the core of the agenda, it was essential to keep both, work and proclamation, in a unity of action since everyone was convinced of the assertion that "...both incoherency and divisions have been for Protestantism the great stumbling blocks that have hindered the progress of the kingdom of God, particularly in our countries."

The enthusiasm felt by all moved the Conference to endorse the recommendation that an "Evangelical International Federation" be constituted, with the mandate that all unions, councils and national federations that might be established, as well as the churches in Spain and Portugal, be included in the new ecumenical body. It is evident that this decision was somewhat premature, as is shown by the fact that the idea did not materialize then. However, it was kept alive as an aspiration in the minds and hearts of many, that finally took shape thirty-five years later with the organization of UNELAM, as will be seen later.

During the rest of this period, the most significant event was the setting up of national councils or federations of churches. The evidence that the right time had come for taking this step is shown by the fact that--within this decade--most of the national councils in existence today were established. These are: Brazil, Mexico, Cuba, Chile, Peru, Rio de la Plata region (Argentina, Uruguay and Paraguay), Colombia, Guatemala, Costa Rica, and later Honduras, Nicaragua and Panama. Puerto Rico had been organized much earlier.

The basis was thus set for the beginning of the third stage in which the united efforts at national level would be enhanced.

III. The Stage of Continental Initiatives and Cooperation

At the beginning of this period, the organization of the first truly continental ecumenical movement undoubtedly deserves to be cited as an outstanding achievement of the Protestant youth, who, as a result of the First Latin American Evangelical Youth Congress, held in Lima in 1941, organized

ULAJE, the Latin American Union of Evangelical Youth (which later changed the word "evangelical" for "ecumenical"). A detailed reference to this can be found in the article written for the special number of the Journal of Ecumenical Studies (Volume 16, Number 1--Winter, 1979) commemorative of the 40th anniversary of the First World Conference of Christian Youth, entitled "The Impact of Amsterdam 1939 on Latin America").

As we have mentioned previously, at the beginning of the forties, the basis was established for a decisive action in favor of greater cooperation and unity at national level, and, subsequently, at continental level as well.

With respect to the interdenominational national bodies, it can be said that their structures were strengthened, and their aims more clearly stated. In general, these bodies counted with the vision and support of many ministers as well as lay leaders that had dedicated many years to a task for which they had prayed, worked at, and persevered, many of them since their youth.

So it was that at national level the work went ahead both in our aim of getting the largest number of churches and denominations interested in the scope of Christian unity, as well as in the common approach and scope of methods of work. In this way, all the national bodies accepted, some in a larger scale than others, the challenge of common action in evangelization, Christian education, literature and journalism, radio work, the study of different areas within countries or regions as to their situation and that of the church, leadership training institutes and camps, youth work camps with religious emphasis, work among students, preparation and use of audiovisual materials, united social service, etc.

In many cases these activities were not stable, but depended on special circumstances, such as counting with the needed trained leaders, financial resources, and so on.

Due to limitations of space, we will not make a detailed description of this vast process, but will limit ourselves to mention, as concisely as possible, what was achieved in the main areas, with a particular reference to those that attained a continental scope:

Evangelization. In Latin America, the work in favor of Christian unity has always had an evangelistic connotation, in accordance with the text found in John 17:21. This is the reason why we see that the interest in evangelization prevalent in the national bodies of cooperation is also present in an important dimension at the continental level.

In 1930, the CCLA, aware of the compelling need of an aggressive evangelization for the development and growth of the church, appointed a travelling evangelist. His mission, besides preaching, was to encourage the churches in organizing united campaigns of evangelization, keeping in mind particularly the educated people, as it was considered of strategic importance to reach these groups with the message of the Gospel. This task continued to develop and expand with the participation of other evangelists, as well as through the interest shown by the more conservative churches who organized campaigns under the denomination of "Evangelism in Depth." This activity, as well as the cooperation in the distribution of the Bible-- through the Bible Societies which in many countries have by now reached national autonomy--constitute one of the circumstances that have, in a meaningful way, helped the different denominational groups to know and understand each other better.

Radio evangelism: The CCLA also did pioneer work in this field. A special secretary was assigned for this task, with the commitment of giving counsel and advice to the churches on this subject. The extent of this work has reached a remarkable dimension. The fact that people of some twenty countries can be reached in one language has, undoubtedly, been an advantage of great help in carrying out the work. On the other hand, this modern method of reaching the masses has facilitated an invasion of independent programs, many of them prepared abroad, that do not always constitute the best influence for the good of the task of local churches.

Christian literature: At the beginning of this period, in 1941, the CCLA called the first "Latin American Conference on Christian Literature," which took place in Mexico. An exhaustive study was made of the needs and the existing possibilities in this area. After considering all the elements, the recommendation made and accepted was to organize a permanent secretariat in the CCLA to take advantage of and develop all the programs proposed by the meeting. This secretariat promoted and directed the execution of an intensive and thoughtfully analyzed program, in cooperation with national and regional literature committees established in Mexico, the River Plata area, Brazil, Chile, the Caribbean, etc.

Parallel to this, a group of conservative missions and churches also organized similar committees, and celebrated international consultations in relation to Christian literature, although based mostly on missionary boards and institutions, as well as on individuals, instead of on national councils and churches. Their contribution has been wide and positive in the spreading of the written word as a way of evangelizing.

Christian education: At the very beginning, the work in this aspect relied on the World Association of Sunday Schools, as well as on the CCLA. The efforts were concentrated primarily in the preparation and publication of

Sunday School materials, as well as in the work among youth, organizing camps and seminars. Pioneer work was done in this area also, in using audiovisual methods in education as well as in evangelism.

In 1961, before the II Evangelical Latin American Conference (II CELA) the WSSA called a meeting in Huampani, Peru, to study the way of improving their contribution to the task of Christian education in the continent. As a result of this, the Latin American Commission of Christian Education--CELADEC-- was organized, with delegates representing different national bodies and churches. The contribution made by this group has been important in bringing up to date the methods and objectives of Christian education in a revolutionary context such as Latin America has lived in the last twenty years.

Church and Society: The Protestant youth pioneered the search of an awakening of the churches to their social responsibility. In 1941, for their first Continental Congress, they adopted the motto "With Christ a New World." Twenty years later, in 1961, several former youth leaders, inspired by the "Rapid Social Change Study" that was being developed by the World Council of Churches, organized the movement known as "Church and Society in Latin America" (ISAL). This movement made an important contribution to the churches on the continent, giving them study materials and information that helped them to understand better what was going on, politically speaking, so that the churches might try to influence the strong process of deterioration of liberties which the continent suffered especially in the 60's. This movement, of an ample ecumenical basis, for at a time there were even some Catholics participating, showed the way for the development of a very important task that the Protestants, regardless of their denominational affiliation, have undertaken in defense of human rights, in every country and at all levels.

University Students' Work: At the beginning of this period, that is in 1940, work among university students in Latin America was started. This has been a kind of extension work of the World Student Christian Federation. The task has not been easy, partly due to the incomprehension of the churches of the particular characteristics of this type of work, as well as because of the traditional indifference found among groups of intellectuals and university people concerning religious subjects. This group has continued its work with ups and downs, and plenty of suffering due to the unstable politics which characterize the life of almost all the countries in the continent. Apart from this group, the non-traditional or conservative churches have also worked and continue to do so, in rendering witness to the Lord in this field.

Continental Conferences: It would take up much more space than we have to analyze the important number of conferences that have taken place in these years. Therefore, we will briefly mention the conferences that had the official support of the churches: The First Latin American Protestant Conference, Buenos Aires, Argentina, 1949--I CELA-- From the very beginning of the initiative up to the closing of the Conference, it was the concern and the responsibility of the Latin American churches. That is the reason for accepting to call it the first conference. The two main themes were: "The Latin American Reality and the Presence of the Protestant Churches," and "Message and Mission of Protestantism for Latin America." The conference brought about as a result a "Fundamental Plan of Protestant Action," with priorities and very important goals to be reached in the future work.

Although the conference adopted a complete and interesting resolution on "Interdenominational cooperation," it did not take any action concerning the organization of a permanent body to continue the work. This was the reason for the difficulties that arose, which prevented a second conference to be called, until the middle of the year 1961. This meeting was held in Lima, Peru. Twenty years had gone by from Havana to Buenos Aires; from Buenos Aires to Lima only twelve, but even these were too many.

The II Latin American Protestant Conference, Lima, Peru, 1961--II CELA--showed great progress over the previous meeting. It was officially called by all the national councils and/or federations of churches existing in Latin America at the time, eleven of them. Two hundred people, representing practically every country of the continent, participated. It is interesting to point out that this conference focused its attention particularly in the subject of evangelism. The two outstanding themes were: "Our message" and "Our unfinished task." This conference was no exception in keeping in mind and spirit, as ever, the subject of Christian unity. In fact, the text of the resolution regarding this topic was far more advanced and precise than any other resolution voted in any previous meeting. Some very concrete and bold suggestions were made, to guide the churches to that wider cooperation and unity wanted by all.

Nevertheless, due to the strong opposition of some observers from fundamentalist associations of the USA, the idea of establishing a regional permanent body had to be considered apart from the conference itself. Although the idea was finally approved, it could not be put into practice.

The III Latin American Protestant Conference, Buenos Aires, Argentina, 1969--III CELA--was called by UNELAM. Although it is past the period we are considering, it completes the picture of this type of conference. The most outstanding characteristic of the III CELA was the fact that it marked the arising of a new vision of the social reality in Latin

American Christianity. The conference became aware of the general underdevelopment of the continent, of the need for structural changes in face of oppression, as well as the necessity of commitment to liberty and justice on behalf of the poor and the oppressed. The statement approved by the Conference proposed that "the church needs to promote the impelling and decisive participation of its members, including its ministers, in the process of transformation of the dominant political systems, as well as to work for the replacement of structures of oppression by structures of justice." The III CELA also made clear a deeper and more serious understanding of the presence and possibility of a new and better relationship with Catholicism, undoubtedly due to the different attitude the Catholic Church had assumed as a result of the conclusions reached by Vatican Council II, and the Conference of the Latin America Episcopacy, at Medellin, Colombia, the year before, 1968.

As a resume, we would like to mention that in Havana 1929, the churches were concerned with the issue of religious renewal in a continent under the domination of an ineffectual Catholicism; in Buenos Aires 1949, the legitimacy of the presence of Protestantism in Latin America is affirmed; in Lima 1961, the Church feels established and firm in its foundations and, trusting in its future and in the Grace of God, proclaims that "Christ is the Hope for Latin America;" in Buenos Aires 1969, the importance of assuming more responsibility with regard to the social reality of the continent is accepted, and a firm commitment to fight for the renewal of structures of oppression which limit the liberty and validity of human rights is taken by the Conference.

IV. Period of Seeking for a Permanent Structure of Cooperation

As has been already mentioned, the decision adopted in Lima in 1961 to create a permanent body of cooperation was frustrated. A meeting that was called by "Church and Society in Latin America"--ISAL--in September 1963, in Rio de Janeiro, for a consultation about "Service and Social Action in Latin America," offered the opportunity for the presidents of the national councils of churches from the following countries to meet and deal with this issue: Argentina, Brazil, Chile, Mexico, Peru, and Uruguay. The presidents of Cuba and Puerto Rico, who were unable to attend, sent their total approval for the purpose of the meeting. In this unforeseen way, this meeting, which proved to be a renewed and categorical manifestation of that vocation for unity we have been pointing at repeatedly, stated what was called the "Declaration of Corcovado," reinforcing the conviction that the time was ripe for a decisive step forward on the way of the Latin American unity of Christians, requesting all the bodies of interdenominational cooperation of the continent to "come together in the wish of establishing a Latin American body of cooperation." This request was rapidly ratified by all the councils mentioned, except Peru's--that is to say, seven of them.

As a consequence of this approval the "Comision pro Unidad Evangelica Latinoamericana--UNELAM", was formally established in an assembly that took place in Montevideo, Uruguay, on December 1964. Dr. Emilio E. Castro, at present General Secretary of the World Council of Churches, was appointed as executive secretary. Obviously, UNELAM adopted, for its program, the recommendation which had been adopted at the Lima Conference 1961, in relation to cooperation and unity; this gave UNELAM, naturally, ample support from the churches.

The organization of this Commission of continental scope, that opened a new and creative period, was the climax of the fifty year process we have been describing. UNELAM fulfilled a very useful period of ten years. During that time, many projects of great help were undertaken, that strengthened the understanding of the meaning of the ecumenical unity of the Protestant family of the continent. On the other hand, that same period was a time of social, political, and economic changes and conflicts, in most of the countries of the region. As can be easily understood, it was also a crucial time which brought some minor but annoying disruptions in several of the national councils of churches that somewhat weakened UNELAM. However, far from losing heart, the churches took the initiative of trying to find the way to transform the crisis into a new opportunity for the ecumenical movement to expand, deepen and strengthen its unifying mission. The answer to this attitude came with the decision of the Oaxtepec Conference in 1976--that UNELAM itself had called--to create a new organization not supported by an indirect representation, as was the case with the councils that integrated UNELAM, but by the churches themselves becoming affiliated.

V.   The New Latin American Council of Churches--CLAI

In 1978, sixty-five years after the first meeting held in New York to consider the future of Protestantism in Latin America, the present fifth period begins with the inauguration of CLAI. This new council has celebrated its first ten years, holding successfully its second general assembly in Brazil, with the participation of over one hundred denominations established in all the countries, plus representatives of about another hundred ecumenical bodies. All this has certainly been a highly stimulating and inspiring consolidation.

In closing we must say we feel that CLAI, because of the strong support received from the churches, has taken upon itself all the prevailing tendencies, uncertainties, expectations, and hopes that have been expressed by the Protestant community in the long process we have tried to describe. This drives us to visualize a future full of achievements and evolvement in the development of the task of extending the kingdom of God in this continent, which so urgently needs the Gospel of Jesus Christ.

So be it! Amen.

The Ecumenical Role of Baptists
David S. Russell

I

Baptists and unity. Like many other Christians, Baptists have shown a marked ambivalence where ecumenical involvement is concerned. On the one hand there are some Baptist Unions or Conventions which have very few dealings with any other Christian body or even with any other Baptist body! Sometimes this 'denominational isolationism' is to be explained by reference to strongly held theological convictions; at other times to the fact that, in the past, Baptists have suffered considerably at the hands of the State Church.

On the other hand, in a number of countries they have taken the ecumenical initiative or have provided outstanding leadership in interchurch relationships. They, and the Baptist Unions and Conventions they represent, have played a key role, for example, in their National Councils of Churches, and in a number of cases have been among their founding members. Thus, the Baptist Union of Great Britain and Ireland and the American Baptist Convention were respectively founder members of the British Council of Churches (1942) and the National Council of Churches of Christ in the USA (1950). It is of interest, too, to observe that in recent years two of the British Council of Churches Ecumenical Officers have been Baptists and that American Baptists have had proportionately more secretaries of local and state councils of churches than any other single denomination.[1]

The past 50 years have witnessed too a considerable degree of Baptist participation in interchurch dialogue at the local and national levels. These are too numerous to mention, but we may note as examples the conversations between the Southern Baptist Convention and the Roman Catholic Church in the United States (sponsored by the Ecumenical Institute of Wake Forest University and Belmont Abbey College), between the American Baptist Convention and eight other denominations in the Council of Churches Uniting (COCU), between the Baptist Unions in East and West Germany and other Protestant Churches and between Baptists and Lutherans in Norway. Some have gone further and have shown a strong desire to enter into organic union with non-Baptist Christians as in the Church of North India where one of the 'founding Bishops' is himself a Baptist.

That having been said, it must be acknowledged that the ecumenical issue continues to be a source of tension and division among Baptists generally, even among the churches of those Unions or Conventions which are strongest in their support. Opposition to such involvement was voiced, for example, at the Assemblies of the American Baptist Convention (1960)

---

1. See William H. Brackney, Baptist Life and Thought, 1600-1980, 1981, p.368.

and the Baptist Union of Great Britain and Ireland (1979) when, in each case, several churches seceded. In both instances, however, overwhelming support was given to continuing participation in the National and World Councils of Churches. In the case of the former Convention the right of any local church was affirmed to express dissent and to withhold its financial support from the National Council of Churches. In the mid-1970s a list of such dissenting churches was published which has grown in length in succeeding years so that by 1982 the Convention's Directory listed no fewer than 510 such churches.

There is thus a wide variety of approach among Baptists to the ecumenical movement. It can be said with some confidence, however, that the vast majority, whilst remaining unconvinced about actual organic union with other Christian bodies, renounce 'isolationism' and are eager to co-operate with their fellow-Christians in their understanding and in their furtherance of the Gospel. Perhaps the greatest measure of involvement is to be found in the work of interdenominational organisations whose aim is that of evangelistic or missionary outreach.

It will be clear from what has been said that it is impossible for any individual to speak in the name of all Baptists or to identify with any degree of accuracy their 'ecumenical' role worldwide. I shall accordingly not attempt to do so, but rather try to give what might be called 'a testament of ecumenical experience' based on my own ecumenical involvement in the British Council of Churches and as a member of the Central Committee of the World Council of Churches from Uppsala (1968) to Vancouver (1982) and reflecting in particular the British Baptist scene with which I am most familiar and the attitude of such a body as the Baptist World Alliance on whose General Council I served for many years.

Baptists and the World Church. Within the diversity of Baptist attitudes to ecumenical relationships, several broad statements may be made which express the mind of most British Baptists and may reflect also the minds of others[2]:

First, baptism is to be seen within the context not only of personal faith but also of the faith and unity of the Church.

Secondly, that unity expresses itself in a fellowship that is visible to all. It is not enough to refer to some 'spiritual' Church over against the 'visible' Church as we know it. Our prayer and goal should be that of 'visible unity,' though this is certainly for most Baptists not the same thing as 'union' or 're-union.'

Thirdly, Baptists are part of 'the one, holy, catholic and apostolic Church'.

> 'The basis of our membership in the Church is a conscious and deliberate acceptance of Christ as Saviour and Lord by each individual...It is this vital evangelical experience which underlies the Baptist conception of the Church and is both expressed and safeguarded by the sacrament of believers' baptism'.[3]

Fourthly,

> 'It is in membership with a local church in one place that the fellowship of the one, holy, catholic Church becomes significant. Indeed, such gathered companies of believers are the local manifestation of the one Church of God in earth and in heaven...Such a local church, however, is not to be viewed as

---

2. See 'The Baptist Doctrine of the Church: statement adopted by the Baptist Union Council, 1948', in Ernest A. Payne, The Baptist Union: a Short History, App. X, 1959; and Baptists and Unity, a report received by the Baptist Union Council, 1967.

3. 'The Baptist Doctrine of the Church', 1948.

"self-sufficient"...It is part of a greater whole in such a way that insufficient regard for the totality of Christian witness is to be regarded as an indication of a deficiency in churchmanship'.[4]

Fifthly, this 'totality' is not to be limited to one's own denomination. The question that must continually be asked is, How far does this 'totality' extend? In particular, does it include common recognition, joint witness and joint action? The answers to such questions as these are particularly relevant in two areas of ecumenical concern in which Baptists have a pronounced involvement - the evangelistic and missionary outreach of the Church and the practice and meaning of baptism. We shall look at each of these two 'areas' in turn in sections III and IV.

The Baptist World Alliance. Most Baptist Unions or Conventions (136 in all) are members of the Baptist World Alliance, formed in London in 1905. They are to be found in 143 countries, with a membership of around 36 millions which probably represents a community strength three times that figure.

It is not a body with 'Church-power' exercising authority over its member bodies. It is rather a loosely-knit organisation which serves, inter alia, as an agency for propagating Baptist principles and tenets of faith, but which may 'in no way interfere with the independence of the (member) churches'. Accordingly it can play no decisive role in the affairs of any member church, and this applies where ecumenical involvement or commitment is concerned. This was well illustrated at the Alliance Congress in Copenhagen just prior to the establishment of the World Council of

---

4. Ibid.

Churches in 1948. The relationship between the Alliance as a World Confessional body and the emerging World Council of Churches was discussed, but it was made clear that it was not the responsibility of the Alliance even to advise on such a matter. Each Union and Convention must make its own decision and was at liberty so to do. Notwithstanding this, however, the officers of the Alliance have deemed it right and proper to be represented by a fraternal delegate at meetings of the WCC's Central Committee and to share in the discussions there.

Besides this, the Alliance, in recent years, has entered into constructive dialogue with other Confessional bodies such as the World Alliance of Reformed Churches and the Lutheran World Federation and, through its Commission on Co-operative Christianity, with the Roman Catholic Church. At the present time consideration is being given to the possibility of conversations with the Mennonite and Anglican communions also. In addition, the Alliance has from time to time accepted invitations to send fraternal delegates to the World Assemblies of several such bodies and in so doing has maintained and strengthened ecumenical links. Given its diversity of membership, however, and the acknowledged lack of 'authority' on the part of the Alliance, it has to be confessed that ecumenical dialogue at the 'Confessional' level is of necessity somewhat limited in its effectiveness.

II

Baptists and the World Council of Churches. Eight Baptist Unions or Conventions were among the founder-members of the World Council of Churches: the Northern (later, American) Baptist Convention, the two

National Conventions of the United States, the Seventh Day Baptist General Conference, the Baptist Unions of Great Britain, New Zealand, Holland and Burma together with the Chinese Baptist Council. Since that time two Unions - those of Scotland and Holland - have withdrawn. Others have become members so that at the present time their number stands at nineteen:

American Baptist Convention
Bangladesh Baptist Sangha
Baptist Convention of Nicaragua
Baptist Union of Denmark
Baptist Union of Great Britain
Baptist Union of Hungary
Baptist Union of New Zealand
Bengal-Orissa-Bihar Baptist Convention
Burma Baptist Convention
Church of Christ in Zaire (Baptist Community of Western Zaire)
Church of Christ in Zaire (Episcopal Baptist Community of Africa)
Evangelical Baptist Union of Italy
National Baptist Convention of America
National Baptist Convention, USA, Inc.
Nigerian Baptist Convention
Progressive National Baptist Convention, Inc.
Samavesam of Telugu Baptist Churches
Union of Baptist Churches of Cameroon
Union of Evangelical Christians-Baptists of the USSR.

These nineteen bodies represent only a small percentage of the 136 Unions or Conventions in membership with the Alliance. On the other hand they represent more than 5 million church members, i.e. about 42% of the 36 million Baptists world-wide. The numerically powerful Southern Baptist Convention in the United States remains outside the WCC and is followed in this by many smaller Conventions, a number of which have strong missionary connections with it, though members of these Conventions, including the Southern Baptist Convention itself, have served on some WCC Commissions.

From an early date Baptists have served not only on the Central Committee and the Executive Committee, but also on the staff of the WCC. In this last category are people like Edwin Espy, Paul Albrecht, Gwenyth Hubble, Victor Hayward, Glen Garfield Williams, Raymond Fung and Myra Blyth. Dr. Williams went on from there to give outstanding service to the Conference of European Churches as its General Secretary for over 20 years. Mention should be made too of Ernest A. Payne who served so effectively as Vice Moderator of the Central Committee and then as a President of the WCC, of Kyaw Than a member of the Executive Committee, of Orlando Costas a valued adviser who did so much to build bridges between evangelicals and the WCC and of Horace Russell of the Jamaican Baptist Union who, though that Union is not a member of the WCC, has been appointed Vice Moderator of the Faith and Order Commission.

Those Unions in membership with the WCC are for the most part in membership also with their own Local of National Councils of Churches. A number of those not in membership with the World Council are also in membership with their National Councils and play an active part in them. In the European Baptist Federation, which represents a region of the Baptist World Alliance, a number of the Unions, whilst not in membership with the WCC are members of the Conference of European Churches and take their full share in the work of that ecumenical body.

Faith and Order. Ever since its inception at the Lausanne Conference in 1927 until this present time Baptists have played a significant role in the Faith and Order movement which in due course was to become an important part of the work of the World Council of Churches.[5] At that Conference they were represented by delegates from the North American Baptist Convention, the Seventh Day Baptist General Conference of the United States, the Baptist Union of Ontario and Quebec, the Seventh Day Baptist Churches of Holland and the Baptist Churches in Germany. The Baptist Union of Great Britain and Ireland did not officially participate but was represented privately by two of its most prominent members, one of whom accepted an invitation to serve on the Continuation Committee. A strong delegation was present at the Second World Conference on Faith and Order, held in Edinburgh in 1937, and at the subsequent Conferences in Lund (1952) and Montreal (1963).

Baptists have been well represented also on the Faith and Order Commission. Of particular interest here have been the prolonged discussions on the question of baptism which has assumed an increasingly important role and in which the Baptists have maintained a theological position distinguishable from that of most of the other 'main-line' Churches. A report on 'The Meaning of Baptism' was presented to the Working Committee on Faith and Order in Spittal, Austria, in 1959 when a noteworthy contribution was made by one of the Baptist representatives on the Commission, Ernest A. Payne. At the Commission meeting in Bristol in 1967 the issue of baptism in relation to the eucharist was seen to be a subject of growing importance, and at Louvain, Belgium, in 1971 the need was recognised for some consensus document to be prepared on baptism, eucharist and ministry. The subsequent Commission meeting in Ghana in 1974 produced the document 'One Baptism, One Eucharist and a Mutually

---

5   See W.M.S. West, 'Baptists in Faith and Order - A Study in Baptismal Convergence', in <u>Baptists in the Twentieth Century</u>, ed. by K.W. Clements, 1983, pp. 55-75.

Recognised Ministry' from which eventually emerged the celebrated 'Lima text' (1982) entitled 'Baptism, Eucharist and Ministry' (see section IV below).

Ever since the Lausanne Conference in 1927, then, Baptist participation in Faith and Order work in general and the Faith and Order Commission in particular has been a significant one and has contributed substantially to that measure of consensus which is beginning to appear among the member Churches of the World Council of Churches.

III

Baptists and missionary endeavour. Since the days of William Carey in the 18th and 19th centuries, Baptists (not least in the United States and Britain) have shown great zeal in their support of 'foreign missions'. Carey indeed has been described as 'the father of the modern missionary movement'. It is perhaps less well known that his emphasis on missionary endeavour was matched by his strong desire to pursue such work in close co-operation with Christians of other denominations. Of particular interest was his suggestion that 'a general association of denominations of Christ from the four quarters of the world' be called together every ten years, beginning with a meeting at the Cape of Good Hope in 1810. 'I have no doubt', he says, 'it would be attended with very important effects; we could understand one another better, and more entirely enter into one another's views by two hours of conversation than by two or three years' epistolary correspondence'. This dream of a worldwide missionary conference had to wait a hundred years for its realization; but it illustrates not only Carey's own wide-embracing spiritual vision, but also the fact that the Baptists' desire for unity owes more to the imperatives of missionary and evangelistic work than to ecclesiastical or ecclesiological considerations.

It was in keeping, then, with their historical witness that Baptists should have shared in the great missionary conference held at Edinburgh in

1910 and in the subsequent formation of the International Missionary Council, accepting the principle of 'comity' which was established to avoid unnecessary competition and duplication of work.

From the Edinburgh Conference, of course, sprang the two great movements of Faith and Order and Life and Work which in 1948 combined to form the World Council of Churches with which in due course the International Missionary Council came to be integrated. It was perhaps fitting that a Baptist leader of world-renown in the person of Ernest A. Payne, at that time General Secretary of the Baptist Union of Great Britain and Ireland, should have played a significant part in bringing the WCC and the IMC together. It was he, together with Dr. David Moses of North India, who was given the responsibility of preparing a report presenting the case for integration. This report, which was essentially the work of Dr. Payne, was published as a pamphlet in 1957 under the title, 'Why Integration?' Its cogent and convincing arguments reflect not only Dr. Payne's astute mind, but also that Baptist tradition in which he stood and of which he himself was such an outstanding example.

This very act of integration, however, brought about as it was with Baptist support was regarded with grave suspicion by some of their number. Their hesitations were illustrated and accentuated by the withdrawal from missionary co-operation of the strong Foreign Mission Board of the Southern Baptist Convention in the United States of America which found difficulty in committing itself to a policy of 'comity agreement' which, it was argued, had not always shown the best results in terms of missionary endeavour.

The coming together of the IMC and the WCC gave renewed impetus to those 'evangelicals' outside the WCC (many Baptists among them) in their own work of mission and evangelization so that, by the

1980s, of the 45,000 Protestant missionaries sent out from North America, for example, only 8,000 were from WCC-related missionary societies.[6] The need was felt early on for a greater degree of co-operation among the disparate 'evangelical' missionary societies. Two events were of particular importance in this regard: the Berlin Conference of 1966 which gave them a new sense of unity and the Lausanne Congress on World Evangelization in 1973 under the leadership of Dr. Billy Graham. An attempt to give structure to 'Lausanne' in the form of a continuing committee, which some might have regarded as a rival to the WCC, was rejected. Conferences on missionary matters have continued to be held, however, and another important Congress is planned for 1989, also in Lausanne. Another organisation, distinct from 'Lausanne' but fully supportive of it, is the World Evangelical Fellowship with its headquarters in Singapore which gives visible expression to evangelical unity throughout the world. With their emphasis on unity through mission, Baptists play a prominent part and provide strong leadership in both these movements.

Evangelism and Mission. 'The Baptist tabernacle', writes H. Wheeler Robinson, 'is not always a graceful structure, but at least we may say this of it, that the twin pillars at its door are evangelism and liberty'.[7] Just as Baptists recognise the missionary dimension of their faith through organised missionary endeavour, so they recognise the responsibility of every individual disciple 'to bear personal witness to the Gospel of Jesus Christ and to take part in the evangelization of the world' (From the Declaration of Principle of the Baptist Union of Great Britain).

---

6 Statistics from an unpublished article by Denton Lotz, 'The Role of the BWA, Baptist National Unions and Conventions and their Efforts in the Cause of Unity in Christ.'

7. H. Wheeler Robinson, The Life and Faith of the Baptists, 2nd ed., 1946, p. 135.

This has sometimes led to the charge of 'proselytism' being brought against some Baptists in ecumenical debate, so keen have they been to share their faith with others and to 'win them for Christ'. Any attempt to engage in tactics which might smack of 'sheep-stealing' - persuading Christians in one branch of the Church, by coercion or some other unfair means, to transfer their allegiance to another - is to be strongly deprecated. But such condemnation must not be used to 'muzzle' the preaching of the Gospel or to deny the right and responsibility of the individual either to share his faith freely with others or, on the grounds of conviction or conscience, to change his or her Church affiliation. Proselytization, which is a disruption of that oneness which is ours in Christ, is not to be confused with evangelization which is of the very essence of Christian witness.

For Baptists, then, evangelism is at the very heart of Christian mission. It is here that their chief emphasis lies.[8] But this mission, though personal, cannot remain private. The Gospel has a societary as well as an individual dimension. Justice, peace and the integrity of Creation take their place alongside repentance and sanctification. This finds good illustration in two contemporary Baptist figures, Billy Graham and Martin Luther King Jnr, the one a world evangelist and the other a world social reformer, the one striving for the salvation of souls and the other for the salvation of society. And yet, to describe their ministries in this contrasting way is to falsify the facts for, in the case of each, evangelism and social action, far from being mutually exclusive, are truly complementary.

This 'holistic' approach has for long been a feature of the discussions at the Central Committee of the WCC; but the fear has been expressed

---

8. See Denton Lotz, 'Baptist Identity in Mission and Evangelism', in <u>Foundations</u>, January-March, 1978, pp. 32ff.

more than once by Baptist members and others that in the years following the Uppsala Assembly in 1968 the emphasis came to be laid increasingly on social and political action to the neglect of the evangelical. Such an emphasis seemed to stand in marked contrast to, say, that of the 1910 Edinburgh Conference and the student movement plea at that time for 'the evangelization of the world in this generation.'

Any imbalance, however, which may have existed between 'the vertical' and 'the horizontal' was, in the eyes of many Baptists, considerably modified by two important WCC documents which appeared in 1975 and in 1982. The first is a Report entitled 'Confessing Christ Today,' presented to the Nairobi Assembly,[9] which emphasizes the need 'to confess Christ alone as Saviour and Lord...in both evangelism and social action' (paras 1 and 3). The second is a statement of the WCC's Commission on World Mission and Evangelism entitled, 'Mission and Evangelism: an Ecumenical Affirmation'[10] which owes much to a Baptist member of staff, Raymond Fung. It is a truly ecumenical document which is at the same time truly evangelical, asserting (in the words of Philip Potter) that 'evangelization is the test of the ecumenical vocation'. The sharp contrast sometimes drawn by Baptists and other 'evangelicals' between 'evangelical' and 'ecumenical' would surely be more easily denied if more of them could be persuaded to take their place within the WCC and in the ecumenical movement generally.

---

9. See <u>Breaking Barriers</u>, ed. by David M. Paton 1975, pp. 43-57.

10. Reproduced in <u>International Journal of Mission</u>, vol. 71, Oct., 1982, pp. 427-451.

IV

The baptismal issue. Baptist understanding of baptism varies greatly in different parts of the world and even within the same Union or Convention. For example, whereas in the vast majority of cases baptism by immersion 'on profession of faith' is required for membership of the Church, in a few countries such as Britain and the northern parts of the United States many churches practise 'open membership', i.e. whereas they practise believers' baptism for new converts, they do not make this a requirement for those joining their fellowship from paedo-baptist churches. This might be interpreted by some as a sign of ecumenicity; it could, however, be regarded by others as a sign of weakness that they are not taking seriously enough the significance of baptism and the relationship between believers' baptism and the baptism of infants. The situation in Britain is probably unique in that in over 60 cases local congregations are in membership with the Baptist Union and with one or more other denominations, sometimes fully integrated and at other times simply sharing the same building. In the case of joint congregations both forms of baptism are used.

One issue that has to be faced by both 'open' and 'closed' membership churches, and perhaps less frequently by 'joint' congregations is a request for believers' baptism from someone who has been baptised as an infant. Here again there are differences of practice and interpretation. Whilst anxious in no way to deny the 'churchmanship' of paedo-baptists, most Baptist ministers would accede to such a request made on the grounds of Christian conviction and conscience, especially if the person concerned had previously made no Christian profession.

An ecclesiological issue. The question is being increasingly asked: How far can the two classic patterns of Christian initiation be viewed as acceptable alternatives? This is not an easy problem to resolve if only because the real issue at stake, for both Baptists and the ecumenical movement generally, is not just a 'practical' one, but a profoundly theological one. It asks the basic question, What is a Christian? and the complementary question, What is the Church? Here is a matter to which the Faith and Order Commission of the WCC might give more urgent attention. It would appear, to some Baptists at any rate, that the World Council may have gone on too hurriedly to consider the nature of the Apostolic Faith in the light of the 381 AD creed, and in so doing may have made assumptions about the nature of the Church which cannot simply be taken for granted. The doctrine of the Church at that time, one suspects, was not quite what it is sometimes assumed to be. Thus, it would appear that many (most?) baptisms up to that point and in the year 381 AD itself may well have been of adult believers. If this is so, it carries with it significant implications for our understanding of the nature of the Church itself.

Of relevance at this point is the difference between 'the Believers' Church', which lays emphasis on personal faith, and those Churches which stress the faith of the community of God's people. Baptists have often been charged, perhaps not unfairly, with individualism and subjectivism in their interpretation of the Gospel and with laying emphasis on personal faith to the neglect of community faith. The obverse, it might be claimed, may be equally true of paedo-baptists. Is there a meeting place between these two lines of approach? Is there common ground between these two bases of belief? This has been the quest of the ecumenical movement, and of many Baptists within it, over many years, and not least over the last 25 years or so.

Louisville, 1979. Ecumenical conversations on baptism reached a significant stage when, in 1974 in Accra, the Faith and Order Commission produced an important document entitled 'One Baptism, One Eucharist and a Mutually Recognised Ministry' (later, in revised form, 'Baptism, Eucharist and Ministry'). The responses of the Churches to this document were considered by a Consultation in Switzerland in 1977 which recommended that the Faith and Order Commission initiate a discussion with Baptists 'to explore the issues involved in the debate on infant baptism and believers' baptism which remain many and complex and need to be addressed at this time if we are to move forward in the agreement on baptism'.   The proposed Consultation took place in Louisville, Kentucky, (1979) with the aim of trying to find possible lines of convergence which might lead to consensus and mutual recognition.

The issues presented there related to the meaning of baptism itself, Christian initiation as a process (including baptism in water in the name of the Trinity, instruction in and confession of the faith and participation in the Lord's Supper), the Christian catechumenate, authority and justification for the practice of baptism, the meaning of faith, the blessing of infants and the question of contextuality.[11]   It was agreed that the practice of believers' baptism is the most clearly attested practice of baptism in the New Testament and, at the same time, that the development of infant baptism is explicable within the developing Christian tradition and clearly witnesses to valid Christian insights.   A Baptist member of the Consultation has summed up its findings in these words: 'The impression gained...was not only a real striving to mutual understanding but a search for perhaps a new approach to bridge the baptismal divide.   Glimpses of this new approach perhaps appeared, particularly at points when the consultation did not start the discussion from the point of view of either infant baptism or believers' baptism but tried to move the discussion into a different dimension.   For example, when the attempt is made to approach the understanding and practice of baptism from the perspectives first, of God's activity in Jesus

---

11. See W.M.S. West, 'A Consultation on Baptism, Louisville, 1979', in The Baptist Quarterly, vol. xviii, no. 5, pp. 225ff.

Christ initiating the Gospel, secondly, of the community of the people of God receiving and communicating that Gospel, and thirdly, the response of the individual within that community to the Gospel, then the issue of baptism, whether infant or believer's looks rather different'.[12]

The Lima text. The Louisville Consultation was one of many tributaries flowing into the mainstream which in 1982 resulted in the so-called 'Lima text' entitled 'Baptism, Eucharist and Ministry.' The Baptist response to it from member Churches of the WCC was one of genuine appreciation, seeing in it a valuable contribution in the Churches' search for mutual recognition. In each response received, however, certain reservations were made which indicate that, although a goodly measure of 'convergence' can be recognised, this falls short of 'consensus', not least in the report's interpretation of baptism and the nature of the Church to which Baptism testifies. Thus, claims seem to be made for the rite of baptism which, in the Baptist mind, belong to the total process of Christian initiation which includes a responsible faith-commitment on the part of the one baptised. This question is closely related to that of so-called 'rebaptism' which, Baptists would argue, cannot be resolved apart from a thorough consideration of the practice of 'indiscriminate baptism' and the ecclesiological question concerning the nature of the Church that lies behind the understanding of baptism to which reference has been made above.

A somewhat similar qualified welcome was given to the sections relating to Eucharist and Ministry. In the case of the former, Baptists found much of the language rather strange within their particular tradition, not least where it interprets the 'unique' place of the Eucharist in terms of the Christian reception of 'the gift of salvation' where the implication seems to

---

12. W.M.S. West, ibid, p. 231.

be that salvation actually comes through participation in the Eucharist - an implication which Baptists would seriously challenge. The subject of Ministry also raised questions on a number of issues such as the fundamental distinction made between 'the ordained' and 'the lay', the assumption of the three-fold ministry of Bishop, presbyter and deacon and the emphasis laid on the episcopate and apostolic succession. The Baptist emphasis is laid on the spiritual nature of the ministry over against the sacerdotal, the competency of the local church in association with other local churches in the recognition of ministry, and the ministry of the whole church and not that of only one man however gifted.[13]

'Visible unity', not least in terms of baptism, eucharist and ministry, may well be a desirable goal, but much thought still requires to be given 'as to what measure of diversity of interpretation and expression is commensurate with unity and as to the proper limits accorded to contextualization'.[14] Baptists who are involved in the ecumenical movement recognise that they do not have a clear answer to this question in terms of baptism, eucharist and ministry, but are eager to try to find a consensus which will realise more fully their participation in 'the one, holy, catholic and apostolic Church'.

The past 50 years, then, have witnessed a greater involvement of some Baptists in the ecumenical movement, but a continuing reticence and even opposition on the part of others. The principles for which Baptists stand, not least that of believers' baptism, have become matters of increasing theological debate in ecumenical circles and are recognised as of no small

---

13. See the (as yet unpublished) response to the BEM document by the Alliance's Commission on Doctrine and Inter-Church Co-operation.

14. Churches Respond to BEM, vol.1, ed. by Max Thurian, 1986, p.74.

importance in the search for that convergence of belief and practice leading to consensus and to that visible unity of Christ's Church which, in all its diversity, is a sign and instrument of God's mission in today's world.

The Ecumenical Role of World-Wide Anglicanism
Oliver Tomkins

One of the achievements of Amsterdam 1939 was that it opened the eyes of many young Christians to the richness of <u>confessional</u> church life. Whilst it is true that the essence of ecumenism is to recognize the face of Christ himself in our fellow-Christians, it is also paradoxically true that we are helped to appreciate the unsearchable riches of Christ through seeing how diverse are the <u>corporate</u> traditions in which individual disciples of Christ are moulded.

Another article here, by Francis House, illustrates how shared liturgical worship can foster this discovery, especially as exemplified by the Orthodox Holy Liturgy. But another window onto Christian diversity is afforded by seeing how individual church leaders bring their characteristic contributions to the orchestrated harmony.

It is a fact that Anglicans have played a part in the total ecumenical movement of this century out of all proportion to the size of the Anglican

Communion in the total Christian community. Let us look at some of the dramatis personae.

The cast must be headed by Charles Brent (1862-1929) then a missionary bishop of the Episcopal Church USA in the Philippines. He had been a delegate at the World Missionary Conference at Edinburgh in 1910 when, at his prayers in the daily eucharist, he was seized by the thought that world-wide co-operation in evangelization was not enough; an equally world-wide initiative was called for to seek the visible unity of all Christian people who heeded the prayer of Our Lord in St. John 17. And so, in due course, was born the Faith and Order Movement. At that same 1910 conference, under the chairmanship of a Methodist layman, John R. Mott, another young Anglican was the secretary, J.H. Oldham, who became the first whole-time secretary of the International Missionary Council (and who lived to be the main architect of the influential conference on "Church, Community and State" at Oxford in 1937; but that is to anticipate a later story). Leading bishops like E.K. Talbot of Winchester and Charles Gore, a great scholar-bishop, symbolized the early ecumenical commitment of the Church of England.

The early days of Faith and Order were a mainly Anglican initiative, (though greatly supported by the Disciples of Christ, USA). It was an Anglican delegation from the USA which visited Rome where "through the great courtesy of Archbishop Cerretti, a formal statement and invitation to (the first Faith and Order) Conference were presented to his Holiness the Pope through Cardinal Gasparri, and the official refusal of the invitation was balanced by the personal friendliness and benevolence of the Pope".

As Faith and Order developed, other Anglicans came to play a leading role in it, but head and shoulders above them all, William Temple (1881-1944).

He had attended the 1910 conference as a young Oxford don; later as Bishop of Manchester and then as Archbishop of York, he succeeded Charles Brent as Chairman of Faith and Order. He died, tragically soon, as Archbishop of Canterbury, in the last year of the war. No other individual played such a key role in all the three strands which are always thought of as inter-twining to form the modern ecumenical movement-- the International Missionary Council (dating from the conference at Edinburgh in 1910), the Faith and Order Movement (with its first World Conference at Lausanne in 1927) and the Life and Work Movement (stemming from Stockholm 1926).

William Temple left his mark upon them all. At the second world conference of the I.M.C. at Jerusalem in 1928, it was Temple who was largely the author of the striking "Message", a brilliant summary of the Christian faith which is to be shared with all the world. At the third world conference of Life and Work at Oxford in 1937 he was not only a leading delegate by virtue of his well-known leadership in England on questions of social concern, like unemployment and international peace, but also he introduced at the conference the report which proposed the merging of "Life and Work" and "Faith and Order" to become the World Council of Churches. But it was to Faith and Order that he gave the larger part of his energy and enthusiasm. Elected to succeed the first chairman, Charles Brent on his death in 1929, Temple presided over all the annual meetings of the Continuation Committee of Faith and Order up until the second World Conference at Edinburgh in 1937.

When the Provisional Committee of the World Council of Churches was formed, there was not the slightest doubt that he was the right man to preside over it. He was equally in the closest touch with the younger generation and in constant demand for national and international student and youth conferences.

Temple's strength as an ecumenical leader consisted in the rare combination of a clear theological and ecclesiastical position and a penetrating insight into other positions. His was a mind which did not need to become a closed mind in order to take a firm stand, and which ever remained open to new aspects of the truth. He could lead his readers or hearers to the deep places, as in his Readings in St. John's Gospel or in his sermons on the Christocentric nature of true ecumenical unity. But he could also show amazing breadth as he sought to summarize complicated discussions in which the most divergent viewpoints had been put forward, and as he sought to remain in touch with new movements of thought in the younger generation. In his own country he has been called "everybody's Archbishop," because he was considered to be a leader of all and a spokesman for all. His position in the ecumenical movement was similar, in that all parts of it and all Churches looked upon him as its leader.

The other Anglican ecumenical leader with a secure reputation in the history of the ecumenical movement is George Ball (1883-1958). It is chiefly as Bishop of Chichester and in relation to the German Confessing Church, to the assistance of refugees from Hitler's persecution and to the ethics of war and peace that his name will live. A shy and self-effacing man, a poor orator yet with a dogged persistence in pressing his point home, he is among the moral and spiritual giants. His personal friendship with Dietrich Bonhoeffer drew him into the heart of the theological and spiritual struggle of which the Confessing Church was the costly focus point. His courageous protests in 1943-44, as a member of the House of Lords, against obliteration-bombing of German cities was much resented by Winston Churchill and other Allied war-leaders but was also seen by others as one of the most shining examples of how Christian fellowship can transcend the bitterness of earthly division. It was natural that, in 1948 when the World Council of

Churches was founded, he should be chosen as the first Chairman of its Central Committee and he guided it wisely through the first decade of its existence.

It would be tedious to go on cataloguing other Anglicans who played a leading part in the Ecumenical Movement from the preparations for Edinburgh 1910 right up to the active roles of the present Archbishops of Canterbury and York. It must suffice to say that almost every theologian of national and international stature in the Anglican Communion was asked at some time to contribute to the work of Faith and Order. Nor must one forget the genius of J.H. Oldham in drawing into the preparations for Oxford 1937 such distinguished laymen as T.S. Eliot, R.L. Calhoun, Sir Ernest Barker or Lord Lothian-- but that is part of a different and wider story, affecting many churches and nations.

If we go on to ask what Anglicanism corporately has contributed to the ecumenical movement, the answer is not primarily in its liturgy, widespread though the influence has been of the Book of Common Prayer. The answer lies rather in the 100-year-old Lambeth Quadrilateral.

At the third Lambeth Conference (in 1888) Resolution 11 read "That in the opinion of this conference, the following Articles supply a basis on which approach may by God's blessing be made towards Home Reunion:

A)   The Holy Scriptures of the Old and New Testaments as "containing all things necessary to salvation and as being the ultimate rule and standard of faith".

B)   The Apostles' Creed as the Baptismal Symbol, and the Nicene Creed, as the sufficient statement of the Christian faith.

C)   The two Sacraments ordained by Christ himself-- Baptism and the Supper of the Lord-- ministered with unfailing use of Christ's words of Institution, and of the elements ordained by Him.

D) The Historic Episcopate, locally adapted in the methods of its administration to the varying needs of the nations and peoples called of God into the Unity of His Church.

The Lambeth Quadrilateral re-appears at the Lambeth Conference of 1920 in a context which is strikingly contemporary.

To re-read the Appeal to All Christian People of Lambeth 1920 can be a ground for despair. All the right things were said nearly seventy years ago. And they are being said still. The unity we seek is no mere human invention, it already exists.

> "It is in God, who is the perfection of unity, the one Father, the one Lord, the one Spirit, who gives life to the one Body. Again the one Body exists. It needs not to be made nor remade but to become organic and visible...We have only to discover it, and to set free its activities."

Mission and renewal alike demand unity. "The Faith cannot be adequately apprehended and the battle of the Kingdom cannot be worthily fought while the Body is divided." Unity is not uniformity, it is a rich diversity. This passage has not been excelled in subsequent pronouncements. The vision which rises before us is that of a Church, genuinely Catholic, loyal to all Truth, and gathering into its fellowship "all who profess and call themselves Christians", within whose visible unity all the treasures of faith and order, bequeathed as a heritage by the past to the present shall be possessed in common, and made serviceable to the whole Body of Christ. Within this unity Christian Communions now separated from one another would retain much that has long been distinctive in their methods of worship and service. It is through a rich diversity of life and devotion that the unity of the whole fellowship will be fulfilled.

The Lambeth Quadrilateral re-appears as paragraph VI of Resolution 9, slightly re-worded from the 1888 version.

"We believe that the visible unity of the Church will be found to involve the whole-hearted acceptance of:--

"The Holy Scriptures, as the record of God's revelation of Himself to man, and as being the rule and ultimate standard of faith; and the Creed commonly called Nicene as the sufficient statement of the Christian Faith, and either it or Apostles' Creed as the Baptismal confession of belief:

"The divinely instituted sacraments of Baptism and the Holy Communion, as expressing for all the corporate life of the whole fellowship in and with Christ:

"A ministry acknowledged by every part of the Church as possessing not only the inward call of the Spirit, but also the commission of Christ and the authority of the whole body."

The story continues, right through to the recent Lambeth Conference of 1988. But our theme here is the Anglican contribution up to the Amsterdam Youth Conference of 1939. It was a combination of gifted individuals and a corporate tradition which had long stood for the visible unity of all Christ's People. Later historians must judge whether that continued to be the case!

The Leavening Process of Ecumenism
Raymond M. Veh

The word "ecumenical" is derived from the Greek language. It denotes "the inhabited world." In the past 50 years it has taken on a somewhat different connotation. It is used in this late twentieth century to signify a sense of "Spiritual togetherness."

Use of the word "ecumenism" today conjures a way of life in its religious entirety. The word is freighted with more meaning than the much-used words of unity, cooperation, internationalism. Is this not due, in part, to the fact that Christian young people who met at Amsterdam, Holland, July 24-August 2, 1939, from 70 different nations around the world became "ecumenical" in that they achieved an experience which permitted them to sing the challenging verse

"In Christ now meet both east and west,
In him meet south and north;
All Christly souls are one in him
Throughout the whole wide earth."

For that First World Christian Youth Conference surprisingly large delegations of persons, totaling 1,775 delegates and visitors, at great sacrifices of time and money, came together to give witness to the reality of a common calling. Only belief in "Christus Victor" (Jesus Christ as the Lord and Saviour of humankind) could ever have brought together such a diverse group of young people and leaders.

Here were Scotch lads in their kilts and skirts. Here were youth from the East Indies in turbans and gowns. Here were long-whiskered Russian Orthodox exiles wearing clerical robes and gold crosses. Here were Japanese delegates (23 of them) with silk kimonos and obis. Here were Bulgarian and Roumanian lads and lassies in their colorful national costumes. For the most part the delegates from East and West appeared as might any of the youth in our western churches. Western clothes have pretty well become the adopted dress around the world.

It was a miracle of God that this Conference could take place at all. In a world of tensions, hates, and threats, even with war (World War II) likely to break out at any time, youth circumscribed all, believing that God in Jesus Christ our Lord has called all nations and races in this world to his service, to communion with him, and to his Church. Certainly one outstanding feature, possibly its most notable one, was the fashion in which a conscious Christian fellowship was developed among the youth present. On the return home of these representatives the ecumenical stance experienced inevitably would reach into all areas of the world.

No recountal of this Conference could be given without mention of the profound impression left by the worship services. They were memorable experiences. Planned with utmost care and through the use of programs printed in three languages, it was possible for those speaking in other tongues to participate wholeheartedly. A variety of services permitted every type of worship-- ritualistic, evangelistic and informal mission. The fervor with which this huge gathering sang the hymns of the Church is unforgettable.

Varied services were typical: Free Church, French, a formal Lutheran service; a simple African service; a centuries-old Orthodox Church liturgy with a 10-voice male chorus (Russians-in-exile from Paris); a strangely-beautiful Indian (India, Burma, Ceylon) service, an American service, and a Saturday evening preparatory service for Sunday's communion in four "kerks" in Amsterdam.

The leavening process of ecumenism permeated with profound and lasting value the Bible Study weekday morning hours. Two diverse viewpoints surfaced in these groups: 1) the delegates with the continental theological attitude which, in exalting the Supreme God and the Church, evidenced a certain pessimism with regard to man, his worth and his powers; 2) the delegates with the western attitude who are not gravely concerned over theological implications but lay great stress on the practical expression of Christianity. The confusion did not make for division, for the youth of all nations were in Amsterdam to seek the truth in religion as well as God's will for the world. Out of conflict of viewpoints there gradually emerged a kind of higher order and a genuine spiritual enrichment for all.

Discussion groups were held weekday afternoons from 4:30 to 6:30. Forty-three groups studied seven main topics: 1) World of Nations; 2) Nation and State; 3) Economic Order; 4) Education; 5) Race; 6) Marriage and Family Life; 7) Church and World Mission. It was the writer's privilege to share in one of the groups of category Seven. In addition to the detailed work carried on in the Biblical and discussion groups, the delegates took part each day in plenary sessions which informed and incited many to gain wider concepts of ecumenism.

In the group and plenary sessions the Biblical emphasis made a deep impression on youth from many areas of the world. A young Swiss delegate in one impassioned plea summarized the importance of this emphasis by stating:

> "Amsterdam must not have been in vain. What we would wish to have learned here is to listen freshly and more faithfully to the Bible, that is, to the Lord of the Bible. And we have seen how good it is to study the Bible together. Youth from all nations are returning home with a determination to become acquainted with the experience which God reveals for his children in the Bible."

In many instances, it was evident that the spirits of the delegates were bruised by the plain facts of the current history which all were experiencing in Europe. The suspicion and hate and warmongering among the nations was felt keenly. War--or the absence of permanent peace--was a crucial issue in the world in conflict of which delegates were a part. Every delegate felt a deep strain of guilt for the world situation. "We have sinned," we said, "because we have stayed within the bounds of self and altogether within the world. Our resolve was to be done with self-centeredness, to make God's will supreme, and to become instruments of social betterment because we are His instruments of ecumenism."

It was evident that "Christus Victor", the theme of the Conference, was become reality in the lives of many delegates. Most delegates came with a sincere desire to learn more about Jesus Christ and the Church. Delegates quickly perceived that the "Let's-get-together-and-be-good-fellows" attitude would not be sufficient in this Conference. There swiftly developed an awareness that only through prayer and spiritual struggle can there be unity and real ecumenicity. Each delegate searched his own relationship to God, the Church and his fellowmen. The personal responsibility to go into home communities all over the world and to be constructive builders of Christ's kingdom became the high resolve of every sincere delegate.

The leavening process wrapped up in the Conference theme had become reality in the lives of those who had caught the real essence of ecumenism. Let us see how this is revealed in forthright present-day situations:

--Sponsorship of soup-kitchens in multiple communities for the hungry.

--Acceptance of black women ministers in southern and northern areas.

--Reconciliation commissions at work in Central American countries.

--Presentation theatrically of biblical parables and faith musicales.

--Promotion of "Talk-to-Me" telephone reassurance programs for latch-key children.

--Extending hands of reconciliation and love to the Russian nation and to the Moscow Patriarchate.

--Movement toward purposeful membership of denominations to the Consultation of Church Union (COCU).

--Sponsorship of ecumenical rehabilitation programs to drug abusers and criminals.

--Meeting emergency appeals from money to be used by Middle East and African Councils of Churches.

--Making Christian witness in the economic order through small prayer and Bible study groups in offices or factories cutting across professional status.

--Bringing groups of persons with varying professions together for special jobs such as the Peace Corps.

--Giving support to the Christian family through therapeutic fellowship groups, counseling centers, and camping programs.

--Supplying staff and special programs for local churches in resort areas, coffee-house ministries, the National Parks Ministry.

--Undergirding ministries to parents of retarded children, narcotic addicts, counsel for divorcees, 24-hour emergency services.

--Identifying in churches of varying denominations the many different types of people God has chosen to work his Way in the world. An unknown leader suggests this could help all ecumenists "come a little closer to one of the great truths of the Christian religion, which is that getting ready for life in Heaven with God has the interesting consequence of getting us ready for life on earth with each other."

--Nurturing Christian journalists who will be bound by a vision of the Kingdom peripheries, have a sensitivity to the integrity of other cultures, have the ability to stand in the shoes of someone else, and a clear understanding that all people are citizens of God.

--Pursuing any or all of the above thrusts will lead to other and multiple social visions which will come into reality in the future as the leavening process of ecumenism grips more and more people, regardless of sex, class, race, ethnic origin.

After fifty years since that momentous Conference took place, no one can adequately summarize the abiding consequences of this gathering. But one thing seems certain: the experiments of young men and women of varied races and classes together on absolutely equal terms, talking over their problems together, living in Christian fellowship on high levels, discovering possibilities in varied types of worship, commitments to making Christ conqueror, provided new advances for the ecumenical movement which must reverberate through decades to come.

One thing is certain: THE 1939 FIRST WORLD CHRISTIAN YOUTH CONFERENCE WITH SUBSEQUENT CHRISTIAN YOUTH GATHERINGS HAVE BEEN, AND WILL CONTINUE TO BE,

IMPORTANT IN CREATING A GROWING ECUMENISM--AND IN DEVELOPING LEADERSHIP FOR THE ONGOING ECUMENICAL MOVEMENT. (From the 1988 WSP Calendar).

It is inevitable that all significant gatherings must come to a close. On the last afternoon of discussion groups of the World Conference of Christian Youth in Amsterdam, Holland, the 40 youth and leaders in our group, who represented 15 different nations, were about speak their "goodbyes". The leader summed up concisely the prime points of the 40 hours of discussion we had had together. In simple but earnest language he began to expand the walls of our meeting room in the Oberrealschule (high school) building until we began to see how our little group was related to the whole world. He outlined the program which Christian youth must follow in the spirit of "Christus Victor", emphasizing the necessity for a reconstructed social order in which men and women are no longer separated by class or race or national antagonism. As he talked his voice deepened into a vibrant quality and the faces of these youth from the four corners of the globe lit up with renewed hope and high purpose.

Then, when it was evident that though we had come from many backgrounds we were returning to those with oneness in ideals and commitments, the leader quoted, "I saw God wash the world last night." It had been raining in sheets all day, but the sun was now edging through the dripping leaves with a golden beauty. (It was six o'clock but the sun is high in the sky at that hour on a summer afternoon in Amsterdam). As he quoted the concluding lines,

> "I saw God wash the world last night,
> Ah, would he had washed me
> As clean of all my dust and dirt
> As that old white birch tree,"

each person in the room seemed to be making it his or her own prayer. Then we all stood, joined hands, and sang together, "Blest Be the Tie that Binds." The tune was familiar to us, and the words in many languages fitted it perfectly.

Quite without previous planning, the meeting had worked up to an unforgettable climax. It was as if we were standing on the mountain of spiritual imagination where we could see al the kingdoms of the world and the possibility of transforming them into the Kingdom of God. FOR A MOMENT WE GLIMPSED THE GREAT SOCIAL FORCES WHICH MUST BE RE-DIRECTED IF THIS VISION IS TO BECOME A REALITY.

We yielded to the personal commitment which such a talk implies. AND WE KNEW WE COULD NEVER AGAIN BE QUITE THE SAME SONS AND DAUGHTERS OF GOD.

Humbly we said our "Goodbyes."

It was a quiet, meditative group who on the afternoon of August 2, 1939--50 years ago--saw the momentous Conference close under the leadership of Dr. W.A. Visser 't Hooft, then General Secretary of the World Student Federation, later General Secretary of the World Council of Churches. As the end of this twentieth century approaches, we are sensing visibly the need of enlarging the scope of the entire ecumenical Christian movement of our day.

1) We must come to realize a proper sense of humility in a world which confronts us with problems we are unable to solve in our own puny strength.

2) We must come increasingly to rely upon God to aid us in the problems which have their sources in powers over which God alone has control.

3) We must utilize the groundwork based on virile and active ecumenism at work in scattered areas through the 50 years past for the 50 years aborning.

Amsterdam's challenge of "Christus Victor" remains constant for the reuniting of Christendom that God's will may be done on earth as it is in heaven--for then only will Christ be Victor indeed.

Our Common Calling in the USA Today[1]
Robert S. Bilheimer

From college experience in the World's Student Christian Federation, including Amsterdam '39, until now, my life has been caught up in the ecumenical movement. Throughout, the core of continuity has been a sense of vocation, or, better, of common calling, intensely personal for me, but not merely individualistic. Rather, it has conveyed a communal sense of direction. The communal element has simultaneously involved both Christians of other churches, and Christians of other peoples and nations. The sense of direction has been invigorating: a sense of being with these Christians for the purposes of witness in the world and of achieving some visible unity with them. Thus the common calling in Christ, the ecumenical calling, contains the most exhilarating vision I know, and the most stimulating renewal or rebirth that I can conceive.

---

1. Note: This article draws upon a forthcoming book, Breakthrough--The Power of the Ecumenical Tradition, William B. Eerdman's Publishing Co.

The ensuing paragraphs set forth four claims. First: our churches today possess the priceless gift of those who respond to our common calling. Second: in the USA, this priceless gift is in danger. Third: our common calling suggest certain basic responses to the danger. Fourth: we consequently have an almost impossible task.

I. The Priceless Gift

In 1939, when we gathered at Amsterdam, the beginnings of the ecumenical movement were comparatively slight, yet unusual, dramatic and of high potentiality. International conferences had been held, most recently in 1937 on Church, Community and State, as well the same year as the second world meeting on Faith and Order. In 1938 a convention had been held in Utrecht to draw up a constitution for the proposed World Council of Churches, and the dramatic Third World missionary conference had met in Madras at Christmastime. For nearly half a century, the World's Student Christian Federation had worked with productive effect. Moreover, a Biblical-theological renewal, arising first in Europe in the interwar years, had gathered worldwide, interconfessional force.

We need not rehearse the course of world history or church developments since 1939, save to say that awareness of a new world and in it a new church situation has now become all but commonplace. I wish, however, to stress that within the world situation characterized by global consciousness, global relationships and a sense of global destiny, and within the ecumenical church situation as symbolized by the World Council of Churches and by the impact of Vatican II, we in the churches have been given a priceless gift.

My own observation of this gift has come from national and regional work in the USA, but I have no doubt that it is also worldwide in extent.

It is a fact of church life, so obvious that its importance and character of priceless gift almost escapes notice. It is the fact that

> The ecumenical Roman Catholics, Eastern Orthodox and Protestants have more in common with each other than any of them have in common with the non-ecumenical membership of their own communions.[2]

Furthermore, my own experience leads me to state this more sharply:

> What the ecumenical Roman Catholics, Eastern Orthodox and Protestants have in common with each other is more fundamental than what they have in common with the non-ecumenical membership of their own communions.

These two formulations, however, do not quite tell the whole story. The further, underlying factor, the ecumenical glue, is the realization that in some recognizable measure "Church" exists in other confessions among other peoples. At the Second Conference of Christian Youth in Oslo in 1947, for example, the Dutch-Indonesian war caused immense strain between the Indonesian and Dutch delegates until, especially after a dramatic public address by Visser 't Hooft of Holland, they were led to recognize one another in Christ. Such drama was not confined to political conflict: it took place as confessions confronted one another, each with long histories of antagonism or estrangement behind them.

In every ecumenical experience I have had or been a part of heard tell about, this recognition of one another in Christ has been liberating and the source of intense excitement. It means that I am member of, and caught up in, the People of Christ in the varied church confessions in the USSR, in the Third World, in the peoples of the West and the Islands of the Sea, and

---

2. This formulation, including the succeeding sentence, appeared in People, Programs and Papers, a publication of the Institute for Ecumenical and Cultural Research, Collegeville, Minnesota).

that the People of Christ among these peoples know that I am a part of the same People, and all are participants in world history and in church history.

Dawning, this recognition supplies a new bond among the people upon whom it comes. Invariably, they have attributed the ecumenical bond to the Holy Spirit of God-in-Christ at work in the Church and in the world of today. Remarkably, this bond does not produce a sense of discontinuity, obliterating the confessional or national ties, but rather denies that these ties are final. The new bond in Christ thus transcends the old ties. Held by the new, we are not trapped in our own histories of nation or church, but find a vivid, commanding sense of participation in world and church history. In this way, the new bond is stronger and more important than the old, for in it the old is not diluted but renewed and transformed.

This is the priceless gift: the worldwide binding of veritable multitudes from the Roman Catholic, Eastern Orthodox and Protestant persuasions, a binding in which they have more in common with one another than they have with those whose loyalties are still imprisoned within their own churchly, national or cultural traditions.   That no organizational structure fully embraces the whole testifies to the present day fact that the power of the ecumenical bond is not institutional but of the Spirit, personal and communal.

II. In the USA, Danger.

In the USA, ecumenism is vital, and found in a variety of forms. Among them the following may be the chief:

--Issue-oriented ecumenism, in which people of many church affiliations gather to promote common convictions. Movements for justice and peace, the women's movement, race relations, ecological concerns, civil rights, gay and lesbian rights, the sanctuary movement, do not exhaust but illustrate the character, scope and interests of this vital force of ecumenism today.

--The ecumenism of councils of churches, local, state, and national. This is the historic form of US ecumenism, having been started just after the turn of the last century among mainline Protestant churches. Now, it includes Orthodox and Roman Catholic participants, and is greatly, though not exclusively, concerned with the issues indicated above and with other forms of ecumenism in this listing.

--The ecumenism of the Conference on Church Union (COCU).

--The ecumenism of church mergers.

--The ecumenism of the Roman Catholic bi-laterals, international in character, but with US participation.

--The ecumenism of conservative Protestants: Billy Graham, Youth for Christ and the current televangelists suggest the wide variety of this category.

--The ecumenism of publications: books of Biblical studies, theology, church renewal, spirituality, social witness and ecumenism itself; liberal, mainline and conservative magazines and quarterlies of both historic and fugitive stature; and newspapers.

--The ecumenism of the academy, including college and university courses and graduate training for professional Christian vocation in denominational or interdenominational institutions, and the professional associations of those engaged in such training.

--The ecumenism of institutions and movements concerned with church renewal, sometimes confessional and frequently interconfessional.

The point of this doubtless partial listing is not only to acknowledge the assets, variety, energy and resources of ecumenism in the USA today, but also to point strongly to its danger. As to its asset side, I thank God that ecumenism in the USA is not dead, ingrown or stuffy, but as vital and widespread as the above list indicates.

At the same time, I am bound to point to its danger. Each variety of ecumenism tends to draw interest and commitment to itself. Issue orientation, for instance, evokes such passion for each of its causes, that the very passion becomes a blindness. Too greatly "my issue" becomes No. 1. Even if there are many varieties of Christians at work on the many issues and aspects of ecumenism, there is scant sense of the whole.

The danger can be described by the "forest" and the "baby." We are in danger of such a focus upon the particular ecumenical trees that we do not see the totality of the ecumenical forest. We are also in danger of throwing the baby of ecumenical coherence out with the bath of ecumenical energy.

Indeed, one wonders whether that has not largely happened. Within this extraordinary variety, one questions whether the basic meaning of ecumenism has not been lost. Has the pluralism of US society itself captured the ecumenical enterprise, stripping away the sharp edge of our common calling? It appears so to me.

III. Basic Needs

In this situation, three needs stand out.

First, an appropriate form of a "confessing church." Some may reply, "What's that?" Others, remembering the confessing church which began in Hitler's Germany and spread through much of Europe, may reply that that cannot be emulated in U.S. society, half a century later. To that I respond: "Of course not. But the confessing church movement of yesteryear had enormous influence in the growth of ecumenical consciousness, and in this context is worth attention today, especially in the U.S.A."

To appreciate the power of the confessing church development, and its influence upon the ecumenical movement, one needs to recall the general situation of church, society and state in Europe. Since the Enlightenment, the old Corpus Christianum, the partnership of church, state and society in "Christendom," resulting from the fourth century settlement with the Emperor Constantine, had been under attack, and was eroding. The decisive moment in this process was the rise of secular, scientific, militarized totalitarianism in Germany, deep in the heart of Europe and the former Corpus Christianum.

This was an end-time development in personal and church life. A whole, historic world had come to an end. With immediacy, Christians were faced with the ultimate decision between Christ and Hitler. From an alliance with the state and society, the confessing church was put in radical opposition to both. Therein lies its contemporary significance. In freeing church life and Christian witness from alliance with society, it sharpened the distinction between Church and society and clarified the role of church in society.

This confessing church was not alone. From the turn of the last century onward, student movements had addressed the secularism of the universities, touching thousands who responded to a world-wide vision of the Church. Since 1928 (Jerusalem), those concerned with world missions had perceived that a sweeping secularism had made the western churches missionaries among their own peoples, and ten years later (Madras, 1938) this view developed into a dramatic sense of the worldwide People of God embattled, yet called to increased vigor in its world mission. The pressure of war deepened these convictions to an intense world-wide sense of being "partners in obedience."

Thus in a broad sense, through the ecumenical enterprise itself, the "confessing church" became a worldwide pattern, a kind of overall norm. This, in turn, produced the essence of the ecumenical calling, namely to confess Christ together in a wondrous, communal partnership among the varied peoples of the world.

In the USA, the ecumenical calling has been generally welcomed and understood within the American context of democracy and the separation of church and state. In the sense of an alliance between Church and State, the historic Corpus Christianum never existed in the USA. That meant, however, that for the most part we in the USA were a bit too complacent about the consequences for European Christians of the disappearance of their Corpus Christianus. We could, and in effect did, always listen with interest, and say, "It must involve an enormous shift in perspective." But this difference in experience, the difference between a newly felt discontinuity between Church/state/society in Europe and the continuity of Church with democratic society and state in the USA was deceptive.

One noted, again and again, that we Americans were too ready to welcome the European shift, and failed to see its implications for our own life. One can put it this way, that especially in the formative post-war years, when the US was at its high point of international, liberal leadership, we Americans somewhat hid behind our separation of church and state, saying that the European shift was not our problem, that we had solved that problem long ago. Frequently we Americans too readily failed to notice that our church/state separation did not automatically carry with it a correlative church/society distinction.

True, in the European sense, the USA never had a Corpus Christianum, a church/state partnership. But in an American sense we did. The virtual fusion between Church and the American Way of Life became an American form of the European Corpus Christianum. In this American form, church and state were separated, but culture, democracy, economics, the good life and Christianity were largely fused. And still are.

In this sense, the first basic need in fulfilling our ecumenical calling is a clear-headed, strong juxtaposition of the identity of the People of God in the USA with the culture and society of the USA. The list of "ecumenisms" given above reveals deep, urgent concern with aspects of US society, and all together they represent no small measure of "distance" between their participants and US society. Yet fragmentation among them is apparent, no more so than in the tendency of their adherents to politicize churches and interdenominational agencies in the interests of particular causes. Precisely here, the problems of the forest and the baby begin to be felt.

The most urgent need calls for a coherent confessing church movement within the churches of the USA, its witness born of faith and of consciousness of the distance between Christ and all societies including that of the USA.

The second basic need is a Biblical, theological renewal appropriate to our time. There will be many views of what "appropriate to our time" entails and should be. I do not offer a prescription as to what is involved, save for one point.

The Biblical-theological renewal of the thirties and forties, which had such dramatic effect upon the ecumenical movement, seemed especially to have had the issue of loyalty in mind. My first experience of that was in WSCF circles in college over the question of the relation of secular values to Christ. In Europe the issue was fundamentally the same, but loyalty in its political form came strongly to the fore. This focus upon loyalty produced strong emphasis upon the Lordship of Christ. Those then involved did not have a hierarchical issue in mind; they were, rather, concerned with the problem of loyalty and the circumstances in which loyalty was tested and expressed.

In the USA today, however, the issue is different. A few years ago, the Minnesota study of church life, Faith and Ferment[3], showed how profoundly an individualistic subjectivism reigns in church life, whether the church was or was not highly structured. Habits of the Heart[4] confirms the same for the whole culture. In the churches, this amounts to a subjectivism of personal preference, a "do it yourself religiosity." So entrapped, we Christians seem to merge into the general society, save that we go to church.

This suggests a different need than that which gave rise to the earlier search for the meaning of loyalty. Our problem concerns identity, namely the meaning in its Biblical and theological sense of Christian identity in our surroundings and habits of subjectivity. Granted that problems of subjectivity/objectivity usually focus upon knowledge and knowing, it nevertheless appears to me that now, in our current USA church situation, we need a concerted Biblical, theological renewal as to our sense of being, of what it means to "be" in Christ, of the nature of identity in Christ. This would counter our devastating subjectivity in life not only with the claims of truth in Christ but also with a clearly recognizable communal identity in Christ.

The third basic need is for a more nuanced and better balanced relationship between "movement" and "structure" in the USA ecumenical church situation. The church has historically required a combination of

---

3. Faith and Ferment, Joan D. Chittister O.S.B. and Martin E. Marty, Robert S. Bilheimer, ed. Collegeville and Minneapolis, 1983. The Liturgical Press and Augsburg Publishing House.

4. Habits of the Heart, Robert N. Bellah, et. al., New York, 1985, Harper & Row.

movement and structure. An early example is monasticism, which was first a movement into the desert and then into communities, both in reaction to, if not protest against, immoralities within both society and the Church. Monasticism made its point, to put it mildly, and itself became subject to reforming movements within the structures of the great orders. Movements of theological thought, of church reform, of missionary and social responsibility have followed ever since the desert fathers. In 1948 (WCC) and in 1965 (Vatican II), the ecumenical movement was made a part of church structure, again illustrating this historic rhythm of church life.

Today, in the USA, the balance between structure and movement in things ecumenical is too severely skewed. Movements of genuinely ecumenical concern thrive either too much outside of the churches, or seek too strongly to politicize the church structures in favor of the particular interest of the movement concerned. Theological renewal becomes theological battle as structure sees itself threatened; or structure, geared to the "effectiveness" of the institution, sees theological renewal as irrelevant, leaving theological inquiry too isolated in the academy where too frequently it becomes only esoteric. Church "social action" is too frequently confined to "statements" or local church program planning, that is, social action becomes, like Biblical and theological groups, institutionalized; or on major occasions it becomes a matter for the action of a single denomination or confession, without effort to make it ecumenical.

I wish to stress a single point. Many of the great ecumenical concerns, concerns which can be put in a single word or phrase, like mission, unity, social action, theological/Biblical renewal, exist in present day church structures, but they lack the force and coherence which the common calling of the ecumenical movement supplies. One reason is the skewed balance between "movement" and "structure." At present, either structure too strongly co-opts movement or movement lives too much in bits and pieces outside the structure. Ecumenism with coherence enough to be noticed and guts enough to have impact will need to find and maintain a balance between movement and structure within the church and among the churches.

IV. The Almost Impossible Task.

The "confessing church" does not belong only to the past of Hitler's Germany and Europe. It exists today in Eastern Europe and the USSR, in South Korea and the People's Republic of China, in the Philippines, Latin America, North Africa, Africa south of the Sahara and South Africa, to mention some areas where strong pressure evokes clear confession. Even so, it is not made easily and "the cost of discipleship" weighs heavily.

As regards the freedom to make clear and strong confession, our situation in the USA is far easier, yet in a further sense it is all but devastating. It is devastating because the American hedonism of success eats at our souls and erodes our discipleship. This erosion dulls, weakens, and ultimately blinds us to the summons of the Christian prophetic tradition. And is it not this erosion which has allowed even the ecumenical forces to forget, neglect or so re-interpret the apostolic mandate in our faith, that evangelism has been left mainly to TV tricksters? The do-it-yourself religiosity within our churches lacks certainty in its voice.

How to be the church in this situation? In what terms to be the People, the Body, in this society, so large with possibility, so fraught with devastation as to be almost impossible to comprehend? At the present time, the answer is apparently given by the varied forms of ecumenism that we listed at the beginning of this article and by the many people and groups who quietly serve the poor, the downtrodden, the afflicted and prisoners.

But is that enough? Is it enough to say "I can't do everything, this is my 'issue,'" whether the issue be of social or ecclesiastical import? I do not believe it is.

The power of the ecumenical movement, of the ecumenical tradition, lies in the vigor of ecumenical wholeness. When the general public thinks of religion, I suspect it thinks of: what I do about religion; what the televangelists do about religion; what a conservative Pope does about religion. On a happy occasion, the US Catholic bishops make the front page, latterly with fine statements regarding nuclear weapons and the economy. But so far, neither the general public nor the church public knows the authenticity, power and helpfulness of a visible ecumenical tradition. One does not have to be overly concerned with the evening news and the front page, although one does not denigrate their power. I am concerned far more with the apparent absence of ecumenical witness in the USA of our time, with the apparent absence of voice, action and life together on the part of the real but hidden ecumenical reality in US church life.

That reality is what we started with. The ecumenical movement, of auspicious beginnings, has developed beyond all initial expectations. But in the USA its most far-reaching manifestation is largely hidden, hampered by its invisibility. The ecumenical Roman Catholics, Protestants and Eastern Orthodox who have more in common with one another than they have with the non-ecumenical members of their own traditions exist in telling numbers. My own experience tells me that they want and need one another: the excited explosion of ecumenical recognition in Christ takes place all the time. But these people in the towns and the cities and the regions of the country need voice, the voice of common speech and common action. Can they, can we, find it?

Diary of a Politician from Experiences in the Ecumenical World
Lessons to be Learned
Olle Dahlen

1. Berlin, August 1939

When leaving Amsterdam a couple of Swedes went to Berlin. On a sightseeing tour the guide said: "We are now passing the Olympic Stadium. We have bells in the Tower. We lubricate them well in advance when we are expecting great events. Thus, we have done that now."

We felt the menace. A few days afterwards: Everything seemed to stop. Ecumenical links were broken or at least made very weak. The hope for a better future looked rather distant. Fortunately, we did not expect that it should be so many years to dawn.

2.   The Universities in the Future, 1944

We did not feel that we in Sweden had any opportunity to do something of importance for the Ecumenical work, neither in general between churches nor among students.

After a while, the World Christian Student Federation came with the appeal that Christian student organizations all over the world should start studying the role of the universities in the period after the war. It gave us an opportunity to feel, again, the links that we experienced at the Amsterdam Conference.

3.   New Start Mid-1945

Immediately after the end of the war, the Christian Student Movements in Denmark, Finland, Norway and Sweden started their Ecumenical work. Already in August, a Nordic conference was held in Abo, Finland. It was followed by a meeting in Copenhagen of the Christian Student Leaders in the Nordic countries. There something significant happened which has followed me in my work in politics as well as in Ecumenical encounters.

The scene in one of the opening talks was this: The leader of the Norwegian delegation had played an important part in the secret Norwegian Resistance Movement. He was a theologian, who later became Bishop. He turned to the Finnish delegation, asking: "What were you doing when we were fighting Hitler and you went into war against our allies, the Soviets?"

"We prayed. We did that in our tents, cabins, and trenches. That was the only thing we could do in our situation."

The Finnish answer was as simple as it was effective, and it silenced the attacker. However, at the same time, both in Finland and in Sweden, a heated debate was taking place about what the Allies tried to do with

Finnish law-making. They pushed the Finnish Parliament to adopt retroactive laws, which was forbidden in the Constitution. The purpose was to bring to court Finnish politicians who have involved their country in the second war with the Soviet Union. (In the first war the USSR attacked Finland). Many people thought, regardless if they considered the Finnish policy at that time right or wrong, that the oppression of Finland was totally against the principles which should guide democracies. I was one of them and could not resist the temptation to make a little counterattack on my Norwegian friends, making it my first "outburst" in an international Ecumenical setting: "What are you in the Allied countries doing when your political leaders are now pushing Finland to violate its own Constitution?"

The answer was that they had not thought about that. My reason for mentioning this incident is that it constitutes to me an equally symbolic and important element in discussions about international relations, not only among politicians--but also in the world of Ecumenism. An important task is to be on the move, to try to reform, but at the same time keep a well-balanced mind. There was a lesson to be learned.

LESSON NUMBER ONE

Be careful, always, when in the shadow of a conflict; you are dealing with sensitive and complicated issues. There might be more to it than is said. Do not take for granted what is trumpeted forth in the mass media. Be critical.

4. Church and Society Conference, 1966

For almost 20 years, I did not have much contact with international Ecumenism. Domestic politics in Sweden took most of my time. In the fifties I was elected to Parliament.

My personal interest in international affairs had not disappeared, and in the middle of the sixties opportunities came to involve myself more directly in the foreign policy of my country. I became a member of the Standing Committee on Foreign Affairs in the Parliament and was chosen as its vice-chairman. My first experience with the United Nations came in 1958, as a member of the Parliamentarian delegation to the General Assembly. From 1964 onwards, I attended most Assemblies into the eighties. During some years I was also a member of the Swedish delegation to the disarmament negotiations in Geneva.

This change in direction in politics coincided with direct involvement in Ecumenical affairs. I became a member of the Swedish Ecumenical Council and chaired the Committee for contacts with the Commission of the Churches on International Affairs of the World Council of Churches, CCIA. The came an event of import: the Church and Society Conference, Geneva, 1966.

It was easy to accept the invitation to go to Geneva. For a politician, it was like a gift from heaven to be able to participate in a church gathering when a lot of time, money and energy were spent on careful preparation. The big preparatory volumes made excellent reading, I could not agree with everything, how could one, when even the authors have different opinions. The ground to stand on was solid, that was the key thing. The Conference had a great impact and prepared the soil for the WCC Assembly in Uppsala.

Nevertheless, in some essays there was a lack of understanding of the political dimension of some problems. More input from persons practically involved in political decision-making could have been of value. In most Ecumenical meetings the lack of participation of politicians and experts has been common. This fact is necessary to deal with in view of the future of Ecumenism, and I will come back to it later in this essay.

5. The Beginning of Change of Heading and Style, 1967-68

The next experience came when I, as a Delegate to the United Nations General Assemblies, contacted the CCIA office in New York. I had earlier received some CCIA documentation. The CCIA Pre-Assembly summary of its concern about some items was distributed to the UN national missions and it was interesting. Richard Fagley did an excellent job there.

Some people had informed me that the staff was highly competent and experienced. But it was said that they had their own style. They preferred to deal with persons they were used to, civil servants in the UN and in some administrations, mostly in North America and Western Europe. They had done a very good job in the period after the war. Thus, it was a little difficult for CCIA to realize that it was time for a more open and general approach. And who can blame them for that? To some extent we are all prisoners of the environment in which we have been brought up, sticking to the methods we have seen to be useful. It had been very useful to have a CCIA which often worked rather independently from the churches and from the WCC.

However, the international scene was rapidly changing, as easily recognized in the UN. The new independent nations became larger in numbers and influence. They did not accept that neither the former colonial powers nor the "big" powers should decide over their heads. Gradually the Anglo-American/Western and East European blocs lost majority and influence in the General Assembly. Something similar happened in the Ecumenical world. The churches from the newly independent states gradually grew in influence. The membership of the Orthodox churches had added to the tip of balance in the World Council of Churches away from the Atlantic dominance.

These trends ought to have their impact on the methods which WCC used in its involvement in international affairs. CCIA could no longer be run by a group of Anglo-American individuals, regardless of how excellent they obviously were.

Most people understood this. When Eugene Carson Blake in 1967 was chosen as the World Council's General Secretary, he took up the challenge even regarding the Council's acting in international affairs. It is remarkable that the Professor of Political Science, Dr. Darril Hudson, in his book The World Council of Churches in International Affairs, published for the Royal Institute of International Affairs, 1977, obviously does not understand the reasons behind the changes in the Council's instrument for acting in international affairs. He puts all the "blame" on Blake, writing: "Centralization, originally begun to satisfy one person's desire (Blake) for direct control of all activities, has been continued due to inertia and fiscal realities..." He continues to criticize that these fiscal realities made it necessary to close the CCIA London office by judging: "London is certainly more important in world politics than Geneva."

So far as I understand, it was not a choice between Geneva and London from the point of view that Hudson indicates. When the Swedish CCIA Committee responded to the inquiry from the Council on this matter, we said, of course, there has to be a strong CCIA office in Geneva, despite the fact that maybe it will mean abolishing the London office.

Blake invited me to participate in a Consultation in the Hague which should give WCC advice on the future work of CCIA.

The participants of the Hague Consultation gave the advice that CCIA should continue with some independence but with stronger links to the WCC itself. The changes were accepted by the WCC General Assembly in Uppsala in 1968. The misgiving expressed that CCIA would be led by the nose of the WCC General Secretaries did not materialize. I never experienced that Blake or later on Philip Potter tried to oppress our opinions. On the contrary, in one way or another the CCIA people were always involved when the WCC should act in the sphere of CCIA activities. The truth is that it was usually CCIA which took the initiative and drafted the statements for the different WCC bodies. In the Policy Reference Committees at the General Assemblies and the Committees for Public Statements at the Meetings of the Central Committee the majority was always from CCIA. Even the members of the Central Committee who sat in these special committees were mostly chosen among those who also were CCIA Commissioners.

LESSON NUMBER TWO

Churches have a millenium or two to look back on. This constitutes leaning towards what has been good in their organizational forms, even when it comes to young bodies--like WCC.

In the fifties and sixties there came drastic changes on the international scene, changes which had to influence the Ecumenical world when trying to do business with it. To stick to old forms out of nostalgia could be dangerous. Even the Churches have to read the signs on the wall.

Now to comments on some specific issues on the international agenda during my active involvement in ecumenical affairs:

6.   Consequences of One's Acting, 1969 and Onwards

The first meeting of CCIA, after my election as Commissioner by the WCC GA in Uppsala, Sweden, was in August 1969 in Cambridge. One of the very hot issues was the Biafra war in Nigeria.

There were Christian leaders on both sides of the conflict, a fact which came out in the open in the Uppsala Assembly. The debates in political circles were sometimes heated. I myself had raised the issue in my Parliament.

CCIA was asked to draft a statement for the WCC Central Committee, which was to meet afterwards. It was a difficult task. The sufferings of thousands of persons, especially in the Biafra zone, was big news in the mass media all over the world. That CCIA had to take into account. On the other hand, aid to the Biafrans, of course, also gave them better opportunities to continue the war. The WCC was on the side of peace, which meant an end to the war as rapidly as possible.

In that situation the value of advice from experts and persons with political wisdom came into focus. Two persons of this kind took part in CCIA: two Ghanaians--Mr. A.L. Adu, the Assistant Secretary General of the Commonwealth Secretariat, and Dr. Robert Gardiner, Director of the UN Economic Commission for Africa, ECA. Both of them said: "Of course, the churches have to give humanitarian aid. Of course, this has political implications for the war situation. Of course, that fact ought to be spelled out in the statement; no hiding should be allowed."

Their interventions were so convincing that we all agreed, and later on so did the Central Committee. This openness surely was one of the reasons why the WCC was the first international Non-Governmental Organization which, after the end of the war, was allowed to come in with humanitarian assistance.

The Churches should not try to hide what could be the consequences of their acting. It is much better to indicate what they could be; that is also a sign that you are not ignorant.

7. The Programme to Combat Racism, PCR

During my years at the UN the single act of the churches which was given most attention was when the WCC created the Programme to Combat Racism. I do not know if Senator George McGovern, who chaired the Consultation on the issue, and the other church representatives could imagine what impact the Programme would have in the debates in the UN regarding apartheid and similar issues. Over the years PCR was, time and again, quoted in interventions from a number of Member States. It gave some kind of moral alibi for them in their own righteous indignation. If ever, the WCC creation of PCR was a timely act.

It had lasting effects. When I later became Ambassador-at-Large in the Swedish Ministry of Foreign Affairs, Sweden was not a member of the Committee set up the Economic and Social Council for relations to Non-Governmental Organizations. It is a small committee by UN standards. The Netherlands was a member. The Dutch diplomat in charge of related issues was Dr. Theo van Boven. Some time after my taking office he came to me and said: "With Swedish interest in NGO-affairs and you as the first ambassador ever having such a responsibility, we in the Dutch Ministry think it would be appropriate if we gave up our seat and proposed that Sweden should take it."

It has to be noted as one of the strange facts in history that van Boven in 1983 succeeded me as Moderator of CCIA.

The switch of seats was made. Thus, at the same time I was Moderator of CCIA and sitting in the ECOSOC NGO Committee, part of the time as its Chairman. My distinct impression was that the churches had a good standing among most of the delegations. The delegations from black Africa were in the forefront in occasions when that was of importance. In the Committee we dealt with a number of issues where the religious background of NGO was scrutinized, not always in favourable terms by some delegations. What different WCC Units and other Christian NGOs were doing played a role in this connection.

LESSON NUMBER THREE

Actions have stronger impacts than statements. Deeds are more important than words.

The good image of the churches did not deteriorate with their handling of the civil war in Sudan, that one which ended in 1972.

8.   The Civil Wars in the Sudan

It was Sunday morning, December 11, 1988. We were sitting in the office of the famous scholar, Professor Omar Beshir, Dean of the African Studies Department of Khartoum University. He said, "I am well acquainted with what the churches did to promote peace in our first civil war and how you helped to get the Addis Ababa Agreement in 1972. A crucial thing was the wonderful analysis which the excellent American lady made about our struggle. That was a great piece of scholarly work."

"The American lady" was Reverend Theresa Scherf, half-time assisting the American church in Geneva. Her contribution to the peace process in the beginning of the seventies was a research paper she did for CCIA with the aim of describing as objectively as possible the reasons behind the civil war, why it was fought. To our great joy, both of the parties to the conflict accepted it as a fair picture--despite some rather firm judging--and that was not a small contribution in the long period of talks and negotiations.

She did not take part in the negotiations, but her paper added to the impressions among the parties that the churches only had one thing in mind-- peace.

LESSON NUMBER FOUR

When deemed to be of value, do not hesitate to spell out what you see as the real issues in a conflict. Cool judgments, not antagonistic to any party, are appropriate.

The negotiating job was done by Kodwo Ankrah, the WCC's Refugee Secretary; Burgess Carr, the Secretary-General of the All Africa Council of Churches; and the CCIA Director, Leopoldo Niilus. They performed excellently. It is not the place here to go into the details of that work. For those interested, it is now possible to put these mediation efforts into a broader context. The first Research Report from the Life and Peace Institute, Uppsala, Sweden: "Peaceful Resolution of Conflicts: Non-Governmental Organizations in the International System," is the result of the efforts of political scientist Bo Westas; Duncan Wood, former head of the Friends' office in Geneva; and myself, to give an overall view of what churches and other NGOs have done in this field and what they might be able to achieve in the future.

The peace in Sudan lasted until 1985. Now a devastating conflict is there again. The present efforts for peace are good examples of one of the ideas behind the changes in methods of WCC/CCIA work. The hope was to have more close co-operation with national and regional ecumenical bodies. On the whole, it has proved to be the right approach despite what Darril Hudson predicted. Let me take the collaboration between the Sudan Council of Churches and WCC/CCIA and other ecumenical bodies as an example.   President Niemeri of Sudan in September 1983 introduced new legislation based on Islamic law, Sharia. That was a challenge to Sudanese Christians and other Non-Muslims. The Sudan Council of Churches (SCC) asked WCC/CCIA to express its concern about the situation. I was asked to go to Khartoum to illustrate that and met with a number of key actors in the conflict. Later on, a special WCC delegation went there and did a good job.

Those efforts did not change the situation, and no one had thought that they might. What happened was that the Christians were supported and that the many other Non-Muslims and Muslims who did not agree with Niemeri were assured that there was an international concern about the situation, not the least among Churches.

The co-operation between CCIA and SCC has continued, and SCC has played a very active role as a peacemaker, so far without result. The tragic situation inspired SCC in the fall of 1988 to send a delegation to Western and Northern Europe. The purpose was to raise the level of awareness of the dreadful consequences of the civil war and the drought. They visited churches, ecumenical organizations--and politicians and diplomats.

Even we in Sweden met with delegates. The meeting in Khartoum referred to in the beginning of this section came as a result of repeated invitations from SCC to us at the Life and Peace Institute in Uppsala to come to Sudan and familiarize ourselves with the situation. They promised to set up meetings with influential persons. That story will be told later on in this paper.

I have taken Sudan as an example of co-operation between a national Ecumenical Council and the WCC/CCIA. There are a number of similar experiences involving not only National Councils but also Regional

Ecumenical Councils, like the All Africa Conference of Churches, the Christian Conference of Asia, the Latin American Council of Churches, and not least, the Middle East Council of Churches.

LESSON NUMBER FIVE

The world cannot be run from either Moscow or Washington, or from the United Nations in New York or the WCC in Geneva. In co-operation with churches on the spot lie the best opportunities for achieving results.

9. Promoting Human Rights

The CCIA record on its activites in the field of Human Rights is a proud one. Dr. O. Frederick Nolde was the first CCIA Director, from 1946 to 1969. Even before the establishment of CCIA Nolde was active in promoting Human Rights. It is a historical fact that Nolde played an important role as Chairman of the group of NGOs assisting the UN in drafting the Universal Declaration of Human Rights. That story is reported in Nolde's book, Free and Equal, published by WCC, 1968.

During his years CCIA intervened in many cases concerning Human Rights. However, this is my story, and I will not try to report on their work. I will briefly describe some of the elements in the new contribution WCC/CCIA tried to give from the beginning of the seventies.

Some time ago, I was asked by the European Commission of the World Alliance of Reformed Churches to read a paper at its meeting in Brno, Czechoslovakia, "Human Rights from the North-South Perspective." I wrote the paper in the form of a letter to Allan Boesak, the President of WARC, thus the personal tone as I quote the part on how it began:

> In this connection something happened which has had a profound personal Christian meaning for me. I was asked to be the chairman of The Commission of the Churches on

International Affairs (CCIA). The election was to take place at the Central Committee meeting in Addis Ababa in January 1971. I should, of course, have given a lot of thought about what I saw as the main responsibility for CCIA, but I did not do that. Thus, I was unprepared when the CCIA staff a couple of weeks before the Central Committee meeting asked me in Geneva what I saw as of specific importance for the CCIA to concern itself with in future.

In retrospect I am very grateful that the Lord has different ways of working, even through people who have not been doing their duty. On the spur of the moment my answer to the question was: Human Rights, adding not only the problems of religious freedom and political rights which we in the West have been pressing for, but the whole spectrum, i.e. also civil, economic and social rights.

We have to be very careful to indicate that we have been used by God. For me it seems obvious that the Holy Spirit used my experience in the UN about the whole problem regarding Human Rights and at that moment in Geneva with the CCIA staff put a spotlight on that experience and made me see the role of the churches.

Obviously the spiritual situation was the same for the CCIA staff, Leopoldo Niilus and Dwain Epps. There was no need for argumentation pro et con. We agreed to propose to the Central Committee a fresh start for the WCC in dealing with the Human Rights problems on a broader base. The Committee agreed and authorized the CCIA to do the job in cooperation with others.

In my letter to Boesak, I gave several reasons why to report in this fashion. One was that it might be of interest for the record how the new approach began because the Central Committee agreed with us and authorized CCIA to do the job in co-operation with others. But there was also a lesson to be learned.

LESSON NUMBER SIX

The experience gave me the inspiration to write to him:

> <u>Knowledge and insight</u> are necessary elements also for the Holy Spirit. The three of us who were sitting there in Geneva discussing what WCC/CCIA ought to take up as a responsibility, <u>we knew about the problems,</u> and we were aware of our own shortcomings and those of the churches. Our potential but slumbering knowledge was used.

10. The St Polten Consultation, 1974, and the WCC General Assembly, 1975

The CCIA staff put in an incredible amount of excellent work, together with other staff members and some key advisers from different countries in order to prepare for "Human Rights and Christian Responsibility," the St. Polten Consultation in Austria, 1974. After more than two years of preparation, we came together from all corners and tried to dig as deeply as possible in the vast area of Human Rights and the Responsibility of the Ecumenical World.

The WCC GA in Nairobi in its decisions regarding Human Rights built on the report from St Polten. There is, however, one incident from the Assembly which ought to be analyzed.

As could be easily foreseen, during the last days of the GA the question of Religious Liberty in the Soviet Union was brought to the floor. It was said by some US and West European delegates that the churches in the USSR were not given the possibility to work as freely as in other parts of the world. They were called "victims of political oppression." Of course, that was right, although some of the arguments for that opinion were not so adequate.

The tension rose in plenary and in the Policy Reference Committee, which had to deal with the issue. The delegates from the Soviet Churches were unhappy, sorry and angry. The issue was not brought up in co-operation with them. They felt exposed. I remember saying to one of my American friends: "I think it is a bad method to punish the victims." They should have been assisted, not brought unprepared to a public court.

The Committee met in the afternoon. It was necessary to invite them to an open hearing and the Committee room was crowded. It was one of the most unpleasant and tense meetings I have experienced in WCC. A draft statement was presented, unfair and totally unacceptable to the Soviet delegates.

Two things were lacking in the draft: Efforts to understand the situation for the churches concerned, and ignorance about the fact that Religious Liberty cannot be dealt with separately from Human Rights as well as from the political system in each country. Realizing that, I used the dinner break to write a new draft, praying that it might ease the tension and bring the groups together.

More hours of heated debate followed in the closed meeting of the Committee. When in the small hours it became complete chaos, I asked for the floor and read my draft. Rapidly there was a consensus that it could be used as a basis for a resolution.

A formal drafting group was appointed, consisting of T.B. Simaputang of Indonesia, Alexey Buevsky of the USSR, and William P. Thompson of the USA. They polished the draft and presented it in plenary. In this the record of the Assembly is correct. As this occasion is one of the not so many where I have been able to assist in crucial situations of that magnitude, I might be forgiven for including the above. Simaputang asked me if I would like to be mentioned in plenary as the one who had made the draft.

Since at that time I was Ambassador-at-large in the Ministry of Foreign Affairs (US State Department), I did not think it would be good to be exposed in public; thus, my answer was "no, please!" Now, the story can be told, without bad consequences, I suppose.

LESSON NUMBER SEVEN

Violations of Human Rights, including Religious Liberty, matters of specific human beings, persons who can be easily identified. When the "victims" are taking part in a Church meeting, the first act is to have an open talk with them. One can never be sure of agreeing, but it is imperative to try. (In the Central Committee meeting in Berlin, 1974, a church leader from the Philippines answered the accusation against the dictatorship rule of President Marcos with "he is a gift from God". No meeting of the minds was possible). Not trying to meet is against the true spirit of Christian community.

The churches are doing a disservice to oppressed people when they mostly concentrate their efforts on the victims of violations of Religious Liberty. All persons have equal value. All of us are God's children, are we not?

11.   Centralized and Decentralized Activity

The above has given an example of the co-operation between a central organ for church activity in international affairs like CCIA and the Sudan Council of Churches. The present CCIA Director Dr. Ninan Koshy and the staff have been able to continue on that road. The Roman Catholic Church has some distance to cover before it realizes that the world cannot be run from Rome.

To continue with Sudan. As mentioned above, the Life and Peace Institute in Uppsala was asked by SCC to come to Sudan and study the situation. First a word about the Institute.

Archbishop Olof Sundby of the Church of Sweden (Lutheran) took the initiative to invite leaders to Uppsala, 1983. The purpose was, for once, to gather church leaders together in order to consider the responsibility of Christianity against the threat of human survival, specifically the threat to peace from modern weaponry.

They came, Orthodox, Roman Catholic, from the Reformed tradition, "liberals," middle-of-the-road persons, Evangelicals. As a political scientist, I consider it the most representative gathering in Christianity during the past 1600 years, or at least the past 900 years. It was said that there would be just this conference, and that no new ecumenical body should come out of it. However, Rev. Dr. J. Andrew Kirk, the representative proposed by the Lausanne Committee for World Evangelization to sit in the International Preparatory Committee, which I chaired,
came up with the idea of a Christian Peace Institute.

The Conference sent a Message to the Churches which included the following:

> We appeal therefore to the churches...to develop peace
> education programmes. These programmes should encourage
> Christians to think theologically; to search out the causes of
> conflict; to explore Christian concepts of non-violent resistance
> to evil; and to trace the connections between disarmament and
> development. To this end the possibility of creating an
> international Christian peace institute should be explored.

To make a long story short, there has been since 1985 the Life and Peace Institute in Uppsala, with the purpose called for. It is both international and ecumenical, trying to "bring Christian perspectives to bear on situations of conflict by stimulating peace research within a framework of interdisciplinary cooperation, mainly among theology and the social sciences."

I think this is an example of the need for the Churches to <u>dig deeper, to be more specific and expert-like in their approaches to international problems</u>. The reports from the Institute are now starting to be published: the one mentioned above, "Peaceful Resolutions of Conflict," "Statements on Peace and the Authority of the Church," and "The Militarization of Space."

Going back, the leader of the Institute's Project on the Horn of Africa, Rev. Sture Normark and myself went to Khartoum and met with present and former Cabinet Members, opposition leaders, diplomats, church leaders, persons with different religious backgrounds, and so on.

Over the years of conflicts in the Sudan, there have always been three major elements:

(a)   The underdevelopment of the South.

(b)   The ethnic dimension, Arabs versus Africans.

(c)   The religious tensions between Muslims on one side and Christians and other Non-Muslims on the other.

Depending on the actual political situation, one or the other of these elements has dominated.

We came back convinced that this time the religious tension had dominance. The Prime Minister, Sadiq el Mahdi, promised in 1986 when he took office to repeal the Niemeri, Sharia-based laws. He has not done so, which has created growing tension. People do not like to have two classes of citizens: Muslims and Non-Muslims.

This is a brutal illustration of an increasing concern of mine. "Religion as Causes of Conflict," which is another of the Institute's projects, is timely. Even we, as Christians, have to take it seriously. We are part of the problem, either by creating it--to some extent--or by not trying hard enough to solve it.

We have to build up co-operation with other World Religions. This is easy to say as it is difficult to achieve. But there are causes of such a magnitude that one cannot avoid becoming heavily involved. It has to be done, bearing in mind that there is often more than one element of a conflict. As in Sudan, often the underdevelopment of one region is crucial. As in the USSR, the whole political climate has to be taken into consideration, not just caring for our fellow Christians.

LESSON NUMBER EIGHT

In this world of ours, it is no longer possible for a country to live exclusively for itself. We are all in the same boat--in a rocky sea--and will survive or perish together.

Christians must--together with other World Religions, together with representatives of different ideologies--try to build an international ethos based on common responsibility. There is an urgent need for at least a minimum amount of ethics, large enough for a new kind of international as well as national behaviour. This platform has to be common for all groups who share the same intentions. We Christians do not have a monopoly on how to build that common platform. We have to involve ourselves with others in these efforts.

There is a need to work on this in central bodies, whether they are political, religious, or other kinds. At the same time, problems differ from country to country, region to region; thus, decentralized work, by regional and national bodies of the same character, is urgent.

We Christians have a right to be proud of our heritage. But we have also to be humble, recognizing that, in building a better society, all others have the same right to be recognized in the common work for humankind.

Reliving Amsterdam
Gerald Hutchinson

Amsterdam has been laying fresh claim on me lately. Maybe the
anticipation of 50th Anniversary is doing it, or maybe it is natural for anyone
fifty years later to be remembering and evaluating.

The influence became apparent long before the Conference itself for
preparations and sponsoring agencies drew people together from diverse
sources. So YWCA Secretary Baptist Florence met Anglican layman Garth.
When Garth and I joined the crowd for Amsterdam, Florence and the other
sponsors stayed home. But their marriage, their home and their influence
in church and community has been a delight far beyond either Anglican or
Baptist circles. A few months ago Garth sent me a picture of the Canadian
delegation calling for help in trying to put names with faces. We were
disturbed to realize that having been so closely involved then, we could not
remember now. That search for people awakened other enquiries: What

were we doing there? What happened there? If we can't even remember our own delegation, was it important at all?

That search for memory of persons revealed something else important to me. I started looking for notes, memos, lists, pictures--any of the clutter one brings home. I felt quite bereft when I realized I had none at all.

Amsterdam is inseparable from war. The heaviness of anticipation hung over us, many delegations were hampered by restrictions, the splendid visions of youthful enthusiasm and ecumenical sharing only seemed to illumine the prospects of a dark and violent future. Many of us from North America lived with an innocent naivete, and wondered about the pessimism of the Europeans--but on the other hand, we learned enough to be shocked at a Dutch host, the head of a major Travel Agency, who told us, "There won't be any war! It's all paper talk."

Amsterdam initiated a host of young people into the tensions of Christian belief and intention in the midst of hopeless or almost hopeless destruction in the human community. Then, having shared in the rich and diverse resources of the Christian community, having been inspired by the Orthodox choir, having sung hymns in French, German and English all at the same time, having seen far beyond into a Promised Land...we scattered.

Many times I have wondered what happened then. We would never be able to forget what we had known together, but were now thrust apart into differing national interests and into the limiting confines of local congregations. The war was upon us with such divisive and devastating force that even friendly correspondence was almost eliminated. The Dutch Delegation sent out a Christmas letter, Geza Soos sent a Christmas card from Hungary, Vessela Tsoneva wrote two rather despairing notes from Bulgaria, and I have a most charming scrap of birch bark with a Christmas candle signed simply Hypatia of Lithuania. How I cherish them! If the same group of people had been summoned to meet in 1949 what response could there have been?

For my part, I visited relatives in Britain, and went to the Glasgow docks August 25 to board the SS California. "Ye ken, the boat is no' sailin'" he said. The California had become a troop ship. Knowledgable friends helped me to secure passage on the over-crowded Athenia, leaving Liverpool on September 2. My long time friends, Professor Gerald Cragg and his family, were the only Amsterdam people I knew on board. By Sunday morning we were well out into the North Atlantic. About 11 a.m. we were informed of the Declaration of War with Germany. Groups of anxious people counted the lifeboats, and talked of What-if-a-torpedo? and what would be the outlook for single young men on a boat overcrowded with women and children. About 7:30 p.m. the torpedo hit, pierced the side below waterline, shattered a section of cabins, and invited the sea to rush in flooding the ship. Our Captain said it was the first shot of the western war-- and a damned good shot too! Hours of scramble and confusion, into lifeboats, rowing heavy boats in the heavy swells, and finally rescue freighter and rope up the towering sides. Five hundred of us, including the Craggs, were landed in Galway, thence to Glasgow, and eventually home. It has been a part of the Amsterdam experience for me--and of course is the reason I have no notes, or lists or memos. We escaped with what we had in our pockets--all else was gone. And in that experience, the realization that every one of our companions had dispersed into something new, many into unimaginable scenes of violence and privation. How many survived? I wonder.

The war naturally affected our reporting of Amsterdam. While raising funds to get to the Conference, I promised to report on my return, so a heavy schedule was ready for me. But now the fresh emotions of war took precedence. I could never talk about Amsterdam without first satisfying the demand for the Athenia. And the questioning was of the same nature--"If the Christian Youth of the world were there, why did they not produce a plan of peace for the world? Is there a Christian hope in a world of war and dying? What should Christian youth be doing now?"

Since I was recuperating from active TB in 1938 enlistment in the Services was out of the question, and continued with my Theological Studies with the influences of Amsterdam expressed through the Student Christian Movement and Church youth groups. When John R. Mott visited Edmonton the Amsterdam people were prepared to meet him. By 1943, I was ordained, and invited to become the National Secretary of the SCM of Canada.

The implications of Amsterdam were everywhere and immediate. The World's Student Christian Federation and the SCM's had been heart and center of the Conference and were naturally involved in its consequences. Profound planning and anticipation occupied many of the leaders offstage and in back rooms. It was realized for example that the WSCF office in Geneva might well be isolated or over-run so the office was dispersed--Helen Morton to monitor an office in New York, Robert Mackie to Toronto, with Visser 't Hooft in Geneva.

So when I moved from Edmonton and my prairie home to Toronto, Robert and Dorothy Mackie, and their son Steven, were already established. I was facing new responsibilities of national and international scope, and look back with amazement and gratitude for the supporting influence of these wise and world-aware people, not only in the six Toronto years but into the retirement home in Scotland, Steven's work in St. Andrews, and even into Grenada. And the influence continues on through correspondence with the amazing Helen Morton.

I think now that the most significant influence for me was the changed attitude towards other churches. In any given community, churches are often rivals, marked by jealousy for one's own tradition, and critical suspicion towards others. I cannot say that this has entirely disappeared but Amsterdam had demonstrated the great wealth in diversity. Orthodox Churches had been entirely alien to me but the Paris Choir and Prof. Leo Zander won my heart and admiration. Hymns in French deeply moved me, and so did Philippe Maury through WSCF years. Consequently in my work in the Canadian scene it became entirely natural to respect the work and tradition of others, and to seek common cause wherever possible. The formation of the Canadian Council of Churches made sense, and was achieved because some of each of the churches had been together at Amsterdam.

From Toronto I returned in 1949 to my western roots to undertake an extensive rural ministry in an area of particular need. A large heavily-wooded area based on grey-wooded soil had always frustrated attempts to farm it, until soil scientists had completed their research and demonstrated a method of successful cultivation. The whole area was ready for change and growth of population. So my intention was to settle in for an extended period. I had no idea that the Amsterdam experience would have any bearing.

For several decades there had been migrations of European peoples to gain a fresh start in Canada. Some were able to get established on better soil but many with meager resources were inevitably drawn into the unproductive and cheaper land. They pitted their skills against heavy odds. At the time of my arrival there were quite discernible blocks of national groupings. Each family held individual title to their land, but they settled as close to each other as possible and for a long time retained the identity of their language and customs. Very few of them were able to establish a church in their own tradition. The United Church of Canada had developed an open stance to community anyway, so it was expected that I would be somewhat available for weddings, funerals, and sometimes for worship.

A group of Hungarian Presbyterians attempted to have occasional services in their own language, served by a young Minister based in the city of Edmonton. We became good friends in a kind of shared ministry. I commented one day that I had previously known only one Hungarian churchman. I had known Geza Soos at Amsterdam. "Geza Soos!" he said, "he is my best friend!" That simple encounter of two people was not only a joy, but a source of strength in the realization that there is a dependable network of persons, maybe a seamless robe of relationships with sustaining power.

My Ministry involved meeting with seven congregations in scattered undeveloped communities with very diverse cultural backgrounds. Less than 15% were of Anglo-Saxon origin. I discovered a common base in the Apostles' Creed, and found my own college training helpful but the encompassing warmth of diverse groups in "The Amsterdam Congregation" provided confidence and understanding.

So much for looking back and tracing some outcomes. Could a similar Conference be convened now? What would be an equivalent in the contemporary scene?

We seemed to accept without question that Europe was Home Country, source of tradition, base of the Christian Church. The combining of European traditions was World Church and the vision was glorious. But the devastations of the next few years changed that outlook. European nations were battered with destruction and impoverishment. North American nations shared wealth and people but without being harmed, and in the process developed great national confidence and industrial strength. In 1946 Church leaders were attempting to take stock. A consultation of Church, Military and Political leaders was convened in London to which my SCM position gave me a place. After many had had their say, a young American officer startled many and antagonized some by saying,

> "Gentlemen, it doesn't really matter any more what Britain thinks, or what Europe thinks. The United States has the power, and the decisions rest with us."

He seemed like a brash young man, but there is not a nation in the world now that is not affected by American decision and influence. Surely there has never been a developing Empire so directly linked with evangelical fervour and the projection of national righteousness. TV evangelists and others have made such far-reaching use of communication channels. Religious movements originating in the United States and incorporating the dynamics and technologies of the new world have quickly become world-wide institutions with pervasive influence--far-reaching Pentecostalism of many kinds, Mormons, Witnesses, Adventists. In Canada we have come to recognize in almost every community, the traditions of European-based churches (including European-based churches developed in the United States, and extended into Canada), and a whole variety of American-based groups and fellowships. The European-based groups follow the Amsterdam tradition, meet quite easily in Ministerials and Councils. Some American-based groups meet with them cautiously, others maintain an entirely separate cause. Can you imagine now trying to assemble a representative gathering of all who honour the name of Jesus?

We had many races of people at Amsterdam, but there was an obvious dominance of English, white, Western--and their traditions. The balance would be different now. Maybe Africa would be an alternative stage. I do not mean that there is a new Alexandria arising to challenge Rome or Geneva or London or Canterbury. I do not see the means or the combination of institutions that could be ready to stage a contemporary Amsterdam. But I do see a vast continent of peoples with growing power and confidence, asserting their right to belong and to be recognized, and finding both insight and support in their churches.

Maybe the new Amsterdam would be convened around a common concern rather than around a common tradition or place. Social justice, refugees, environment seem more important than denominational loyalty and tradition for many dedicated people. And many are finding insight and instruction in the Bible contrary to the established custom of the recognized churches. I think it was Visser 't Hooft who remarked that "the churches are all united in the Bible--until they open it." The Bible is being opened and read.

Perhaps the new Amsterdam would need a much stronger inter-faith perspective. We seemed so confident then that the Christian faith was the obvious truth for the world. By now we are much more aware of the virility and integrity of world religions from the quiet appeal of the Buddhists to the challenge of Islamic Fundamentalists. In Alberta a few years ago, some Roman Catholics and Protestant groups took real satisfaction in making common cause in what we called Inter-Faith. We were surprised one day when an East Indian Hindu walked into a meeting, delighted that he had found a relationship he had been seeking! He was welcomed all right, but we simply were not ready to be "that Inter-Faith."

Many readers will have recognized by now that in remembering aspects and qualities of the Amsterdam Conference, I have been reflecting the perspectives of a young western Canadian student. Obviously the mature leaders and planners would have quite different insights and evaluations.

It may well be that nothing comparable to Amsterdam of 1939 is appropriate now, or even possible now. If the name of Jesus, and the claim of Christus Victor, served to unite us then, it would not now. It is as though the Church failed to get a patent on the name of Jesus, and the use of the name of Jesus, so that everyone may use it much as they wish. Sometimes in blasphemy, or even blasphemy down-graded to the status of slang in everyday conversation. The proclamation of the saving power, the Lord and Saviour is prominent in entertainment of all sorts, in athletics, as well as in the multi-million TV promotional ventures. The name of Jesus is a powerful commodity if you know how to use it. And many do know how.

We must recognize too that many are responding with integrity to a spiritual power in Jesus' name which they encountered and experienced outside of the churches, and could not find in the traditional churches--just as though the Holy Spirit had escaped the confines of the known Church, and was moving freely as the wind "where it will."

If the unmanageable diversity in expressions of Jesus' name, and the significance of his person, makes it too difficult to assemble a World Conference, it may at the same time open new perspectives for the continuing ecumenical imperative in many different ways, in various settings and with differing groups.

I have already stated that relationships amongst the European-based groups seem easier now. Recently a mature couple, employed in a rural community of Lutheran neighbours, decided to be married, and to the delight and satisfaction of their friendly neighbours, asked if they could be married in the local Lutheran Church. The church was kept heated but closed except for one service per year. Shortly before the wedding, with all announcements out and plans made, their plans for an officiant were changed, and they had no one. So, as an old-timer retired clergyman well-known in the community, I was invited and was entirely satisfied with the wedding as proposed. So a United Church Minister faced a Baptist groom with a Roman Catholic bride in a Lutheran Church. And everyone seemed delighted. There is much more to be done, especially in a time of increased willingness, in the shared resources of the Churches sharing the European background and traditions.

The ecumenical imperative requires us to share whatever we can with the Assemblies, Fellowships, Gospel Churches and Peoples Churches that have developed in the same communities--even in single race and single language communities. These are all serious and earnest expressions in the name of Jesus, and his spirit is shared in these people.

The ecumenical imperative calls us too to respond to the non-English speaking, and the non-white appearing people who are now present in almost every community. We are no longer single race communities, or single language communities, but our traditional congregational experience still limits us to "people like us," as though we were a social club built around common characteristics. Any kind of "different person" has difficulty in the group. A Ukrainian Catholic friend joined the Armed Services, and in Montreal without question went to the Roman Catholic Church. Perhaps because of his inner sense of inferiority, perhaps because of attitudes in the people he happened to meet first, he felt entirely unaccepted in the French group, and returned after the war alienated from the Church. The diversity of the world has come into the community but not often into the church.

The ecumenical imperative would not be well served now with the theme Christus Victor--not because it is untrue but because it suggests inappropriate implications. It reads like the banner of a victorious army, or a conquering Empire. If he is Victor, and if we are his, then we are the victors too, aren't we? There have been occasions in Christian history where that was the meaning, and symbols were developed to express that meaning. But not now. The European nations with long traditions of Christianity battered and destroyed each other in war, and were humiliated in the realization. The Christian churches exalting the name of Jesus developed a long and deep prejudice against the Jews who had not accepted or honoured him, were thought to have rejected him and been responsible for his death. So exalting Jesus seemed to mean despising the Jew. The Church was profoundly humiliated as the Holocaust finally exposed to the world that a Christian prejudice and blindness had contributed to the savage death of a people. And with the humiliation, the realization that Jesus had not been honoured by the prejudiced presentation--quite the contrary.

A dogmatic group of theologians laid out their demands as to what the Church must be doing, ending with the declaration "Christ must be obeyed!" Which is to say, we speak for him, you must obey us. A senior Anglican clergy once told me that he had been many years in the church before he realized that when the Bishop told him that something was "God's will," he was really hitting him with a club. Would we now say, "Jesus the liberator," "Jesus the Suffering Servant?"

The ecumenical imperative must surely require us to devote much more attention to an acceptable way of recognizing and honoring the person of Jesus, as contrasted to our insistence on believing what we have said about him. We have learned a great deal about the environment in which Jesus lived; his century does not seem so long ago or far away. The Biblical sources have been so thoroughly researched that we can now more clearly see him in his human dimension. The faith is that he was, in his person, the revealer of God, the God of all creation and of all peoples. We must see him in relation to all the peoples of the world. If it were really true that he rose from the dead, and that his loving Spirit and presence was poured out for all mankind, we have fresh perspectives now for asking, what access had he then to the native peoples of this continent? Had they any means of being aware of his living and questing Spirit? And he any means of making himself known? Or did the Living God--the Risen Lord--the Holy Spirit-- gain access to these people only when we imported the knowledge?

An Asian Christian addressed himself to this question recently at a Conference under the title "Jesus, an open truth." He encouraged his listeners to consider and experience in a more open way than we had ever done before, the truth that is Jesus..."As a Christian I must say that Jesus is my Saviour. I cannot say that Buddha is my saviour, but I also cannot say that God has nothing to do with, or to say from, Buddha...We cannot understand our Christian faith in a ghetto called the Christian Church."

I have no idea whether anyone will be able to assemble a new version of Amsterdam, and can hardly imagine how it could be. But we learned and demonstrated that when people cross traditional barriers, and meet person to person with each of them being faithful to what he knows, that profound and lasting influences flow out through those people. I truly wish that I was now at the beginning of a Ministry rather than nearing the conclusion. Not because I missed something and want to try again; not because there has been any lack of amazement, joy and worth in these fifty years, but because there seem to be so many exciting vistas opening before us.

World Ecumenism and Churches under Communism
Blahoslav Hruby

Some radical changes in the Soviet Union brought about by Mikhail Gorbachev's glasnost (openness) and perestroika (restructuring) and by the process of de-Stalinization of the Soviet system offer an opportunity to examine the subject of world ecumenism and world Communism. Keeping in mind these changes, let us turn our attention to the role of the ecumenical movement in the relationship toward the churches in Communist countries since the foundation of the World Council of Churches (WCC) in Amsterdam in 1948.

The World Council of Churches established contacts with the churches in the USSR and other Communist countries in Europe, and invited them into membership. The fact that all those churches were under strict control of their respective Communist governments presented no serious obstacle during those negotiations. The Soviet and other Communist governments did not object to such contacts because they realized that they could exploit the presence of their churches in the WCC to support Soviet policies and peace propaganda.

In order to protect the membership of those churches in the WCC, its leadership always sought to avoid any pronouncements or public discussions of internal affairs and in particular of the violations of religious freedom and human rights in the Soviet orbit. Whenever an attempt was made to discuss such issues at meetings of the WCC's Central Committee, it was stopped by the WCC leaders with a warning that "the Russians might walk out." Any debate concerning such issues in the WCC's Central Committee was a taboo.

It was not until 1975 that this silence was broken at the WCC General Assembly in Nairobi, Kenya. A public discussion of the religious situation in the USSR was forced there after the local press published an appeal addressed to the WCC delegates by two members of the Russian Orthodox Church, the Rev. Fr. Gleb Yakunin and Lev Regelson. This created the greatest sensation at the WCC Assembly in Nairobi. As could be expected, the delegates from the USSR publicly denied any violations of religious freedom in their country but were unable to prevent the first public discussion of this issue by the WCC. And their walk-out in protest did not last more than a few hours. Unfortunately, even after the revelations contained in Yakunin's and Regelson's appeal the WCC continued its silence regarding the violations of religious freedom and human rights in Communist countries.

On several occasions when the WCC leaders prevented the Central Committee from taking any action in behalf of the persecuted in Communist countries, I gathered among the delegates 40 or 50 signatures for protest cables addressed to the Soviet and other Communist governments. These appeals were picked up by news media and I am happy to say that such appeals helped numerous victims of persecution, particularly those in prisons and labor camps, of which we received many testimonies.

One can only wonder how many more of our fellow believers behind the Iron Curtain could have benefited from an action in their support proclaimed by such an imposing religious body as the World Council of Churches. It is true that in some isolated instances its representatives intervened in accordance with their concept of "quiet diplomacy;" however, its results turned out to be less than impressive. Communist leaders were, and still are, far more responsive to the squeaky wheel method of protest.

In this context I should like to mention the National Council of Churches in the USA (NCC) and the periodical <u>RCDA-Religion in Communist Dominated Areas</u>. This publication was founded in 1962 by Dr. R.H. Edwin Espy, Dr. Paul B. Anderson and myself in order to provide authentic information about the religious situation in Communist countries. At that time the National Council of Churches was eager to establish contacts with the churches behind the Iron Curtain, which lead to an urgent need for a publication that would inform about the church-state policies, laws, regulations and problems concerning religious bodies in Communist countries.

The first official delegation of the NCC to the churches in the USSR in 1962 received briefing documents prepared by Dr. Anderson and myself. After its return, the participants recommended that the publication of such documentation continue and consequently, Dr. Espy, then the General Secretary of the NCC, asked Dr. Anderson and me to publish <u>RCDA</u> under the auspices of the NCC's International Affairs division. This effort was supported financially and morally by the United Presbyterian Church, the Orthodox Church in America, the Episcopal Church, the Greek Orthodox Church, and the Moravian Church. Dr. John Coventry Smith (United

Presbyterian Church), Archbishop Iakovos (Greek Orthodox Church), Dr. Paul C. Empie (Lutheran National Council) and Dr. John Groenfeldt (Moravian Church) were especially encouraging of the new project.

It was a very modest beginning. The budget always presented a problem because of very limited financial support from U.S. denominations. Nevertheless, RCDA provided information not available anywhere else in the English-speaking world. It published documentation and materials both from official Communist sources and from the dissidents; some of these documents are now recognized as landmarks in modern history of the church in Communist countries. In addition, RCDA served as textbook in many U.S. and foreign institutes of higher learning.

However, its battle for survival at the NCC became so critical that in 1972 the NCC decided to terminate its publication. I regarded the discontinuation of RCDA a betrayal of the believers in Communist lands who were being harassed, persecuted and discriminated against because of their faith and whom our publication helped in deed. My solution was to create a non-profit organization that would continue to publish RCDA. Dr. Espy agreed to release RCDA to the newly organized non-profit Research Center for Religion and Human Rights in Closed Societies, Ltd. I have served as its executive director since its inception and edited RCDA with the help of scholars, theologians and political scientists.

Thus, RCDA has marked its 27th year in the Interchurch Center at 475 Riverside Drive, New York City. I should like to stress and gratefully acknowledge the financial support provided by the Glenmede Trust Company.

RCDA is appreciated for the authenticity of its documentation, but also criticized for presenting unflattering evidence about the situation of religion and human rights in Communist countries, which allegedly "hurt" the image of Communist governments as well as detente, ecumenical relations and the East-West dialogue. While certain Western churchmen were bending backward in their effort not to offend Communist governments, representatives of the churches behind the Iron and Bamboo Curtains privately encouraged and even urged us to keep presenting the unvarnished truth about the religious situation in their homelands. For instance, in his public statements the late Metropolitan Nikodim, the spokesman of the Moscow Patriarchate, would never admit any religious persecution in the USSR; however, privately he expressed to us his appreciation for our work and admitted using RCDA to support his arguments with Soviet authorities. Several other church representatives followed similar tactics; however, I mention Metropolitan Nikodim because he can no longer suffer any harm for this revelation.

For the past 15 years the NCC has not provided any support--whether moral or financial--for RCDA. It is not a matter of wounded vanity on our part if we feel that RCDA deserved more recognition and appreciation not only from the NCC but from various denominations. It is our great satisfaction to see that the Soviet media and General Secretary of the CPSU, Mikhail Gorbachev himself, now confirm what RCDA has been saying these past 26 years, namely, that the believers in the USSR had been treated in the past as third-class citizens, deprived of their civil rights, persecuted, harassed and subjected to arbitrariness by state authroities. Far from hurting the ecumenical relations, RCDA has prepared the ground for radical changes in favor of religious bodies in the USSR, for instance, by publication of a secret document on the Party's control of the Russian Orthodox Church, of analyses of Soviet laws on religion, of appeals by dissident clergy, etc. These materials should have provided the NCC and the WCC with sufficient ammunition in the struggle for the believers' rights. The ecumenical movement represented by the WCC and the NCC was in error when it restricted its contacts with churches in Communist countries exclusively to the state-recognized (registered) churches and ignored the churches without state license, and when it refused to protest publicly against the discrimination and persecution of its believers.

Although the recent developments in the USSR and some other Communist countries give us good reasons for cautious optimism, it would be foolish to consider them a panacea and a happy end to all problems related to the situation of human rights. For one thing, Gorbachev's position remains precarious in view of the internal opposition and of the dismal economic conditions that his perestroika failed to improve. Secondly, we have witnessed in recent months a revival of the ugliest forms of antisemitism tolerated, if not fully supported, by the Soviet government. Freedom of religion continues to be denied, for instance, to the Ukrainian Catholic (Uniate) Church. Soviet Evangelicals and Jews remain on the periphery of Soviet society and thus far have not benefited from any substantive concessions on the part of the government. The anti-Muslim campaign in Soviet Central Asia has been stepped up recently. There is a strong possibility that it will drive the Islamic population in that area into the camp of fanatic fundamentalists of the Khomeini type. We are witnessing a religious and ethnic explosion in various areas of the USSR, and it is a moot question whether Gorbachev will be able--or want--to resolve all such grievances in a peaceful way.

Therefore, it would be premature to succumb to euphoria and declare that religious freedom has been restored in the USSR. It would be equally wrong to discount or disparage the reforms initiated by Gorbachev. This should offer the ecumenical movement represented by the WCC and the NCC an opportunity to press the USSR government for genuine equality of believers and non-believers, of all religious denominations--Christian, Jewish, Moslem and Buddhist.

I should like to underscore that changes in public attitudes in the USSR are preceded by changes in the persuasion of individual citizens. For example, Georgi Malenkov, Stalin's long-time secretary and for a brief period his successor, was the first Soviet leader to be buried with full rites of the Russian Orthodox Church. He had spent many years in virtual exile in Central Asia. Upon his return to Moscow he found a spiritual home in a church where he performed a public act of penance and later served as an elder of the congregation. He died in January 1988, but his death had not been reported in Soviet media for weeks and all references to his religious funeral were omitted.

The editors of RCDA were informed that when Brezhnev's coffin was being carried out from the Kremlin, Mrs. Brezhnev turned to Patriarch Pimen with a request for a blessing of her husband's body. The Patriarch was taken aback, but she insisted: "He was baptized--so he was a Christian!"

Gorbachev himself comes from a family of churchgoers, although he and his wife are committed Marxists. Yet it seems that his government will follow the policy of toleration toward the church, although it is not clear whether this attitude will apply to all religious bodies and whether it will not just co-opt the church (specifically, the Russian Orthodox Church) in order to control and manipulate it even more.

The world ecumenical movement should observe the changing policies in the Soviet orbit and protect the interests of churches, particularly because the thaw in church-state relations is not in evidence everywhere, as confirmed by a recent display of police brutality unleashed against a peaceful gathering of Catholics in the Slovak capital of Bratislava. Opportunities for ecumenical intervention and even quiet diplomacy exist in cases where dissidents and especially believers are still being harassed by the police, languishing in prisons, labor camps and psychiatric institutions; where citizens of nations forcibly annexed to the USSR are struggling to retain their national and religious identity; where minorities (particularly in the USSR, Bulgaria, and Rumania) are being deprived of their language, traditions, culture and faith and doomed to annihilation.

RCDA hopes that a turning point in the ecumenical movement has been signaled by the election of Fr. Leonid Kishkovsky, RCDA's Vice President, to the office of the President of the NCC for the 1990-1992 term. We welcome this decision as we are aware that the religious situation in Communist countries will continue to be a challenge to which the ecumenical movement must publicly respond in a more positive way than in the past.

Ecumenism in the Black Church
Chester Arthur Kirkendoll

Fifty years ago the First World Christian Youth Conference met in Amsterdam, Holland. The meeting opened in August of 1939. As a delegate to that conference, representing the Christian Methodist Episcopal Church, I can recall the tremendous feeling of confidence this experience instilled in me. My confidence was fashioned by the knowledge that the church universal was making progress in a positive manner. The feeling I experienced was that the church universal, the true Church of God, was moving forward toward ecumenism and that I was playing a part in that movement.

As I recall, during the late 1930's the world was tottering on the brink of economic destruction and global war. The years following 1930 were dominated by the great international economic depression. This depression almost ruined world trade and brought many nations to the verge of bankruptcy. The tensions in domestic affairs led to a marked turn toward dictatorial forms of government and to widespread repudiation of financial and moral obligations by nations in a concerted effort to solve domestic problems.[1]

The German war machine was cranking up for the ultimate encounter. The German government, under Adolph Hitler, formally denounced the clauses of the Treaty of Versailles concerning her disarmament. Tensions were high throughout the entire world. There were few people in the world who did not believe that war, global war, was imminent.

Yet, in the midst of these chaotic conditions, a successful attempt was made by the Christian forces in the world to bring together the youth of Christendom in a conference of great magnitude. With the chaotic conditions that were evident all over the world, this Christian Church conference suggested that there was still hope. A half century later, as I reflect upon the church universal and upon the Black church in particular, I am pleased with what I see taking place in the Christian world. Today I see a sense of growth that is decidedly positive, both in the world church outlook as well as in the outlook of the Black churches of this country.

A semblance of peace is imminent in the world. Christians must always grasp these moments of peace if we are to save the world from man and for Christ. The United States and the Soviet Union have signed treaty agreements ending some phases of nuclear proliferation. The Middle East war between Iran and Iraq is tapering off. The trouble spots of the world are not as feverish as they have been. And, to my amazement and pleasure, the church is growing at a very positive rate. Truly, we can say that God is still in control of this world.

---

1. Langer, William L., An Encyclopedia of World History, Houghton-Mifflin Co., Boston, 1968, p. 1125.

I want to believe that Christians are realizing, as a direct result of the teachings of the New Testament, that diatribe, that is to say, bitter and abusive criticism and division, is not only unfortunate, but a scandal and a sin as well. Robert M. Brown, in his book entitled The Ecumenical Revolution, notes that the New Testament is void of a justification for the denominational system that is rampant today.[2] There is no room for competition within the framework of Christian living. Brown says that "the notion of denominations, let alone huge blocs of Christians, severed from full unity with each other is foreign to its (New Testament) pages."[3]

Paul wrote to the church at Ephesus and decried disunity. He said, "there is one body and one Spirit, just as you were called to the one hope of your calling: one Lord, one faith, one baptism."[4]

To the Galatians Paul expounded, "as many of you as were baptised into Christ have put on Christ. There is neither Jew nor Greek, there is neither slave nor free, there is neither male nor female; for you are all one in Christ Jesus."[5]

Finally, Paul exclaims his ecumenical view of the church in his first letter to the Christian church at Corinth. "Each of you says I belong to Paul, or I belong to Cephas, or I belong to Christ. Is Christ divided?"[6] That is the question we must look at as we consider our discourse on the way Black denominations work in a spirit of harmony and a spirit of love.

---

2. Brown, Robert McAfee, The Ecumenical Revolution, Doubleday and Co., Garden City, N.Y., 1967, p.9.

3. Brown, p.9.

4. Ephesians 4:4-5.

5. Galatians 3:27-28.

6. 1st Corinthians 1:12-13.

To speak about ecumenism in any form is to talk about dedicated membership in God's church. We, in fact, ask this question: What does it mean to be a member of the church? This becomes the question that requires an answer, regardless of the race, color, or ethnic origin of the congregation. Johannes Weiss states that a member of the church is a unique breed of person with special characteristics.

Specifically, Weiss says that

> ...membership in the community does not depend so much upon the mere wish to join, nor upon external measures such as the paying of a contribution or an entrance fee, as upon the wholly supersensual experiences of the conferring of the spirit of baptism. In this experience the 'calling' is completed and the election receives visible expressions.[7]

Once persons become members of the Church, not a church, they must immediately be made cognizant of the oneness of all believers. If we are one in Christ, we are, in effect, ecumenical in our outlook.

In the "Preface to the American Edition" of the Official Report of the Oxford Conference, there is a passage which emphasizes the restoration to meaningful, contemporary usage of the word "ecumenical." This preface was written by Henry Smith Leiper, an ecumenical pioneer, who later became an associate general secretary of the World Council of Churches. His statement was that:

> In the generic sense Oxford was Catholic, meaning, of course, universal, all-inclusive, interracial, supernational. A better word, less subject perhaps to misunderstanding, is the one so frequently applied: Oxford was ecumenical. That old word from the Greek was reborn and brought back into circulation,

---

7. Weiss, Johannes, Earliest Christianity, Vol. II, Harper & Brothers, New York, 1959, p. 622.

along with the fundamental idea for which it stood in the early Christian centuries...the idea of the whole household of faith.[8]

The main thought here is that ecumenism is a concept supporting the whole household of faith. Most books on ecumenism tend to deal with either the Protestant story with all of its inherent views or with the Catholic perspective. This paper will not try to cover either of these perspectives alone, but rather it will explore a segment of the Christian church that has its own uniqueness.[9]

This paper will investigate a portion of the household of faith, the Black church. It will show their functioning together as a unit and the consistency of their interaction.

For the last 50 years the Black church has been a symbol of togetherness. This is a fact that is, without equivocation, irrefutable in every way. The rationale for the togetherness hinges upon the need for unity in the face of the social and civil struggles that engulfed this country in these turbulent years.

These years have seen a remarkable and radical change in the conditions of the life of Black Americans in particular and for Blacks in general around the world. The spirit of Black Americans fifty years ago was one of what was termed the "Double V." This stood for victory at home as well as victory abroad. "This slogan became immensely popular in Black communities, and reflected a growing urge to rid the world not only of Hitler but of the racism of Hitlerism."[10]

---

8. Mackay, John A. Ecumenism, Prentice Hall, Inc., Englewood Cliffs, N.J., 1964, p.7.

9. Brown, p. xv.

10. Tindell, George B., America: A Narrative History, W.W. Norton & Company, New York, 1988, p. 1197.

The struggle against racism continues to be the struggle of Black Americans. One of the most obvious efforts to overcome this movement is ecumenism, first within the Black church itself, and then within the church universal. The civil rights movements of the 1950's and 1960's made some inroads into the problem. We still have a distance to travel and ecumenism may be the vehicle that we will be able to use.

Just a step back in history needs to be taken to make us totally aware of the ecumenical spirit in the Black church. This is not a new venture, but it is a recurrence of an historical perspective. Ecumenism is inherent, in one sense, in the very nature of the Black church.

Black people have been, from the very first time they were brought to this country, joined together in their religious attitudes. James Olson indicates to us that when slaves came they adopted Protestantism, but gave it their own sense of direction. He indicates that they "imbued it" with an emotional flavor that was uniquely their own.[11]

All Black churches of today have a similarity that is unique to themselves. "This root of parallelism stems from African musical rhythms and dances, from voodooism and from a great amount of folk culture," says Olson. The parallel of Protestantism to their own cultural background appealed to the slaves. They enjoyed the revivalistic, rhythmic, joyful flavor with its "handclapping, rhythmic body movements, public testimonies, and conscious presence of the Holy Ghost" as their incentive.[12]

This thread of commonality that runs through all Black churches gives vent to the strong rationale for working together on the part of the Black

---

11. Olson, James Stuart, The Ethnic Dimension in American History, Vol.I, St. Martin's Press, N.Y., 1979, pp.43-44.

12. Olson, p.44.

congregations. Though they are quick to preserve their identity--Methodists, Baptists, Presbyterians, Congregationalists, members of the Church of God in Christ--yet they are also quick to function together in a spirit of unity as the need arises. This is the true ecumenical spirit that permeates the very heart of the Black church today.

During the early development of America "the Black churches were influential forums where leadership could be developed and grievances freely expressed," says Olson.[13] It was in the setting of the church that men felt a sense of dignity and self worth. It could be said that the church was the institution that gave Black men a point of leverage to allow them to move some of the injustices and inconsistencies that were hampering their progress in the world.

Most Black people joined the Baptist or the Methodist churches because these institutions were known to be havens for the poor. Even the poor whites were members of these denominations as well. The sophisticated, erudite, white property owners attended the Episcopal Church, the Presbyterian Church, and the Lutheran Church. There were some Blacks who attended these high church services as well, but not in numbers significant to be counted. Another reason for Black membership in Baptist and Methodist Churches was because more white persons in these communions sponsored the development of Black clergy. These and other factors were responsible for the large influx of Black people into these churches.

Olson suggests that even during the ante-bellum period there was a sense of unity on the part of slaves as it related to religion and church functioning. Through church attendance and through the inherent devout

---

13. Olson, p. 153.

doctrinal teachings of these religious bodies, the slaves were able to vent the frustrations of bondage. They were able to unite in a sense of common mission and recognize themselves as individuals regardless of their social status.[14] This was a spirit of ecumenism in the history of the Black church that holds us today.

Because of this spirit developed by our forefathers, there exists in Black churches today a platform upon which the Rev. Jesse Jackson can now stand and expound. He can stand in a congregation made up of representatives of all Black denominations and all Black churches to make us aware that "we are somebody." Our forefathers cut across denominational lines to bring a sense of individual pride to the worshipper.

To look at the Black church collectively is to look at a form of ecumenism that is active. Admittedly, there are many and varied denominations within the Black community. It is noted that many of these denominations are offsprings of each other. But there is a oneness in the Black church, a oneness that supersedes the variety and gives a sense of unity to the concept of the Black church and all that this term implies.

Black churches and particularly Black clergy have a comradery that bespeaks a sense of ecumenical cooperation in its highest form. Ministerial alliances exist that encompass all denominations functioning and working together for the good of the Black community. In 1968, during the march in Memphis by sanitation workers for equity in job security and income, it was noted that Dr. Martin Luther King, Jr., a Baptist minister, and several ministers from other denominations, including the late Bishop B. Julian Smith, a bishop in the Christian Methodist Episcopal Church, and Bishop

---

14. Olson, p.157.

J.O. Patterson, Senior Bishop of the Church of God in Christ, were together marching for justice and the rights of the people.

Black churches are intricately involved in religious groupings other than ethnic organizations. Their membership and participation in such groups as the National Council of Churches, the World Methodist Council and the World Council of Churches adds credence to this view.

There are thirty-two churches that are a part of the National Council of Churches of Christ (NCC) in the U.S.A. Of this number, six are historically Black denominations. The Black denominations of the NCC include the African Methodist Episcopal Church (AME), the African Methodist Episcopal Zion Church (AME), the Christian Methodist Episcopal Church (CME), the National Baptist Convention of America (NBC), the National Baptist Convention, U.S.A., Inc. (NBCUSA), and the Progressive National Baptist Convention, Inc. (PNBC). This makes up more than sixteen percent of the total membership in the NCC.

Black church participation in these national and world organizations has grown tremendously over the last fifty years. Representatives from Black denominations have assumed and continued to hold positions of leadership in these prestigious religious organizations.

Functionally, the ecumenical spirit is shown through Black church representative's involvement in the decision-making process of the NCC. Twice a year, delegates from all the communions in the NCC meet as the governing board. This includes, of necessity, the Black representatives from their respective churches who join in setting policy, in approving budgets and in setting program priorities. Like an extended family, board members mark the achievements of each other's churches, share occasional sorrows, have a common organizational history and sometimes disagree even while working together in a spirit of ecumenism moving toward common goals.

Black church persons have served in every capacity of leadership within these organizations, including President, Vice-President, and Recording Secretary. I served as the Recording Secretary of the Governing Board of the National Council of Churches for one term which was a three year period. The work I did, and the service of other Black leaders testifies to the involvement of Black leadership in the world and national church bodies.

Within the NCC there is a growing movement toward ecumenism. This growth is seen in the commitment to the visible unity of the church. One example of this is that the communions in the Council have pledged to talk with each other and to challenge one another in mutual accountability and to cultivate relationships with Christians who are not members of the Council.

One of the key elements that guides the NCC is the move toward ecumenical learning. An attempt to grow in our knowledge of one another in Christ. We become enriched and feel closer to each other as a result of our learning the history and faith stories of other denominations. This is true ecumenism in action. The NCC has an ecumenical agenda which focuses its energies on the present pressing needs and challenges of the ecumenical movement in the U.S. The churches, including the six Black denominations, of whom ecumenistic commitment is integral, express that commitment in many ways. Locally, their congregations cooperate with other congregations. Their regional bodies participate in state and regional ecumenical agencies. They are also involved in church unity talks with other communions.

Since 1978, Black church leaders, clerical and laity, have been resourced by the National Council of Churches of Christ in the USA to effect greater cooperation across denominational lines. The purpose was to inspire, inform, and work with these churches so that they could provide viable solutions for the problems caused by racism, sexism and classism.

This movement is known as Partners in Ecumenism (PIE). It makes very clear the purpose of Black ecumenism. It comes together in eight regional conferences and there have been seven national conferences held by the organization. The purpose of these conferences is to determine the issues that are critical for Black persons. It determines how these issues can be addressed by Blacks working ecumenically within the Black church and as well as by Blacks, Hispanics, Native Americans, Asians and whites working together.

Some of the goals this organization (PIE) is attempting to accomplish include the following. First, it seeks to conduct a national conference with workshops relevant to full involvement of the PIE constituency in the ecumenical movement. Second, it seeks to facilitate the establishment of PIE chapters in local areas throughout the country. Third, it serves as a network information agency for Blacks, Hispanics, Asians, Native Americans, along with other religious communities, informing these groups of the work of the NCC, the WCC, and explaining how these organizations interconnect with PIE. Fourth, it attempts to identify resources, human and other, that will assist in bridging the gaps between racial and ethnic groups. Fifth, this organization plans to explore the connections between racism, sexism and agism and how such issues impact upon the minority entities of this nation. Finally, it seeks to bridge the gap between Black Americans and Africans hoping to network Black churches and their communities internationally.

This organization holds annual meetings to facilitate ecumenical relationships. Its 8th Annual Conference will meet in Washington, D.C. in the Spring of 1989. The theme of the conference will be "Witnessing Ecumenically to a Divided World." PIE will be addressed and complimented on its work by such distinguished individuals as the Rev. Jesse Jackson, Governor Michael Dukakis, Bishop Desmond Tutu, Allan Boesak, and representatives from both the Democratic and Republican National Committees. Scheduled to be present at the conference are representatives of both Houses of the United States Congress. Those representatives who have indicated that they will attend include Representatives Walter Fauntroy, Louis Stokes, Roy Flake, and William Gray, along with Senators Edward Kennedy, Pat Schroeder, Frank H. Murkowski, John Glenn and Howard Metzenbaum. The ideals and purposes of this organization further exemplify the fact that the Black church is not inward in its perspective. The ideals reveal that the Black church, indeed, has a world perspective, and the purposes prove that Black churches are, in a real sense, ecumenical by their very nature.

Another movement that Black churches have worked together in for several years is the Consultation on Church Union. Four churches instituted this organization in the United States in 1962. The four churches that initiated the movement toward church union were the United Presbyterian Church in the USA, the Protestant Episcopal Church, the Methodist Church and the United Church of Christ. Growing quickly to ten denominations by 1967, COCU worked throughout the 1960's. Three Black churches were added to its membership, the African Methodist Episcopal Church, the African Methodist Episcopal Zion Church and the Christian Methodist Episcopal Church. These churches worked with COCU in developing an agreed-upon theological foundation. During the 1970's, while the theological sections were being revised, COCU created experimental projects in shared mission and worship in various parts of the country. The AME, AMEZ, and the CME churches were all a part of these projects. The consultation developed an ecumenical sense that went beyond simply working together.

Working as another example of ecumenism, it organized groups to wrestle with such humanity-dividing questions as racism, sexism, and handicapism.

In the late 1970's and early 1980's, COCU entered the third era of its life. It met to envision and agree upon what the shape of the ecumenical body would be in the future. The "COCU Consensus" is the result of this agreement. This Consensus asks that each church, "by formal action, recognize the following:

> 1.   an expression, in matters with which it deals, of the Apostolic faith, order, worship, and witness of the church,
>
> 2.   an anticipation of the Church Uniting which the participating bodies, by the power of the Holy Spirit, wish to become, and
>
> 3.   a sufficient theological basis for the covenanting acts and the uniting process proposed at this time by the Consultation."[15]

It should be noted that the leadership of this Consultation is interracial. Black church representatives have served and continue to serve as leaders of the organization.   Presently, Dr. Vivian U. Robinson, a member of the C.M.E. church, serves as the President of the Consultation on Church Union. In addition, three bishops of the C.M.E. church (Bishop Elisha P. Murchison, Bishop Caesar David Coleman and Bishop Marshall Gilmore) have functioned as members of the executive committee of COCU. In every venue, in every clime, the Black church has made inroads toward ecumenism.

---

15. "In Common," Consultation on Church Union, Newsletter, Vol. XVIII, No.1, June, 1988, p.1.

Being a part of COCU is a tremendous step forward by the Christian church in general and the Black churches in particular. Six churches have already approved this "COCU Consensus," "by formal action." This includes the CME church, which approved this agreement during its 1986 General Conference in Birmingham, Alabama. The two other Black denominations in COCU, namely the AME and the AMEZ churches, also have approved this giant ecumenical step in their General Conferences during the Summer of 1988.

The churches represented in COCU include the following:

the African Methodist Episcopal Church
the African Methodist Episcopal Zion Church
the Christian Church (Disciples of Christ)
the Christian Methodist Episcopal Church
the Episcopal Church
the National Council of Community Churches
the Presbyterian Church USA
the United Church of Christ
the United Methodist Church

Collectively, this ecumenical organization constitutes more than twenty-two million Christians working in harmony, to bring the work of God to its fruition on earth. It represents Black churches and non-Black churches, functioning together, for the uplifting of Jesus Christ.

As a footnote to COCU, two of the Black denominations within that organization are actively pursuing a course that will ultimately lead to merger. The African Methodist Episcopal Zion Church and the Christian Methodist Episcopal Church are presently in dialogue concerning this merger. Committees on merger have been appointed and both legislative bodies of the respective churches have tentatively approved merger dialogue. It is possible that within the next several years this merger may be consummated. It will, of necessity, accentuate the idea that, not only should there be only one Black Methodist body, but also that there is really only one body in Christ Jesus our Lord.

One of the most relevant indicators of the reality of Black ecumenicalism was the effort in theological education that took place in Atlanta, Georgia. In 1959, four major Black denominations came together to form a theological center that would train its collective ministry. This is the Interdenominational Theological Center (ITC). The four denominations that originally founded and formed the ITC include the African Methodist Episcopal Church (AME), the Christian Methodist Episcopal Church (CME), the Methodist Episcopal Church Central Jurisdiction now the United Methodist Church (UM) and the National Baptist Convention (NBC).

The ITC stands today as one of the premier theological schools in the nation and uncompromisingly as the finest within the Black community. The institution holds membership in the United Negro College Fund and is fully accredited by the Southern Association of Colleges and Schools. Uniquely, this was one of the first academic institutions that received immediate accreditation at its inception. The rationale for this action resulted from the fact that all of the seminaries that created the ITC were fully accredited as the merger was consummated.

Today the ITC stands forth as a monument to Black theological education. The center has grown from four to six schools and their supporting denominations. These include the A.M.E. Church (Turner School of Theology), the C.M.E. Church (Phillips School of Theology), the National Baptist Convention (Morehouse School of Religion), the United Methodist Church (Gammon Theological Seminary) and the Church of God in Christ (Mason Theological Seminary). The ITC is a revolutionary achievement in ecumenical functioning to bring together varying ideologies in one place and to have them function under one roof and with one direction. The ITC symbolizes the motto of the United States of America very well, E PLURIBUS UNUM, which means "in many, one."

The ITC is a role model for Black ecumenism. It shows, without question, that there is an affinity that Black churches have with each other. This merger of schools clearly indicates, to all who are observant, that ecumenism is more than a catchword. Ecumenism is a reality, demonstrated in the institution that was created to allow the members of God's household of faith to function, to learn, and to serve together. Ecumenism has not excluded from its agenda the women of the church, nor it from theirs. The Black church has recognized contributions of women, and through ecumenism has worked to provide networks in which the women of the church can exchange ideas in programming and can develop a deeper knowledge of Christ and Christian fellowship. During the last fifty years, women have worked attempting to extend their ecumenical activities by using global perspectives and initiatives. This, in turn, has led women to become more deeply aware of human needs and of the injustices that run rampant in our world and has helped women acquire a unified strength to correct some of those needs.

Black church women have been involved with the Federal Council of Churches in America, the World Day of Prayer, the Council and Cooperation between the United Methodist and Christian Methodist Episcopal women, the International Council on Religious Education, the National Federation of Colored Women's Clubs, the National Council of Negro Women, Inc., the Board of Missionary Education, Church Women United, and the World Federation of Methodist Women. Women in the Black church have long been associated with women in other churches, women who have had a deep and genuine concern about the rights and responsibilities of human beings.

United Church Women (now Church Women United) are women of deep and sincere religious principles. They fought hard for the open church where all people could celebrate having gained the right to salvation through Jesus Christ. These women believe that unity is the key to strength and success. Women of all faiths--Methodist, American and National Baptist, Greek Orthodox, Lutheran, Catholic, Reformed Churches of America Presbyterian--believed in justice and opportunity for all in every endeavor in life.

Dr. Mary Ross, National President of the National Baptist Women, served as Vice President of United Church Women. Mrs. Clair C. Harvey, a Black professional woman from Jackson, Mississippi, served as National President of the organization. Dr. Thelma Adair and Dr. Sylvia Talbot have served as National Presidents of Church Women United. Mrs. Alfreda Bunton of the Christian Methodist Episcopal Church served as a member of Christian Causeway, a project of Church Women United. This service took Mrs. Bunton into the South America countries of Chile, Peru and Brazil, expounding the gospel.

Because of the enormous number of young women at the bottom of the ladder of social and economic change, WICS, an organization of interfaith, interracial volunteer women, came into being. Incorporated in December, 1964, this venture grew out of the four largest women's groups in the country, namely: the National Council of Catholic Women, the National Council of Negro Women, the National Council of Jewish Women, and Church Women United. In 1965, WICS signed a contract with the Federal Government to screen young women for the Job Corps. Volunteers gave over six million hours, without compensation, helping 60,000 young women from poverty areas. In seventeen Job Corps centers, young women between the ages of sixteen and twenty-two were being educated in work skills, basic education, home and family life, health education, guidance, and counseling. Each young woman was given an allowance each month, plus room and board, clothing, medical and dental care. Black church women have strengthened ecumenical initiatives through denominational affiliations with the National Council of Churches. Especially effective is the Women's Caucus of the Council, where issues involving women of all races, creeds, and religions are brought to the forefront and presented to the Council for discussion, resolution, and affirmation. The Caucus has given unity and cohesiveness to the struggles women have for finding their places in the church and for using their God-given talents to promote the mission of the church.

The World Federation of Methodist Women (WFMW) is a unique organization, having a membership of over seven million women, comprising sixty-two units in sixty countries. They are headed by a Black African Methodist Episcopal Church woman, Mrs. Edith W. Ming. The WFMW is an excellent example of ecumenism at its finest. Working with women all over the world, the federation seeks to further the cause of education, human rights, social, political and economic justice, religious affirmation and opportunity, and international peace throughout the world. All of its work is done using a Christian approach to these problems. The late Mrs. Artisha Jordan of the African Methodist Episcopal Church also served as President of the World Federation of Methodist Women.

Black church women have been able to further the ecumenical ideal through their relationship with the Consultation on Church Union (COCU). The women of COCU, through the National Fraternal Council of Church Women, an auxiliary of the Fraternity of Black Methodists Units, have stressed the Christian women's responsibilities in this age of transition in the home, in the community, and in the church. As earlier mentioned, in

December, 1987, Dr. Vivian U. Robinson, of the C.M.E. Church, was nominated to head this prestigious body. She was the first Black woman to be so honored as well as being the first woman and the first lay person to serve in this capacity. Black church women have participated in scores of other organizations and agencies. Agencies like the Bread of Life, the World Council of Churches Ecumenical Decade, Churches in Solidarity for Women, and Urban Consultations. Black, brown, red, yellow, and white hands have pulled together in unity for the cause of Jesus. Women have learned that when a cause is for Christ, working with and through the Holy Spirit, goals are set in the right direction. They have learned that the ultimate success of those goals and the ultimate blessings of the projects and people for whom those goals and projects are set are best exemplified in Jesus. Women and men of the church have learned that the road to travel is the ecumenical route. When all are working together to accomplish the same goal loads are lighter, grasps are stronger, and much is accomplished in making Christ known and in building the kingdom of God here on earth.

It should be noted, by way of summary, that there are other ecumenical organizations within the Black church community. These include the Congress of National Black Churches (CNBC) based in Washington, D.C., and the National Association of Black Clergymen, which is based in New York. Each of these organizations play a vital role in bringing about ecumenical relationships between the various constituencies of the Black church.

Within the Black church, there is a very viable ecumenical effort in motion. Evidences are clear to document this reality. The past fifty years have been very prosperous for the Black church. The world has seen a growth in the interrelationship of Black congregations in many areas. With all the factors that we have highlighted in the above statement, it is very apparent that Black churches are seeking the support of their associates in working for the kingdom of God.

It is noted on old Spanish coins that there was an inscription which read: Ne Plus Ultra ("No More Beyond"). These coins were in circulation when Spain was one of the major powers in Europe during the 14th century. But, with the birth of the Columbian era, the passion for discovery, and the ultimate success of the Spanish nation in exploration and discovery, a new motto was drafted. This motto was inscribed on the new Spanish coins. This new motto read, Plus Ultra ("More Beyond").

As I reflect upon the cooperative spirit that flows from the Black churches presently, I cannot help but feel that there is "plus ultra" in the relationship of Black congregations. Surely there is "more beyond" for the black churches to achieve with respect to ecumenical endeavors. The hope and the prayer of the Black church is not "ne plus ultra," but our aim is "plus ultra."

The future aim of the Black church, in a collective sense, is to promote a fellowship and a sense of unity that will allow them to act together. A unity that will provide the churches with opportunities to make the Church of Christ truly one church, united and together, in one accord.

There is no desire to become a bureaucratic union with control over each unit. The future of Black ecumenism is realistically found in the spirit that presently exists. That is the spirit of cooperative love, coupled with a willingness to work together, with all of God's people, for the glory of the Lord and Saviour, Jesus Christ.

ACKNOWLEDGMENTS

I would like to thank Dr. Arthur L. David, Academic Dean of Lane College and Pastor of the Mother Liberty C.M.E. Church for the research assistance and word processing of this paper. Without the invaluable assistance of this scholar, the attempt to put a paper of this magnitude together would have been in vain.

Special thanks also to Dr. Thelma Dudley, immediate Past President of the Women's Connectional Council of the C.M.E. Church for the information she shared relative to the work of Black church women in ecumenism. Without her assistance, this paper would have been less than complete.

Ecumenical Witness for Peace
Phillips P. Moulton

The First World Conference of Christian Youth, at Amsterdam in 1939, produced no startling new theological formulations, position papers, or programs of action. In these respects it could not be expected to go beyond the Oxford Conference on "Church, Community and State" of 1937. The aim of Amsterdam was different. It was to expose youth leaders to the ecumenical cause and inspire them to commit themselves to it. That it had this effect to a remarkable degree is made evident in the symposium published in the Journal of Ecumenical Studies to commemorate the 40th anniversary of the conference. It is confirmed in the symposium of which this essay is a part. Under the superb leadership of its organizing secretary, R. H. Edwin Espy, the conference made a striking impact on its participants, many of whom emerged as leaders in their denominations and in the ecumenical movement. They played major roles in the deliberations on issues of war and peace in the last half century.

Starting with Oxford conference as a base, my purpose here is to note significant statements of the World Council of Churches (WCC) from its formation in 1948 through its Sixth Assembly in 1983. I shall then examine relevant Roman Catholic, Methodist, and Presbyterian studies in the United States and suggest issues that need further attention.

The Oxford report on "The Universal Church and the World of Nations" stressed a major problem facing peacemakers: the unwillingness of nations to relinquish sovereignty by submitting international conflicts to arbitration by a tribunal with jurisdiction over the contending parties. The issue was highlighted forty-five years later in Jonathan Schell's book The Fate of the Earth. Another contribution to Christian thinking made by the Oxford report was its brief reference to "the unequal distribution of natural bounties" as a cause of war. It planted the seed for a major emphasis of the 1980s on justice.

The central problem that has beset all later church conferences dealing with peace was posed by Oxford. It recognized that the delegates could not agree as to which of three irreconcilable positions Christians should take: the pacifist rejection of all war, the obligation to participate in wars that are considered "just" on the basis of certain criteria, or the granting of such great authority to the state as to require taking up arms for one's country unless one is absolutely certain that it is fighting for a wrong cause. In reading the Oxford report, one is impressed by the contrast between justification of some wars and the statement that "war is a particular demonstration of the power of sin...and a defiance of the righteousness of God as revealed in Jesus Christ and him crucified."

The First Assembly of the WCC, in 1948, followed the Oxford precedent in confessing that war "is a sin against God." Also like Oxford, the Assembly stressed respect for international law. It was greatly affected by the use of the atom bomb and the totalitarian nature of modern war. Noting that war "has greatly changed," it brought Christian thinking beyond Oxford by challenging the concept of the just war.

The Second WCC Assembly (at Evanston in 1953) asserted: "It is not enough for the churches to proclaim that war is evil. They must study afresh the Christian approaches to peace." The Assembly made a positive contribution to the ongoing dialogue by claiming: "Peace means far more than mere absence of war; it is characterized positively by freedom, justice, truth, and love." The key word is "justice", which has been emphasized increasingly since then. The phrase "peace with justice" appears several times in reports of the Third Assembly (at New Delhi in 1961).

The concern for justice was the focus of the World Conference on Church and Society convened by the WCC in Geneva in 1966. Its tenor was in accord with its title: "Christians in the Technical and Social Revolutions of Our Time." The conference marked a turning point in the life of the WCC--from an emphasis on order to an advocacy of social change. This reflected the influence of young people, who were involved in the social struggles of the times. The participants included a higher percentage of youth delegates, as well as of lay persons and Third World leaders, than had attended previous WCC meetings.

The Fourth WCC Assembly (at Uppsala in 1968) reflected the new thinking of the 1966 conference. It called for greater justice in race relations, development, and economic life and explored the connections between injustice and the threat of a major war. It urged greater unity and cooperation among churches in order to meet these challenges effectively. Influenced by representatives of the historic peace churches, led by Quakers Barrett Hollister and Wilmer Cooper, the Assembly took a major step forward. It instructed its Central Committee to "explore means by which the

WCC could promote studies on nonviolent methods of achieving social change." Responding to that mandate, a thorough two-year study was conducted by a Working Committee on Church and Society, whose report was accepted by the WCC Central Committee in August 1973. Entitled "Violence, Nonviolence, and the Struggle for Social Justice," the report remains one of the most perceptive treatments of this vexing problem.

The Fifth WCC Assembly (at Nairobi in 1975) was influenced by the Working Committee report of 1973, by youth counterculture movements, and by liberation struggles in many nations. By this time, under the leadership of Eugene Carson Blake and Philip Potter, WCC programs were increasing their emphasis on action and were focusing more attention on the Third World. A statement by the Assembly on "The World Armaments Situation" decried the increasing pervasiveness of militarism. It urged the WCC to press for disarmament and for the churches to declare "their readiness to live without the protection of armaments."

Section V of the Assembly dealt directly with "Structures of Injustice and the Struggles for Liberation," noting that violence embedded in the institutions of society is as destructive as the overt violence of revolutionary movements. Greater awareness of institutional violence led to emphasis on the human rights that were increasingly being violated. At Nairobi and in the following years, young people kept pressing their elders to become more radical in espousing the cause of the poor and challenging militarism. This set the stage for the deliberations at the next WCC Assembly on justice, peace, human rights, and the integrity of creation.

A contribution of the Sixth WCC Assembly (at Vancouver in 1983) was an incisive analysis of the Cold War. It decried the distortion of priorities as huge funds were poured into destabilizing weapons systems while millions starved. It asserted, more emphatically than previous Assemblies, that justice is a prerequisite for peace and warned that the arms race posed a serious threat to our environment. It then called on member churches to commit themselves to a united struggle for justice, peace, and the integrity of creation, seen as three aspects of a single whole. This effort, it claimed, was a moral imperative for Christians, not to be evaluated simply by its effectiveness.

The Assembly went beyond previous Assemblies by adopting a statement made by an ecumenical Hearing at Amsterdam in 1981 that "the churches must unequivocally declare that the production and deployment as well as the use of nuclear weapons are a crime against humanity and that such activities must be condemned on ethical and theological grounds." It also categorically rejected nuclear deterrence "as contrary to our faith in Jesus Christ" and urged Christians to "give witness to their unwillingness to participate in any conflict involving weapons of mass destruction or indiscriminate effect," whether nuclear or conventional.

The traditional criteria of a "just war," or simply the application of international laws, especially those concerning the immunity of noncombatants, would rule out most modern wars. The gap between the pacifist who is opposed on principle to all war and the just-war theorist has become narrower with the advent of modern weapons (nuclear and non-nuclear) of mass destruction. Yet the number of those who identify themselves as pacifists has not increased as much as the Vancouver declarations might lead one to expect. One who makes a reflective judgment during a conference of committed Christians who are accustomed to thinking in ethical terms cannot always be expected to maintain that judgment in the different atmosphere of one's home community. On social and economic issues, a marked hiatus generally exists between the views of church leaders, including clergy, and most of the laity.

Each WCC Assembly took account of ecumenical, denominational, and youth conferences, as well as of preceding Assemblies. The above sketch of major WCC statements up to 1983 reflects the views of many thoughtful Christians in addition to those of official delegates. We turn now to some of the more comprehensive reports issued by church bodies from 1983 to the present.

Most assessments of church pronouncements have been made from a just-war point of view. I hope to shed new light on some of the major issues by considering them from the perspective of a pacifist who is opposed on principle to killing, and hence to all war. In 1983, the U.S. Roman Catholic Bishops issued their pastoral letter: "The Challenge of Peace: God's Promise and Our Response." This was the result of a thorough study over a period of years by a committee that consulted some 150 experts, including government officials, military personnel, peace activists, Biblical scholars, and political scientists. Its purpose was to challenge U.S. Catholics "to join with others in shaping the conscious choices and deliberate policies" required to influence decisively the course of the nuclear age.

This document was rightly acclaimed as making a significant contribution to the cause of peace. It stimulated its readers to think more deeply and in several respects challenged U.S. foreign policy. Recognizing the perilous situation of humanity, it opposes Pentagon plans to prevail in a protracted nuclear war. It also opposes first-strike weapons and plans. On the positive side, it favors a weapons freeze, a comprehensive test ban, and the elimination of short-range nuclear weapons. An important section calls for more study and consideration of nonviolent methods of defense.

The world will be much safer than it is now if the changes advocated in the pastoral letter take place. My main criticism derives from the constraints upon the bishops. Their conclusions must accord with papal teachings, and their strong deference to tradition leads them to a "moral acceptance of nuclear deterrence," albeit "strictly conditioned." Three main conditions are expressed. The first is that "proposals for prolonged periods of repeated nuclear strikes...in nuclear war are not acceptable." A second is that "the quest for nuclear superiority must be rejected." The third is that "nuclear deterrence should be used as a step on the way toward progressive disarmament."

For further light on the conditions set by the bishops and the question of whether they are being fulfilled, let us look at the statement they issued five years later. In June 1988, they brought their offical position up to date by unanimously approving a "Report on 'The Challenge of Peace' and Policy Developments 1983-1988." This was produced by the bishops' Ad Hoc Committee for the Moral Evaluation of Deterrence. Its task was to assess whether the conditions of the pastoral letter are being met, and to express to the National Conference of Catholic Bishops "a judgment on the moral status of deterrence."

The Report advocates "measures which still very much need to be undertaken to meet the conditions" of the 1983 letter. These include far-reaching changes in the policies that guide nuclear arsenals. Then it lists nine criteria for "a more secure and morally justifiable basis for peace" that it grants are not currently being met. Four of these criteria are that deterrence must not be based on direct targeting of urban populations, on weapons that have "a credible first-strike posture," on "the risk of the preemptive use of nuclear weapons," or on arsenals that "far exceed the requirements of survivable second-strike deterrence."

The Report states also that "reason, morality, and faith combine today in opposition to the idea that nuclear war fits our traditional understanding of justifiable use of force." Despite this admission, the Report reaffirms the acceptance of nuclear deterrence, while cautioning that it merits only "strictly conditioned acceptance." We shall take a closer look at this apparent lack of consistency and logic after briefly surveying how other religious bodies have grappled with the issue.

The predecessor to the United Methodist Church (UMC) was the first denomination to establish a task force to deal with war and peace issues. The UMC has remained in the forefront of denominations that maintain an active and consistent witness for peace. This it has done through official and unofficial channels. Herman Will, who devoted 37 years to international affairs programs with the UMC, has documented this involvement up to 1984 in the excellent 279 page volume The Will to Peace.

One of the most significant treatments of the nuclear crisis is the book containing a "Foundation Document" and a three-page Pastoral Letter issued by the UMC bishops in 1986. Entitled In Defense of Creation: The Nuclear Crisis and a Just Peace, the volume is commonly referred to as the Bishops' Pastoral. It seeks, with considerable success, to utilize the insights of both pacifism and just-war theory. I shall note some of its major emphases, and focus on its position regarding nuclear deterrence. To augment its usefulness for those with different points of view, I shall indicate where its judgments differ from those of the pacifist, roughly characterized as one who is opposed on principle to all killing and seeks to avoid preparation for, or participation in, war--either for aggression or defense, for domination or liberation.

The title of the document points to a fruitful context for exploring these issues--stewardship of the creation with which we are entrusted. Among other merits, this approach clarifies the common ground peace activists share with environmentalists. A central theme of the document is the integral relationship of peace to justice. Its depiction of the many ways justice is offended in our militaristic society is quite comprehensive.

The Methodists, like the Catholic bishops and the Presbyterians, call for serious study of nonviolent, civilian-based defense as a possible alternative to military defense. As a constructive alternative to the arms race, the document calls on the United States and the Soviet Union to take independent initatives in reducing armaments, accompanied by invitations to reciprocate. This could pave the way for a comprehensive, systematic method of arms reduction. The document recommends the procedures of the McCloy-Zorin Agreement signed by the United States and the U.S.S.R. in 1961 but never implemented.

Both just-war theorists and pacifists have welcomed In Defense of Creation. Insofar as it is taken seriously and its suggestions followed, it will take us a long way on the road to peace. Yet pacifists should be aware of points at which its message differs from theirs. On page 37 it applies just-war criteria to condone wars that "seek the restoration of peace with justice, refrain from directly attacking noncombatants, and avoid causing more harm than good." On page 25 it states: "Human sinfulness is, according to Scripture, a warrant for defense against enemies"--presumably by military means.

Regarding the moral justification of nuclear deterrence, the document reads: "Deterrence must no longer receive the churches' blessing, even as a temporary warrant for the maintenance of nuclear weapons." Then it continues:

> "The interim possession of nuclear weapons...requires a different justification--an ethic of reciprocity as nuclear-weapon states act together in agreed stages to...eliminate their nuclear arms. Such an ethic is shaped by...a vision of common security...rather than mutual terror."

Does this differ from the Catholic stance? In certain respects it does. The Methodists reject the policy of deterrence and any use of nuclear weapons. The Catholics leave the door open for possible retaliatory use in a limited exchange. To the Methodists, "deterrence" implies hostility and terror. Like the Catholics, they would keep the weapons temporarily; but with their retention based on reciprocity rather than deterrence, they envisage a less adversarial stance. Both sets of bishops favor eliminating the weapons by mutual agreement in phased withdrawals. Both reject total unilateral withdrawal--the Catholics because they want the allegedly deterrent effect of the weapons and believe they facilitate progress towards disarmament, the Methodists because withdrawal might "tempt other countries to develop or expand their own nuclear arsenals, thereby increasing the risk of nuclear war." The Methodists do not suggest what action the nation should take if it is attacked during the interim period.

The General Assembly of the United Presbyterian church in the U.S.A. has issued statements on war and peace nearly every year since 1937, the initiative for which has usually come from local or regional church bodies. In 1980 the Assembly adopted a document, Peacemaking: The Believers' Calling, which stimulated increased study and action in its constituent churches. Officially the denomination sanctions military defense, while recognizing freedom of the individual conscience, which may lead to conscientious objection to military service. Nonviolent, civilian-based defense is recognized as offering real promise and being worthy of further study, although not yet widely enough accepted to be advocated as a national policy. Official pronouncements increasingly emphasize common security, human rights, and social and economic justice.

Responding to grassroots requests for policy direction, the General Assembly authorized the publication in 1985 of study guides that were used rather widely. Covering a broad range of issues, they focused on the question of whether, in view of the increasing militarization of society and the danger of a nuclear holocaust, Presbyterians should adopt "a stance of resistance" to the state. The Assembly of 1988 expressed its preference for "a stance of obedience to God," which may require cooperation and obedience in relation to the state, or noncooperation and disobedience.

This reflected the long-standing emphasis of the Presbyterian Church on the sovereignty of God, with its corollary that the nation must not be given one's highest allegiance. Although the individual generally owes obedience to the state, if this conflicts with obedience to God, the latter must have priority. The obligation to follow one's conscience might thus lead one to resist the state. According to the 1988 Assembly, resistance should be nonviolent and should preferably be done through legal channels, but may lead one to legitimate acts of civil disobedience.

The 1988 Assembly reaffirmed, as applicable in the nuclear age, its historical acceptance of the just-war doctrine. Declaring that the criteria of proportionality and discrimination cannot be met when nuclear weapons are used, it condemned participation in nuclear war. It went on to ask: "If the use of nuclear weapons cannot be justified...can the possession of them be justified?" It then noted that Jesus "clearly condemns revenge. Yet deterrence is based on the threat of massive retaliation."

In still another way the 1988 Assembly recognized the complexity of this issue. Quoting a previous Assembly statement that nuclear deterrence could be morally defensible only on the basis of "buying a little time to work for peaceful alternatives," it added that even as an interim ethic the moral case for nuclear deterrence "has been undermined by unrelenting arms escalation." Strange as it may seem, the Assembly thereupon rejected immediate unilateral disarmament on the ground that such a change in a stable arms relationship could be dangerous. Having reached this conclusion, it advocated seeking "to effect a change in national policy as rapidly as possible." Like the Catholics and Methodists, the Presbyterians have responded to the crisis of our time with a good deal of thought and action.

Governing bodies and task forces of other denominations have engaged in similar studies and projects aimed at a more peaceful world. In the United Church of Christ, several years of work culminated in the UCC officially proclaiming itself a Just Peace Church and publishing a 160 page book with that title in 1986. The Joint Commission on Peace of the Episcopal Church issued comprehensive reports in 1982 and 1985, and the Episcopal Diocese of Washington, D.C. published The Nuclear Dilemma: A Christian Search for Understanding in 1987. The latter was produced by an unofficial Committee of 16 persons who met frequently for two years and consulted a wide range of written works and experts. The growing Baptist peace movement culminated in an epoch-making International Baptist Peace Conference in 1988. Similar studies and movements in other denominations could be cited.

Because the Christian calling is so demanding and the influence of secular society is so pervasive, I do not anticipate unanimity in the immediate future. The ethicist Edward LeRoy Long is probably correct, however, in stating that "a higher degree of consensus has developed about the moral illegitimacy of deterrence by nuclear threat." The most authentic Christian statements were probably those issued by the WCC Assembly in Vancouver, whose call for commitment to Justice, Peace, and the Integrity of Creation (JPIC) has met with a favorable response by church bodies world-wide.

As the denominations follow the WCC lead in focusing on JPIC, they continue to face the question of what the Christian stance should be. By "Christian stance" I refer to the position individual Christians, denominations, and ecumenical bodies should take. I do not try to solve in this essay the complex question of the relationship of the Christian position to national policy, although I assume that Christians have as much right as others to affect that policy. Nor do I presume to offer an ideal solution to the dilemmas we face. My aim is to raise questions and make proposals to be considered further.

The paradox is that church bodies declare in unequivocal terms that war, particularly nuclear war, is evil. They generally condemn any use of nuclear weapons. Yet they usually oppose unilateral disarmament, which implies approval of possessing the weapons. The Catholic bishops justify possession on the basis of conditional approval of deterrence. The Methodist bishops justify it by "an ethic of reciprocity as...states act together...to eliminate their nuclear arms." Although possession is considered an interim condition pending multilateral disarmament, all agree that the interim will necessarily be a long one.

As long as a nation possesses nuclear weapons, it is possible that they will be used; the longer they are possessed, the more probable this becomes. The church bodies virtually agree that any use will very likely escalate to a nuclear holocaust. By rejecting immediate unilateral nuclear disarmament, the churches may be sanctioning the worst of all possible sins. Why do they take this position?

Although some denominational statements have reached the point of disavowing moral justification for nuclear deterrence, others still accept it. It is hard not to be influenced by constant repetition of "peace through strength" concepts. I shall therefore deal at some length with deterrence before suggesting other reasons church pronouncements generally reject unilateral disarmament.

We should note first that insofar as our weapons are a deterrent, they deter a danger that we have created. In 1969, to enhance deterrence, the United States deployed multiple independently targeted reentry vehicles (MIRVs). Faced with this new threat, the Soviet Union rushed to do likewise. As a result, we were less secure than before. But defense strategists then pointed to U.S. MIRVs as deterring Soviet MIRVs--which, to some extent, they did. If, instead of deploying the new "deterrent," the United States had proposed a ban on MIRVs, the Soviet Union would almost certainly have agreed. Their technology was behind ours, their overburdened economy needed relief, and they have a realistic fear of the holocaust such weapons bring closer. We would be much safer today had we gone this route. This type of scenario occurs nearly every time the United States gets a new weapon. (As of this writing the forthcoming Stealth bomber and Trident D-2 submarines are being heralded by U.S. strategists as our new deterrents).

My next point is more significant: Nuclear weapons are more likely to precipitate a war than to deter it. Obviously, the weapons would tend to deter a potential aggressor in one type of situation. Let us assume that policymakers in the Kremlin were deliberating in the absence of a crisis and that they were completely rational and had ample time for reflection. Assume also that they believed peaceful coexistence could probably not last forever. Hence they were considering a first strike. Yet they knew that however massive their attack, the United States would still have enough nuclear warheads to obliterate them and the entire Soviet Union.

In such circumstances, our nuclear weapons would have a deterrent effect. The Soviet leaders would probably decide not to attack. But how realistic is such a scenario? The likelihood of a war beginning in such a calm, deliberate setting is very slight. And here is the problem: Escalating our nuclear deterrent to guard against that one unlikely scenario greatly increases the chance of war starting in any one of several other ways.

In the name of deterrence, we multiply stockpiles of speedier, more threatening weapons, dependent upon highly sophisticated technology. Even when there is no crisis, this adds to the probability of a war being triggered by mechanical malfunction or human error--as when a U.S. ship in the Persian Gulf shot down an Iranian passenger plane. Confronted with this danger, military analysts sometimes refer to devices intended to provide safety in every conceivable circumstance. Unfortunately, accidents sometimes occur because of a series of inconceivable coincidences.

If a crisis develops, fear and tension will mount, impairing human judgment even further. Insofar as one side has the "strength" that is supposed to be a deterrent, the other side will be under pressure to launch a preemptive attack lest its own missiles be destroyed. George Kennan, former ambassador to the Soviet Union, has pointed out that the only real incentive for the Soviets to bomb the United States would be the weapons deployment with which we threaten them. Yet we claim that this enormous striking power is meant to deter such an attack! The ability of the Soviets to attack is provided by what they insist is only a deterrent--their nuclear arsenal. The paradox is that the more we build up our so-called deterrent, the more provocative it becomes.

In still another way, seeking deterrence by nuclear weaponry increases the danger of war more than it prevents it. It encourages additional nations to acquire the weapons. After all, if they provide peace through strength for the United States, why should this not be true for others? Moreover, the possession of nuclear arms has a prestige value that smaller nations covet.

And as the major powers develop the technology to make smaller, cheaper weapons, it becomes easier for other nations to manufacture them.

In the Non-Proliferation Treaty of 1970, the non-nuclear states agreed not to develop nuclear arsenals; the nuclear powers agreed to reduce and eventually eliminate theirs. The failure of the latter to fulfill their pledge gives the former a compelling excuse for pursuing dreams of nuclear glory, thereby increasing the number of flashpoints at which war could break out. Simply in terms of self-preservation, Kennan expressed the thought of many perceptive students of U.S. policy when he said that if we Americans had no nuclear weapons whatever on our soil instead of the tens of thousands that are deployed, he would feel much safer.

Because the policy of nuclear deterrence is so widely accepted, I have spent several paragraphs showing that possessing the weapons decreases, rather than increases, a nation's security. They are more provocative than deterrent. The most serious critique of conditioned acceptance of the weapons, however, is that the policy is immoral. In view of the readiness to retaliate and the consequent loss of life, nuclear deterrence can in no way be reconciled with the spirit and teaching of the New Testament.

Deterrence policy depends on the resolve to retaliate if the nation is attacked. Without question, this threat will be carried out if the attack occurs. The use of nuclear weapons is an integral part of the chain of command. Officers stationed at control desks in missile silos and elsewhere have been conditioned to obey orders. They have so often practiced the steps leading up to the fatal moment that their response will be as mechanical as robots. Some military planners in high places are not even content to wait until the United States is attacked. When they feel sure war is imminent, they will assume that deterrence has failed, and they intend to

strike first. This is well documented in books like The Button by Daniel
Ford and To Win a Nuclear War by Daniel Axelrod and Michio Kaku.

Certainly the readiness to use nuclear weapons cannot meet the
crucial just-war requirements. The first of these is proportionality: "The
damage to be inflicted and the costs incurred by war must be proportionate
to the good expected." This criterion could be met only if the weapons are
not used or if their use was certain to be limited to an extent that is not
credible by any realistic assessment.

The second criterion is "discrimination," which prohibits directly
intended attacks on noncombatants. The deliberate attacks on civilians in
World War II should convince us that this criterion would not be met in a
future war, no matter what military planners declare. Even if "directly
intended attacks" did not occur, the number of civilians killed would be so
great as to make the distinction between "direct" and "indirect" virtually
meaningless.

Another assertion sometimes made to explain why church statements
often reject unilateral nuclear disarmament is that nations have a right to
self-defense. Granting that nonviolent defense would be preferred, the
Catholic bishops justify "lethal force" if nonviolent methods would not seem
to succeed. I find no basis in the New Testament or the most sensitive
ethical writings for condoning killing as a method of defense. I believe the
willingness of Jesus to be crucified and of other martyrs to die rather than
kill implies that defense is not as ultimate a right as the bishops assume. If
defense required the killing that nuclear war would involve, it could have no
Christian justification, even for the sake of freedom or survival. Moreover,
nearly every nation in war claims to be defending itself or its values. In
World War II, Germany and Japan were able to convince their citizens that
they were redressing wrongs that had been inflicted upon them.

Behind any justification of deterrence and self-defense, of course, looms the pervasive fear of the Soviet threat. I have dealt with this at some length in my book <u>Ammunition for Peacemakers</u>. For more expert analysis, I recommend the writings of Marshall Shulman of Columbia University and Dimitri Simes of the Carnegie Endowment for International Peace. Leading Sovietologists are generally agreed that the Soviets would lose much more than they would gain by occupying Western Europe, even if it were possible to do so. As for bombing the United States, it is hard to see what incentive the Soviets would have if they had no reason to fear our attacking them.

The only realistic Soviet threat is to our vital interests. Military action has not served very well in protecting our interests abroad. To the extent that it is effective, it generally benefits only a small elite segment of the population. It too often supports the exploitation of the people and natural resources of other countries. Instead of risking war to protect our access to Middle East oil, we would do better to become more self-sufficient through conserving our own resources and developing alternative energy sources. For the long-term, the best protection lies in developing better relations with the Soviet Union and Third World nations.

Yet realism compels us to recognize that giving up our military threat and becoming vulnerable to threats by others would entail some economic loss. It would involve the reduction of foreign operations and their profits. Such economic loss would probably be more than offset, however, by the enormous savings reducing our arsenals would bring. This would also have the tremendous advantage of keeping us from getting into a nuclear war by military confrontation abroad. Everything considered, giving up our deterrent threat, while entailing some disadvantages, would be beneficial to our legitimate interests.

As for the fact that U.S. nuclear disarmament might tempt other countries to expand their nuclear arsenals, the risk, I believe, would be amply compensated by the greater safety U.S. disarmament would bring. We face a balancing of risks. On the one hand, the United States may retain nuclear weapons for the many years required to achieve multilateral disarmament. This involves the possibility that they will be used. How great the risk will be and whether it will increase or decrease over time can only be conjectured. The crucial point, however, is that the nuclear war to be risked could be catastrophic enough to destroy human civilization. While the risk may be small, it should outweigh all others.

On the other hand, the elimination of nuclear weapons quickly and unilaterally would entail sacrifice and risks. There is reason to believe, however, that it would greatly reduce the chance of a nuclear war, and if it did break out it would be less destructive without U.S. participation. From the practical standpoint, the second alternative would seem to be preferable. From the moral standpoint, if the churches strive for the second alternative, they would seem to be less culpable.

This essay has been dealing with the position the church should take regarding the nuclear threat. It is difficult to take a stance contrary to the pressures of society, especially of the national government. Yet the institutional church and its members, faced with an increasing awareness of the nuclear threat, have gradually become more critical of national policy. How much influence the church can have on the government is problematical; yet it can determine its own stance.

Church young people at Amsterdam fifty years ago and at WCC Assemblies have prodded the church to take positions based less on pragmatic considerations and more on faith. The historic peace churches have exerted continuing influence on the WCC in the same direction. In joint consultations during the last decade, they shared their insights with several mainline denominations, which have been giving the pacifist position more serious consideration than formerly.

Perhaps the time is coming when some of the major church bodies can take a strong faith stance against the possession of nuclear weapons as a deterrent. At two points in their pastoral letter, the Catholic bishops assert that "no end can justify means evil in themselves." This seems to affirm a categorical imperative--that an act may be so wrong that it must not be committed, come what may. Their Report five years later declares: "There is an absolute moral norm which protects the life of innocent persons." These ethical affirmations would seem to provide a basis for opposing the possession of nuclear weapons, that are poised to be fired upon command. This would imply advocating unilateral disarmament as soon as possible. This is a position of faith--that although not all of the consequences can be foreseen, a moral universe will ultimately validate such a stance.

As the churches struggle with these issues, I suggest further examination of several assumptions and attitudes. One is the assumption that killing in self-defense is justified. Another is the tendency to condone retaliation. More attention must also be paid to the concept of stewardship--of what we do with our lives and talents. Regarding the sin of killing, military service requires subjecting one's conscience to the orders of superior officers. A major aim of basic training is to obliterate moral and religious inhibitions to what recruits will do in war. Above all, the implications of Jesus' submitting to the injustice of the cross need further reflection.

Whether or not the churches take the stance I suggest, and until the nation disarms, I advocate a three-fold agenda on which all peace-lovers can cooperate. First we must do everything possible to reduce the immediate danger, primarily by reversing the arms race. This will involve implementing the best proposals advanced by the WCC, Catholic and Protestant spokespersons, peace movement leaders, and retired government and military policymakers who may now speak freely. The INF treaty (to eliminate all short and intermediate-range nuclear missiles from Europe) was a good beginning. Urgent needs at the time of writing are a comprehensive test ban and a drastic reduction of strategic (long-range) nuclear weapons.

Beyond specific measures to reduce the immediate danger, we must intensify efforts to establish the conditions required for a lasting peace. Just as the international scene in a world at war becomes adapted to the war, so now we must create a climate conducive to peace--both internationally and within nations. This would affect the conduct of the economy, education, scientific research, the corporate world, international trade--in fact, practically every aspect of the common life. It would include developing effective, peaceful means to adjudicate international disputes via a strengthened United Nations and World Court and other methods, as advocated by such organizations as the World Federalist Association and its offshoot, the Commission on Respect for International Law. Assuming a gradual reduction in nuclear weapons, the hope is that they would be eliminated by the time these far-reaching changes have occurred.

Yet even if we succeed in all of these endeavors, this will not eliminate the risk of the holocaust. With good fortune, however, these steps should give us time--admittedly several decades--to prepare for what is very likely the only course that will bring permanent peace. The problem is that a conflict may occur at any time that cannot be arbitrated satisfactorily, and nuclear weapons cannot be disinvented. In any future war between major powers, they could be brought back to destroy us all.

This makes our age unlike any that has gone before. Faced with a peril unprecedented in human history, the churches need to explore new ideas. To an increasing extent, people like the psychiatrist Robert J. Lifton are being driven by the harsh realities of the modern world to conclude that in order to survive we must rule out the whole war system as a means of settling international disputes.

Many of us would agree with this conclusion except for one question: If peaceful methods fail, how would we defend our country? There is an alternative, more serious consideration of which has been advocated in both the Catholic and Protestant documents analyzed in this essay. But it will not be adopted overnight. I refer to civilian-based defense (CBD), which relies on nonviolence and the population as a whole, instead of violence and a special category of armed forces. CBD involves the rejection of killing as a national policy and substitutes the threat or employment of active nonviolent resistance to deter or repel a potential invader. This would be part of a larger policy whereby other types of danger would also be met without killing.

Nonviolent action for social change is not without precedent. We are familiar with its use under Gandhi's leadership to achieve independence for India and under the leadership of Martin Luther King in the struggle for civil rights. CBD is the application of such methods to national defense. It is based on the concept that political power resides ultimately in the citizens of a country. Rulers or invaders depend on the cooperation and assistance, or at least the submission and obedience, of the population. Their power evaporates if enough people withhold their support--even in the face of threats or death. The power of CBD consists of the people denying opponents the cooperation they need to accomplish their aims. Such "people power" caused the fall of the Shah in Iran and Ferdinand Marcos in the Philippines.

Most cases of nonviolent resistance have been spontaneous, with little advance preparation. But CBD should have careful, disciplined planning, preparation, and organization, as well as strong commitment to the goal and pacific methods of attaining it. Techniques vary all the way from simple attempts at persuasion to blocking the path of tanks.

CBD would entail cost and sacrifice, but much less so than military defense. Moreover, it would have these benefits:

1. Citizens would be involved in taking more personal responsibility for the welfare of their country.

2. Without the military means to support dictators or rebels, a nation would need to develop a more positive foreign policy.

3. By reducing fear and hostility, CBD would increase international goodwill.

4. It would greatly reduce the risk of nuclear war by eliminating military targets, which are also a threat to other nations.

5. It would provide a model that dissidents in the Soviet bloc could use to improve their lot.

6. It would reduce the incentive for additional nations to develop nuclear weapons.

7. It would release tremendous economic resources to meet social needs.

8. It would practically eliminate the major threat to the continuance of the human race.

9. Above all, we would be living as moral human beings.

The Christian churches have repeatedly declared that "war is incompatible with the teaching and example of our Lord Jesus Christ...a sin against God and degradation of man." They have not always, however, condemned possessing nuclear weapons for the indefinite time required to achieve multilateral disarmament. Yet those weapons could destroy all that we cherish, including ourselves. The merit of CBD is that it may be the key to solving that paradox. We may be able vigorously to oppose war, pursue peace, and propose a practical method of defending our country.

The crucial question is whether we can survive long enough to replace the war system with a system based on a rejection of killing. Perhaps our best hope lies in the possibility of smaller nations adopting such a defense and its advocacy by a few leaders of the major powers. That could produce what Kenneth Boulding sees as a "profound...shift in the nature of the system which carries us over a kind of watershed into a very different social landscape...Where an institution is ripe for delegitimation, a single person, such as Martin Luther King, can have enormous impact."

New Ground for the Churches

Herman Will

Ten years ago in a similar commemorative issue I wrote about developments in international affairs and the response of the churches during the forty years following the 1939 World Conference of Christian Youth. In this article I propose to look at the changes that have taken place in the self-understanding of the churches, in their perceptions of government and society, and in their response to national and world events.

The Churches in 1939

When 1400 youth delegates and leaders gathered in Amsterdam, they faced a world they knew to be on the verge of war. The Hitler-Stalin pact was concluded only a few weeks later and by September Nazi Germany and the Soviet Union had divided Poland and World War II had begun. Some of the delegates who delayed their departure from Europe were caught and had to find other ways to get home, such as signing on as crew on freighters.

The response of Christians and the churches varied during the immediate pre-war period. Many individuals, but few churches, called for collective military preparations to confront Nazism. Many sought for alternatives, especially in the U.S., hoping that a major power which did not enter the war could help to bring it to a negotiated end short of mutual destruction. Still others were either apathetic or fatalistic, apparently regarding the war as inevitable.

The onset of war did not bring with it the enthusiasm and parades that had marked most earlier conflicts. Conscription was in effect; no nation deeply involved attempted to rely on voluntarism for the large numbers of troops required.

A grim and sober mood prevailed in the U.S. Compared with World War I, there were few instances of religious superpatriotism, of selling war bonds or preaching a crusade. Most congregations had service flags with a star for each member in the military forces. Some, like my own church, placed a star on the service flag for conscientious objectors in their memberships who had been drafted and assigned to civilian work.

However, more than 100,000 Japanese-Americans were evacuated from the Pacific Coast to internment centers surrounded by barbed wire and armed guards. Genuine fear of an invasion, abetted by racism and dislike of Japanese competition, resulted in this shameful act for which the U.S. government has finally apologized and promised a long overdue indemnity. Many churches protested and aided the evacuees with storage space and resources, but these efforts were drowned in the temporary hysteria that followed Pearl Harbor.[1]

---

1. Herman Will, <u>A Will for Peace</u> (Washington, D.C.: General Board of Church and Society of the United Methodist Church, 1984), pp. 68-70.

Even before December 7, 1941 the U.S. churches had begun to look beyond the war to the international institutions that would be needed to avert future wars. The Federal Council of Churches (now part of the National Council of Churches) launched a Commission on a Just and Durable Peace headed by John Foster Dulles and staffed by Walter W. Van Kirk and his Department of International Justice and Goodwill.

The Methodist Church's Commission on World Peace actually convened an exploratory conference of more than 200 church leaders on the Bases of a Just and Enduring Peace in June 1941. This was followed by a National Study Conference of the Federal Council in 1942 and another in 1945. Such programs clearly refuted charges that the churches were isolationist because a majority were anti-interventionist prior to Pearl Harbor.[2]

Working for World Order

While the life and work of many of the churches in Europe, Asia, and parts of Africa were disrupted by armed combat, military occupation, and displacement of people, the churches in the U.S. concentrated on educating their members on the need and functions for a world organization. In turn, they sought to mobilize these members to express their support for a strong United Nations. Among the recommendations proposed were universal membership for all nations, limitations on the veto power of the five permanent members of the Security Council, and the establishment of the Trusteeship Council and the Commission on Human Rights.[3]

---

2. Ibid., pp. 79-81.

3. Ibid., pp. 84-85.

With millions dying in a war of increasing mass destruction, Christians were moved by the call to help create a world organization that would make a third world war unlikely, if not impossible. Mainline U.S. Protestants responded as never before and showered their representatives with letters, telegrams and phone calls.

The results were evident in the 89-2 vote by which the Senate ratified the UN Charter. Generally speaking, the Protestant churches of the U.S. have done a good, though uneven, job of following through on their wartime support for world organization. The availability of funds and changes in priorities have affected the consistency of their efforts.

The United Methodist Church has been outstanding in its work at and in behalf of the UN. The erection of the twelve-story Church Center for the UN has provided an invaluable facility for educational programs and consultations and a home for several denominational and ecumenical offices.[4]

Rooms have been made available to the UN and to UN-related activities ranging from educational and exercise groups to monthly teas of the Delegates' Wives Club to memorial services for deceased UN staff to Non-Governmental Organization Conferences. Ecumenical groups such as Christians Associated for Relations with Eastern Europe, the World Conference on Religion and Peace, and the North American Christian Peace Conference have met there periodically. Major program efforts during the Special Sessions of the UN General Assembly on Disarmament lasting several weeks have been based in the Church Center under the leadership of the Fellowship of Reconciliation and with the support of a wide range of groups.

---

4. Ibid., pp. 97-101.

The United Methodist Office for the UN maintains a seminar program for delegations which have come from all parts of the country for the last forty years. Specialized staff are available to resource these seminars and also to follow important regional issues that engage or should engage the UN's attention. The Division of World Peace has played an important role throughout the years, but the Women's Division of United Methodism deserves special credit for the financing of the Church Center's construction, the basing of its international affairs staff in the Center, and for reaching out to the UN community through its hospitality program.[5]

Several other denominations and church-related organizations have maintained officers and observers at the UN of which the Friends deserve special mention for the continuity and effectiveness of their efforts. These denominations and agencies have conducted educational programs and relayed to their constituencies important developments in the international community. The quality and the continuity of this work reflects a commitment and maturity that offers hope for more achievements in the future.

The Civil Rights Movement

The Montgomery bus boycott led by Martin Luther King, Jr., was the spark in an already explosive atmosphere which touched off a social movement and led to societal changes that will remain as a landmark in U.S. history.

Space does not permit any detailed account of the great events that stirred the nation and especially the churches during the 1950's and 1960's. It must be recorded, however, that the civil rights movement galvanized

---

5. Ibid.

black Christians into commitment and action that challenged white Christians to stand up and be counted. Most white Christians never stood up, but grumbled in their pews about civil disobedience even as they realized they could not deny the moral rightness of the changes sought. We should thank God for the stature of the black leadership that emerged and for the prophetic courage of the white leaders--bishops, pastors, laity--who responded by placing their bodies alongside those of their black sisters and brothers.

Looking beyond the civil rights struggle itself, we can now see that the example of large, peaceful demonstrations coupled with selective non-violent actions made a lasting worldwide impression. The overthrow of the Marcos government in the Philippines by huge, non-violent gatherings, the protests against torture in Chile by small, disciplined, non-violent groups, the "Going Home" movement of displaced Salvadorans returning to their villages from refugee camps in Honduras, the non-violent resistance of the South African churches to apartheid, and the recent peaceful demonstrations against censorship of church publications in East Germany--all these have gained inspiration from the civil rights movement in the U.S.[6]

I shall never forget my 1978 visit to the German Democratic Republic where five of us representing the National Council of Churches met with East German church leaders to discuss issues of foreign policy and the nuclear arms race. We were invited to arrive a day early to join in the observance of the tenth anniversary of the assassination of Martin Luther King, Jr. We were wondering at the memorializing of that tragic event, but learned of the tremendous impression left by Dr. King when he visited and

---

6. Fellowship (Nyack, N.Y.: Fellowship of Reconciliation), March 1987, pp. 4-19. Also September 1988, pp. 5-10.

preached in East German churches in connection with his trip to Oslo for the Nobel Peace Prize presentation.

After attending an ecumenical service during which we viewed a slide set on King's life, we were invited to an evening performance of a cantata written by two East German pastors. It was presented by a choir of 75 and an orchestra of 25 musicians in a large and beautiful church. The building was packed with part of the audience standing in the aisles and the foyer.

The cantata was an interpretation of the life of Martin Luther King and centered on the theme of non-violence. Two or three civil rights movement songs were incorporated and the listeners joined in singing with the choir at those points. To see and hear this German audience, mostly under 30, sing "We Shall Overcome" was a deeply moving experience. This cantata and the fact that it had already played 128 times in packed churches was a living testimony to a vital religious faith among many who may not be regular churchgoers.

During my last visit to Cuba in January 1988, we visited a suburban Baptist church pastored by Raul Suarez of the Cuban Ecumenical Council. One of the rooms had been renovated through a gift from a U.S. Baptist and dedicated as the Martin Luther King center. The dedication ceremony was attended by church and government leaders, believers and non-believers. The Center serves as a library and depository for resources on Dr. King and non-violence.

The Vietnam Experience

In 1964 President Lyndon Johnson and his advisers never dreamed of the tragedy they were unleashing when they stampeded the Congress into passing the Tonkin Gulf resolutino. Based on an alleged attack on U.S.

vessels that was never substantiated, this resolution opened the door for U.S. involvement in hostilities without a declaration of war.[7]

The sending of troops to Vietnam and the bombing of the North soon followed. The process of escalation continued as the Viet Cong and the North Vietnamese forces fought effectively against the expanding U.S. military presence. Nearly 500,000 Army, Navy, Marines and Air Force personnel were stationed in Vietnam.

The response of the churches was prompt and forceful. On April 4, 1965, the Clergymen's (sic) Emergency Committee for Vietnam, initiated by the Fellowship of Reconciliation, published a full page advertisement in the New York Times entitled, "2500 Ministers, Priests and Rabbis say: Mr. President: In the Name of God, STOP IT!" The statement described U.S. policy as returning "evil for evil on a multiplying scale" and warned that such methods "will bring the judgment of God upon our nation."[8]

On May 12, 1965, an Interreligious Committee on Vietnam convened 600 Catholics, Protestants and Jews for a prayer vigil outside the Pentagon. Nine representatives met with Defense Secretary McNamara for an hour and a half, warning against further escalation and urging an end to the bombing of the North to get negotiations started.[9]

As the war progressed and the toll in human life and devastation rose, the church leaders spoke out again and again in public statements, private meetings, and at mass demonstrations. Even some who had warned against communist expansion in the 1950's concluded that no possible good that could result from the war justified the suffering and death of civilians,

---

7. Will, A Will for Peace, pp. 117-119.

8. Ibid., p. 121.

9. Ibid., pp. 122-123.

the death and maiming of combatants, the destruction of homes, the poisoning of the land, and the brutalizing effects on the personalities and characters of the participants.

The founding meeting of Clergy and Laity Concerned About Vietnam was held in the apartment of Anne and John Bennett of Union Theological Seminary in New York. By 1968 Reinhold Niebuhr had declared his opposition to the continuance of the war by the U.S., thus dismaying many bitter anti-communists who had used his lesser evil doctrine to justify the conflict. During the middle and later stages of the struggle, more and more members of the Catholic hierarchy called for a change in U.S. policy.

The strong convictions of most church leaders and many members were shared by a large portion of the U.S. citizenry. Widespread grassroots efforts for an end to the war were coupled with a series of massive demonstrations ranging from 100,000 to 500,000 in size. Usually, the churches did not sponsor these demonstrations, but they publicized them among their members and often housed delegations from local congregations in church buildings in the Washington, D.C. area.[10]

In early 1968, the North Vietnamese and Viet Cong unleashed a major offensive throughout the country which was finally defeated, but only after enormous destruction and heavy losses on all sides, including the South Vietnamese and U.S. This led to a reconsideration of policy by President Johnson who ordered a halt to the bombing in most of North Vietnam. He also announced a gradual withdrawal of U.S. forces and declared he would not be a candidate for reelection in 1968.[11]

---

10. Ibid., pp. 137, 148-151, 154.

11. Ibid., pp. 138-140.

This process of reduction of forces was continued under the Nixon administration accompanied by negotiations with the North Vietnamese. Agreement was difficult to reach, so from time to time Nixon stepped up air raids against the North, the most damaging of which occurred just before Christmas in 1972 and evoked condemnations from religious leaders.[12]

In 1973, the U.S. Congress finally voted to cut off all funds for the pursuance of the war. The churches played an important role in that decision for they had formed the Coalition to Stop Funding the War which coordinated the successful effort.

On January 27, 1973, a ceasefire was signed and the military draft ended, on March 29 the last U.S. troops left Vietnam, and on August 15 congressional action terminated all U.S. bombing. However, the U.S. government continued to send shipments of arms to the South Vietnamese despite growing congressional opposition. Finally the North Vietnamese and Viet Cong forces completed their takeover of the country in April 1975.[13]

In the course of the struggle, the bulk of the Protestant churches, as well as many Jewish and Catholic congregations joined in registering their conviction that the war was wrong and unjust. This was a remarkable development. In United States history, the only other war to which such strong opposition emerged was the Mexican conflict. However, the critics of that aggression--including Abraham Lincoln--were not able to halt it, nor to prevent their government from relieving Mexico of more than half its territory.

It is true that the swift victory of U.S. forces in 1848 was harder to criticize effectively than the prolonged struggle in Vietnam which was nightly

---

12. Ibid., pp. 159-160.

13. Ibid., pp. 161-162.

projected on TV screens in almost every home. Still the persistent and persuasive statements and actions of the churches over a decade during which the executive branch of government seemed impervious to calls for some compassion and reason, redound to the credit of the religious community.

The 1972 General Conference of the United Methodist Church by a 57% majority adopted a statement that exemplifies this unusually firm stand of the churches:

> "We have sinned against our brothers and sisters, against the earth and our Creator. We have paid our taxes without protest; we have closed our eyes to the horror of our deeds; we have driven families from their homes into endless lines tracking across the pockmarked earth...

> "God grant that we may say 'yes' to his judgment upon us and our nation, and that the Indochinese, and we, might be delivered out of this anguish.

> "We further call upon the leadership of the United States to confess that what we have done in Indochina has been a crime against humanity..."[14]

The Central American Tragedy

Before the U.S. became deeply involved in El Salvador, Honduras, and Nicaragua, there were warnings from many quarters that such involvement would mean a repetition of the Vietnam experience. These admonitions were not heeded by the Reagan administration for several reasons: the strong ideological bent of key officials, the proximity of Central

---

14. Ibid., pp. 157-158.

America to the U.S., the private investments in the area, and a concern that other revolutionary situations would be encouraged and move in socialist directions.

However, as happened in Vietnam, the strategists underestimated the amount of popular support for the FMLN in El Salvador and for the Sandinista program in Nicaragua. Huge quantities of military supplies to the Salvadoran armed forces and economic aid to the government have not sufficed to end a stalemate in that conflict. Likewise, substantial arms and money to the contras have not achieved enough political unity and military effectiveness to displace or seriously threaten the Sandinista rule. In both situations, however, the conflicts have taken a fearful toll in human casualties and economic suffering.

The National Conference of Catholic Bishops, the National Council of Churches, and many Jewish leaders have repeatedly spoken out against U.S. attempts to destabilize the Nicaraguan government and, by aid to the contras, to overthrow it. They have pointed out the disregard of the popular will, the denial of self-determination, and the violation of international law and treaties that are involved in U.S. policy.

Meanwhile, local churches have become sister congregations to churches in Nicaragua and other Central American countries. Expressions of Christian solidarity through communications and visits have been accompanied by strong support for programs of refugee aid and medical assistance. Hundreds of Christian volunteers have shared in the Witness for Peace effort to reduce violence by getting eyewitness reports of all contra attacks, especially where civilians have been killed, injured or kidnapped.

As U.S. aid to the contras has continued, the Catholic Quixote Center has coordinated efforts to match the aid to the contras with equal amounts of private assistance to the people of Nicaragua in the form of food, clothing, medicines, school supplies, ambulances and civilian trucks. An estimated 1,500 U.S. citizens, most of them religiously affiliated, have been working in Nicaragua in relief, health, and development programs.

Church related and inspired educational efforts can claim a large share of the credit for maintaining a public opinion strongly opposed to U.S. government policy, a fact substantiated by many polls taken over several years. Some observers have even asserted that U.S. combat forces would have been sent into Nicaragua to overthrow the Sandinista government had it not been for Christians and the churches.

While the conflict in El Salvador has not received as much public attention, some congregations have provided sanctuary for refugees, and many have developed ties with Salvadoran churches and sent relief supplies for refugees, as well as medical aid. In the Going Home project, Christians in small groups have accompanied several thousand Salvadorans who have insisted on returning from UN refugee camps in Honduras to their homes, despite the objections and harassment of the Salvadoran military who want to continue to attack freely everyone in certain areas on the chance that they may be guerrillas.

Again, to the credit of the churches and their members, they have faithfully persisted in their humanitarian efforts and have also sought to inform the public that the dire poverty of the people amid the wealth of the rich and the firepower of the military is the root cause of these revolutions. This is a new role for the Christian community in today's world.[15]

---

15. The Christian Century (Chicago, IL: The Christian Century Foundation), Vol. 105, No. 27, September 28, 1988, "Guatemalan Bishops Respond to the Cry for Land," pp. 841-843, Robert A. McKenzie.

The Nuclear Arms Race

Ever since the first atomic bomb was dropped on Japan in 1945, bishops, pastors, theologians and lay people in the churches have been deeply troubled by its use and even more by the growing stockpile of nuclear weapons.[16]

During the 1950's widespread public concern arose over the dangers of radioactive fallout from atmospheric nuclear testing. The heightened risk, especially for children ingesting Strontium 90 in cow's milk, meant that thousands of persons were dying of radiation-induced cancer, anonymous victims unidentifiable in the annual toll.

After nearly three years of a voluntary halt to nuclear testing by the U.S.S.R., the United Kingdom and the U.S., the Soviet Union resumed testing on September 1, 1961 and the U.S. on September 15. When this occurred, there were strong protests from the churches exemplified by the Methodist Council of Bishops' statement terming the testing an "arrogant disregard for human rights" and "a crime against all humanity."[17]

On June 10, 1963, President Kennedy delivered a remarkable address at Methodist-related American University in Washington, D.C. He announced that Chairman Khruschev, Prime Minister MacMillan and he had agreed that high level discussions for a comprehensive test ban treaty would be held in Moscow soon and that the U.S. would not conduct further tests if others did not. By July 25, the negotiators reached agreement on a treaty providing a limited ban on all atmospheric, underwater, and outer space testing. Unfortunately, underground testing became a more serious problem in the development of new weapons than had been expected.

---

16. Will, A Will for Peace, pp. 187-188.

17. Ibid., pp. 202-205.

A gathering of church, peace, farm, business, labor and veterans' organizations held a strategy session with assistant majority leader of the Senate, Hubert Humphrey, to lay plans to support ratification. Petitions bearing 30,000 signatures were presented to the State Department in behalf of the treaty. Former Assistant Secretary of State Francis Wilcox testified for the National Council of Churches and constituent denominations that "...the weight of conviction among leaders and representatives of the churches...show a deep longing and profound conviction that nuclear weapons testing should be ended."[18] The treaty was ratified in the Senate by a roll call vote of 80 to 19.

President Nixon in 1969 proposed a large scale Anti-Ballistic Missile system, allegedly for defense against a possible Chinese attack. The 1968 General Conference of the United Methodist Church had declared that "Anti-ballistic missile systems threaten to accelerate arms spending and heighten tensions dangerously without adding to the security of the nations."[19]

Eight Protestant agencies joined with the U.S. Catholic Conference and the Union of American Hebrew Congregations to set up the ABM Information Center. This center gathered information on issues, kept abreast of legislative developments, published bulletins and resource materials, and coordinated actions of its constituent groups.

The Center was sufficiently effective to draw some congressional fire. One representative wrote the Internal Revenue Service asking an investigation of the non-profit religious agencies engaged in legislative activities. The IRS took no action, obviously not anxious to take on such a

---

18. Ibid., pp. 205-207.

19. Ibid., pp. 211-212.

task, so the member of Congress then wrote asking that the IRS call the attention of the agencies to the law and regulations on the subject, a request with which the IRS complied. Eventually, one ABM system was deployed in North Dakota, but after several years and the expenditure of $6 billion, it was dismantled as ineffective.[20]

The significance of church efforts in support of arms control and disarmament measures was recognized in 1972 when officials of the U.S. Arms Control and Disarmament Agency invited four representatives from religious peace groups to attend the signing of the SALT I agreements at the White House. Unfortunately, the SALT II treaty was never ratified by the Senate because of resistance from advocates of larger U.S. military forces combined with the Soviet invasion of Afghanistan.

Only passing reference can be made to the extensive educational activities of the churches during the Non-Proliferation Treaty Review Conferences and the UN General Assembly's Special Sessions on Disarmament. Religious non-governmental organizations brought the attention of world leaders to concerns of the churches by a major role in publishing the Disarmament Times, submitting proposals to delegations, holding special luncheon meetings, operating coffee house discussion programs, holding large convocations, and sharing in mass public demonstrations.[21]

Finally, the pastoral letter of the U.S. Catholic bishops on the subject of nuclear war, followed by a similar document directed by the United Methodist bishops to their members and, in part, to a larger audience, represented a new readiness of episcopal leaders to exercise a teaching role.

---

20. Ibid.

21. Ibid., pp. 218-221.

Other religious denominations issued carefully prepared statements and launched new efforts to evoke a response from their local churches.

The record of the Christian community in the U.S. in respect to the nuclear arms race still leaves much that could and should be done. Nevertheless, that community has demonstrated a degree of sophistication and a sense of responsibility far in advance of that shown earlier in the century.

Apartheid and South Africa

The history of apartheid and the South African churches' response is too long and involved for the space of this article, and the author has no special competence in this area. Recent important developments, however, deserve attention.

The mainline churches of South Africa, with the exception of the Dutch Reformed Church, have been making statements critical of apartheid for three decades or more, but taking very small steps to oppose it. In the 1950's Father Trevor Huddleston wrote: "The church sleeps on...though it occasionally talks in its sleep and expects (or does it?) the government to listen."[22]

In the 1980's, tensions increased and Soweto became a symbol of the determination of black South Africans to resist apartheid. As the struggle has drawn more international attention, anti-apartheid sympathizers including religious leaders in many nations have pressed banks to end loans and corporations to withdraw from South Africa. Resolutions supported by churches and religious organizations have been pressed at annual

---

22. Christianity and Crisis (New York, NY: Christianity and Crisis), Vol.48, No.12, September 12, 1988, "For the soul of the church in South Africa," p. 288, Charles Villa-Vicencio.

stockholders' meetings to change companies' policies. Students and faculties have persuaded many colleges and universities to divest themselves of stock in businesses active in South Africa; churches and unions have adopted restrictions on the investment of pension funds; and cities, counties and states have established policies directed against purchases of South African goods and placement of deposits in banks involved in South Africa.

The "Sullivan Principles" advanced by Leon Sullivan, a black U.S. clergyman, have been adopted by many corporations doing business in South Africa as a way of breaking down segregation. However, many persons who are specialists on African affairs question seriously the capacity of U.S. corporations to achieve change by such methods.

Most of these steps have been applauded and encouraged by anti-apartheid leaders in South Africa, including religious representatives, though there is dissent from some who fear the economic effects on the black majority.[23]

In February of 1988, seventeen organizations including the United Democratic Front of which Anglican Archbishop Desmond Tutu and Dr. Allan Boesak, president of the World Alliance of Reformed Churches, are patrons, were banned by the government. In June 1988 the government renewed for the third year a State of Emergency and banned the Cape Town-based Committee for the Defence of Democracy to which Tutu, Boesak, and Frank Chikane, general secretary of the South African Council of Churches, are related. Many see this as a way of silencing these three leaders without banning them individually.[24]

---

23. Will, A Will for Peace, pp. 237-239.

24. Christianity and Crisis, Vol. 48, No. 12, September 12, 1988, p. 289.

On May 30-31, 1988, 230 persons representing 22 churches, 17 church organizations, and 21 regional councils met in Johannesburg. The Convocation, called in response to the February banning, set out to involve the churches in a non-violent action program to support the "days of protest" of the principal trade union federation. Long term aims include the freeing of political prisoners such as Nelson Mandela.[25]

On June 29 a statement of 26 church leaders pointed out that the October 26 municipal elections could not be fair under the State of Emergency. The next day the South African Council of Churches annual conference called for all Christians not to run as candidates nor vote in the October elections since to do so would be to cooperate with oppression. This was a punishable offense and the church publication that contained the statement was promptly banned.[26]

A national conference against apartheid had been planned for September 24-25 that would bring together representatives from more than 70 groups. On September 22, the government banned the conference.

The courage and faithfulness of these church leaders--not all churches and church leaders, to be sure--deserve respect, encouragement, and solidarity. Charles Villa-Vicencio of the University of Cape Town has written:

> "The cautious liberal character of traditional church leadership is not well equipped to promote what must be asked for if the present government is to be removed from power. Christians who believe that the Gospel obliges them to confront the forces of apartheid will weigh the cost of confronting a regime that is unwilling to tolerate any form of effective opposition and resistance. These restraints have shaped the moderate

25. Ibid., p. 288.

26. The Christian Century, Vol 105, No. 29, October 12, 1988, "South African Churches Urge Election Boycott," pp. 885-886, Terry Swicegood.

character of the churches over many decades and are likely to continue to do so."[27]

In plain language this means that religious leaders and followers alike are facing a most difficult choice. Are they prepared to risk the ongoing programs and the institutional existence of their denominations and ecumenical bodies by speaking and acting non-violently with prophetic judgment on the pernicious evil of apartheid?

Rebirth in China

Since World War II, Chinese Christians have probably experienced more drastic changes than Christians in any other land. The victory of the Chinese Communist Party in the civil war, the pressures of the Korean conflict, the prolonged struggle in Vietnam, the dark years of the Cultural Revolution when all houses of worship were closed, and now the totally unexpected opportunities of the Deng Tsiaoping era.

Many Western Christians were dismayed at the criticisms leveled at their missionary activities and accomplishments by Chinese Christians in the 1950's. These criticisms were accompanied by the launching of the Three-Self Movement designed to distance Chinese Protestants from overseas mission agencies and to achieve self-support, self-determination, and self-propagation.

Reflections today on those actions might suggest that the insistence on independence and a break with the past may have avoided even harsher treatment during the decade (1966-76) of the Cultural Revolution. Furthermore, the obviously Chinese character of Protestantism today has undoubtedly opened many opportunities for the churches and helped them

---

27. Christianity and Crisis, Vol. 48, No. 12, September 12, 1988, p. 289.

to attract large numbers of people. Similar movements within the Catholic Church led to a break with Rome, the achievement of autonomy and the selection of their own bishops.

The death of Mao Zedong in 1967 and the ouster of the remaining supporters of the Cultural Revolution led to drastic changes in many areas of Chinese life. For the churches, this meant renewed recognition of the freedom to worship, added protection against local violations of such freedom, the return and rehabilitation of church structures, the payment of rent for past building use, the reopening of the Nanjing Theological Seminary and the initiation of several others, the offering of courses in the Bible and theology, and the organization of the Amity Foundation. The Foundation is a remarkable development, for it affords a renewed chance for Christians and others from outside China to contribute funds, materials and personnel to assist the churches of China in special projects above and beyond their own self-support. Social welfare institutions, recruitment of overseas Christians as English teachers in public schools, and construction of a printing plant to produce Bibles, books of worship, hymnals, and religious magazines are a few of the fruits of this new arrangement.

The response of the Chinese people has been astounding. 4,000 Protestant churches now serve an estimated three to four million persons, quite a jump from the 700,000 members claimed in 1949. An estimated 5,000,000 attend Catholic churches compared with some 3,000,000 in 1949. There is also much new interest in Buddhism and Islam.

New ground is also being broken as Chinese Christians establish ties with overseas religious bodies and send and receive visiting delegations. Out of the experience of their tribulations, most Protestants in China are now worshipping in congregations served by pastors of more than one denominational background, using forms of worship that vary widely, and seeking to create a Chinese Christian community that is not fractured by Western divisions over polity or theology.[28]

Soviet Christians at the Millenium

Since World War II, religion in the Soviet Union has experienced occasional periods of increased tolerance followed by renewed repression. Aleksandr Ogorodnikov, a Russian Orthodox dissenter and editor of a samzdat (unauthorized newsletter) wrote in February 1988 that Stalin opened 22,000 churches to use the religious feelings of the people in the war against Nazism.   During Khrushchev's "thaw" and repudiation of Stalinism, new attacks resulted in closing 14,000 houses of worship.

Mikhail Gorbachev's policies of "glasnost" and "perestroika" combined with the millenial celebration of Russian Orthodoxy have opened new horizons for religion in the U.S.S.R.   From Gorbachev's perspective, the churches can provide allies for him in addition to other political/economic reformers and the cultural elite who share the desire for a more open and prosperous society.

There are varying views of Gorbachev's initiatives. Some maintain that they are not sufficiently sweeping or profound. Others see them as offering genuine hope. There is a consensus that Gorbachev or someone like him must remain in charge for ten years or more if the fundamental changes sought are to be institutionalized.

The Russian Orthodox Church has been the principal beneficiary of the new policies, in part due to its millenial celebration. Nina Bobrova of

---

28. Winifred Nelson Beechy, The New China (Scottdale, PA: Herald Press, 1982), pp. 134-165.   For current information, write for subscription information to China Talk, published by the Hongkong China Liaison Office, World Division, General Board of Global Ministries, The United Methodist Church, 2 Man Wan Road, C-17, Kowloon, Hongkong.

the Orthodox staff noted that the Danilov Monastery had been returned by the government and completely refurbished by the church as its Moscow headquarters. Other monasteries have been turned back to the church and are being rebuilt, as well as a convent near Rostov. Seminaries have recently been opened in the Ukraine and Siberia, besides those in Odessa, Zagorsk, Moscow and Leningrad. Church leaders are often speaking on TV and radio.

Talking to the North American Christian Peace Conference in New York in September 1988, Metropolitan Filaret of Kiev emphasized that the millenium celebration had become a major international and interreligious event. Top officials of the Communist Party were present during major observances. Throughout the year there was a broad presentation of information about the churches in the media. It is becoming apparent to the public that Russian culture is a Christian culture.

Closed dialogues with atheists and scientists are occurring on peace, ethics, and morals, not hostile meetings, but a search for ways to develop morality and spirituality within the society. The Orthodox Church maintains contacts with Jews, not only in the U.S.S.R. but internationally. However, it has no special position on the emigration of Jews from the U.S.S.R. which is a civil right of everyone.

While perestroika raises many questions for the church itself, the structure will not change; it is unchangeable. Filaret did stress that the church must respond to new challenges within the society, to new people, to youth, intellectuals and their interests and requests.

New legislation for religious communities is being prepared for publication soon. Metropolitan Filaret expects that it will provide great opportunites for church members and all believers in the U.S.S.R. Some of the coming changes may already be reflected in recent developments.

In a bulletin of the Harriman Institute Forum (Vol. I, No. 7, July, 1988), Edward L. Keenan stated that it is reliably reported that the Orthodox Patriarchate has been approached by Soviet hospital officials in Moscow on the possibility that the church may take some role in hospital administration. Now we learn that an agreement has been signed by the director of a Moscow hospital and the nearby Epiphany Cathedral, to which Patriarch Pimen is related, allowing voluntary service by parishioners to patients. One man and a group of women led by a nun clean wards, change linens, care for bedpans, and sit with and read or talk to the patients. Where requested, a priest may bring the sacraments or come and pray for them.[29]

The role of the churches in Soviet society, especially the Russian Orthodox, and their relationship to government is rapidly changing. How radical and how sweeping those changes may become will, in large part, depend on the initiative of Christians.

Castro and Religion

Fidel y la Religion is the title of a book, in reality a lengthy interview of the Cuban leader by Frei Betto, a Catholic lay brother from Brazil. It has been published in several languages, but especially noteworthy is its Cuban circulation of nearly a million copies in a country of 10,000,000 people. The book was published in Cuba, incidentally, by the Office of Publications of the Council of State. In the book, Castro tells of his baptism and education as a Catholic, his alienation from the church because of its unconcern with justice, and his continuing conviction that Jesus Christ was

---

29. The Christian Century, Vol. 105, No. 33, November 9, 1988, "Perestroika Links Church and Hospital," pp. 1004-1005, Jim Forest.

the greatest revolutionary who ever lived. To this reader, it appears that Castro is anti-clerical, not anti-religious.[30]

Although the overthrow of Batista in 1959 was hailed enthusiastically by the great majority of the Cuban people, the early rejoicing of many faded when Castro made clear that he would attempt to develop a Marxist-Leninist state. Hundreds of thousands of Cubans left their island during subsequent years, many of them church members and ordained pastors.

The Christians who remained became the subject of close government scrutiny for a variety of reasons. Cubans who stayed and were opposed to Castro often gravitated to church congregations where they could find a sympathetic atmosphere in an institution not controlled by the state. Further, security forces were constantly watching for foreign agents and saboteurs who were steadily infiltrating Cuba with support and training from the U.S.

Because of this situation and at times their own involvement, many pastors and priests were sent for a period of several months to agricultural work camps. Some who were implicated in more serious actions served time in prison. They have since been allowed to return to their pastoral work and even to serve in important posts in the churches.

After an initial period of mutual hostility and suspicion, the churches and government settled down to a "live and let live" attitude. Some years ago, the chief of the U.S. Interest Section in Havana, John Fersh, described the churches as "restricted, but not persecuted." The number of Christians who had decided to accept life under socialism steadily increased from a small minority to substantial proportions.

---

30. Frei Betto, Fidel y la Religion, Conversaciones con Frei Betto, (La Habana, Cuba: Oficiana de Publicaciones de Consejo de Estado, 1985). English edition is now available.

In the early 1980's, Castro's attitude toward the churches began to change. He was impressed by the liberation theology of Christians, including priests, who were deeply involved in the struggle for social justice for the poor. During visits to Nicaragua, he met the Cardenals and others who were working to build a socialist society there.

In 1984 Jesse Jackson visited Cuba during his campaign for the presidency. He and his companions spent long hours in discussions with Cuba's top leaders. In fact, the story is told in Cuba that after a meeting with the Central Committee of the Communist Party, Jackson asked the group to grasp hands and then led in a closing prayer! It is noteworthy that he returned from Cuba with about 50 political prisoners that Castro released at his request.

After speaking at the University of Havana during his visit, Jesse Jackson invited Castro to join him for an ecumenical service at a large Methodist Church nearby, a service in memory of Martin Luther King, Jr. Castro accepted and was impressed by the friendly applause that greeted him on his entrance, and by invitation spoke briefly of the significance of Dr. King and the political courage of Jesse Jackson. After Jackson's address and the end of the service, Castro met the Catholic archbishop for the first time. It was the first religious service that Castro had attended since the triumph of the revolution.

In succeeding years, official policy toward the churches became more friendly. Dr Carneado, director of religious affairs for the Communist Party, told a group from the Florida Council of Churches in 1985 that "It is an illusion to think that we can build a new society in Cuba without the participation of the churches." Several U.S. Catholic bishops have visited Cuba and met at length with Castro. Each time they have asked for the release of political prisoners and found that Castro was prepared to do so (and actually has done so) as soon as the U.S. finished processing their visa applications.

More recently, building supplies have been made available for the repair and maintenance of church-owned buildings. The work of Catholic sisters in their homes for the elderly has drawn public commendation from Castro and suggestions that perhaps they should operate more homes because of their caring and efficiency. Mother Teresa visited Cuba and won Castro's consent for a group of four nuns from Europe to work with the terminally ill in homes, hospitals and hospices. A women's prison official has asked for Bibles to place in the library, and church officials are talking of starting a prison chaplaincy.

The period just ahead holds promise for many changes in church-state relations in Cuba. With the renewal of the immigration agreement with the U.S., with negotiations over independence for Namibia and removal of Cuban troops from Angola nearing success, and with serious discussion proceeding over other U.S.-Cuban differences, the prospects are good for improved relations between the two countries.

As the churches gain self-confidence and take the initiative in redefining their societal role as the Catholic Church has been doing, there is every reason to believe that the Cuban government will respond positively.[31]

Christians in the German Democratic Republic

The religious situation in what many loosely refer to as "East Germany" is truly unique. This is the only sovereign ally of the Soviet Union

---

31. The section on Cuba is based on personal contacts and information gathered during my six visits to Cuba between 1960 and 1988.

where Protestants outnumber Roman Catholic and Eastern Orthodox: 6.5 to 7 million nominal Protestants, mostly Lutheran (Evangelical) and jointly Lutheran-Calvinist (Union) with smaller Baptist, Methodist, and other denominations, out of a population of 17 million.

Just as unusual is the existence of the National Front, a coalition of five parties led by the SED (Socialist Unity Party--the controlling communist party). The others are the Christian Democratic Union, the Liberal Democratic Party, the National Democratic Party, and the Democratic Bauern Party. The CDU is the second largest party in terms of membership and has a set quota of seats in the national parliament. It is composed of Christian believers, Protestant and Catholic, some active in their respective churches, others not. The CDU owns hotels, restaurants, and religious book stores, and with this income and membership support it maintains retreat centers and party staff whereby party members are trained in speaking, writing, organizing and Christian ethics. Many small and medium-sized towns have elected CDU mayors.

During a visit to the German Democratic Republic (GDR) in 1978 for a church consultation on the arms race, I became very aware of the interest of the Federation of Evangelical Churches (Lutheran and Reformed) and other Protestant bodies in the concept of "common security" rather than "national security." I also learned of the concern for the rights of conscientious objectors who are now only excused from combatant training and service.

Over the years, East German Christians have participated in international meetings which have supported "rejection of the spirit, logic, and practice of deterrence," have been active in the October "Ten Days for Peace," and have shared in the work of the Christian Peace Conference. The churches have provided room for environmental and human rights groups to operate, and protested vigorously in November 1987 when police raided the Zion Church's parish house in Berlin, confiscated books and journals, and arrested some hangers-on. Eventually, the government returned the publications and conditionally released those arrested.[32]

The five summer Kirchentags (Church Days) in 1988 reflected the growing determination of Christians to share in the shaping of their society. In Halle, the participants sought the "candor to press in critical solidarity for the renewal of our society" and asked for elections with "recognizable options among diverse candidates" and an independent judiciary. They called for the communists to "forswear their monopoly of truth, backed by force, as well as their claim to be in principle socially superior."[33]

In Rostock, the Kirchentag "packed the aisles as well as the pews for the weekend's highly stimulating fare of lectures, seminars and roundtables." Many eminent Marxists shared in the forums and all were questioned sharply by youthful audiences. The "new thinking" of Gorbachev, according to the Rostock organizers, means "a chance for our own political development."[34]

Meanwhile, "perestroika" is being ignored by the dominant Socialist Unity Party which in November 1988 even banned the distribution of the Soviet monthly, Sputnik, because it did "not contribute to cementing Soviet-East German relations and instead contained articles that distort history."[35]

In the summer of 1988, the government (read SED) denied three church papers the right to publish articles about Christian activity in social

---

32. The Christian Century, Vol. 105, No. 28, October 5, 1988, "Protestants and Perestroika in the German Democratic Republic," pp. 870-872, Charles Yerkes.

33. Ibid., p. 871.

34. Ibid.

35. The Seattle Times-Post-Intelligencer, Sunday, November 20, 1988, "E. Germans ban Soviet monthly for 'distortion'".

renewal. The churches are not to speak out about military conscription, foreign policy, expatriation, environmental policy or public education.[36]

While in the GDR in October as guests of the CDU, we were informed that several younger Christians, including some national church staff, had just been arrested in Berlin in a non-violent protest against the censorship of church publications.   Apparently, both church and CDU leaders intervened, for we were assured by CDU officials that those arrested would be released promptly and that charges would not be pressed.

The situation in the GDR will pit a conservative and bureaucratic communist regime which is resistant to change against the growing popular movements aligned with churches whose leaders are seeking ways to reshape a society with which they are very dissatisfied.   International contacts and exchanges have been and will continue to be of great importance to the Christians of East Germany.

Conclusion

In every country discussed in these pages, the churches and the government are working out new relationships through a process of tension, negotiation, concession, and, at times, confrontation. This process will take different forms in capitalist countries with democratic structures from those in socialist countries with one-party governments or from those in South Africa where a white minority dominates and represses a black majority while trying to maintain a pretense of democracy.

With a multiplicity of socialist governments which no longer recognize any one ideological norm, communists are no longer sure of their monopoly

---

36. The Christian Century, Vol. 105, No. 28, October 5, 1988, p. 870.

on truth. Economic failures in both productivity and quality control have left them open to experiments with mixed systems.

At the same time, militant atheism is waning. Many communists now do not argue that religion is necessarily an opiate of the people. Nor do they assume that the churches are always either irrelevant or reactionary. They have seen in the civil rights movement, in the opposition to the Vietnam War, and in the resistance to U.S. Central American policy that U.S. churches can lead in struggles against racism, injustice and intervention. Churches in other countries are resisting violations of human rights, political repression, apartheid, and economic exploitation of human beings and natural resources.

Even as new relationships with government are being hammered out, the churches are necessarily engaged in rethinking their concept of the church and how that affects their actions in society. In nearly all cases Christian leaders are striving for the church to assume a larger responsibility in the struggle for social justice and peace. As they speak and act, these leaders are relying increasingly on non-violent means as consistent with their faith and appropriate for a world terribly torn by seemingly endless violence.

To Christians in many countries the church-state struggle is clearly drawn, but not in the U.S. Many citizens blindly support church-state involvements to which they would strenuously object if they were part of a Christian minority in a predominantly Muslim nation. Too many are oblivious to the contradictions between their religious faith and the policies of government, let alone many social and economic practices in their community life. Thus it may be more difficult for Christians who live in a nominally Christian society and culture to be faithful to their God than it is for Christians who live under an avowedly atheist government.

Struggling for Christian Unity in a Divided City
David S. Burgess

After my retirement from the United Nations in 1977, I have worked as pastor of a small downtown church and as Executive Director of the Metropolitan Ecumenical Ministry (MEM) in Newark, New Jersey--the poorest large city in the United States, according to the 1980 U.S. Census. It is a divided city full of contradictions. Two-thirds of the city's workforce is made of commuters coming in from some suburban town, laboring eight hours in fine office buildings or manufacturing plants and then returning to their suburban homes each night. In contrast, one-third of Newark's population exists below the poverty line. One-fourth receive some form of public assistance. Among the employable youths ages 16 to 21, 46% are jobless. 50% is the drop-out rate in the public schools. For every new housing unit built during the 1980s, three old units are abandoned, bulldozed or dynamited. 8,000 families are currently homeless, and 11,000 families are on the waiting list eager to rent apartments managed by the Newark Housing

Authority (NHA). Despite these conditions and particularly the fast
diminishing number of available and affordable housing units for poor
families, the NHA demolished 817 rental housing units in 1987 and is now
seeking permission from the Federal Department of Housing and Urban
Development (HUD) to destroy over 4,500 more units in five public housing
complexes. HUD has given NHA funds to build only 325 new units.
Meanwhile, City Hall and the cooperating corporate powers, while the poor
are being driven out of the city, have opened the doors of opportunity to
private, for-profit gentrification developers to refurbish old structures and to
build new ones as condominiums and cooperative apartments for sale to
middle-income and upper-income families at prices ranging from $75,000 to
$250,000. In this city of 320,000 people, of whom 200,000 are black and over
75,000 are of Hispanic, Portuguese or Brazilian origin, what should city
churches do to bring a greater measure of justice to the homeless, the poor
and the forgotten?

We cannot answer this question unless we first know the history of
this city and its churches. At the beginning of the 20th century Newark was
a city of many white mainline churches and great industrial promise. Yet
well before World War II and continuing through the racial rebellion of
1967 and up to the present day, the industrialists removed their plants from
Newark and relocated these plants in suburban areas, in other states or
overseas. Paralleling this industrial exodus, most white residents left Newark
and resettled elsewhere, joined local white churches or founded new ones.
At the same time, black families from the South and the West Indies and
during the last twenty years Hispanic, Portuguese and Brazilian families
moved to Newark to live and work here. As a result a great majority of
churches today, except in sections of the North and East Wards, are now
black and generally of Baptist or pentecostal affiliation. Spanish and

Portuguese language churches were founded and dozens of unaffiliated store-front church fellowships sprang up along some of the main streets of the city. Today two UCC churches, three Reformed churches, four United Methodist churches and nineteen Presbyterian churches remain, and a majority of members of these churches are black.

In the midst of a city with so many racial, ethnic, language and denominational differences, how can the diverse churches of this city be brought together so that the cause of Jesus Christ and God's Kingdom can be better served? To answer this complex question, we must first understand the dynamics of what is happening within the life of many churches. In most congregations the pastor is both the shepherd and doorkeeper of his flock. His (or her) chief concerns are the survival of the church in a poor city, steps to increase the number of members and make the church financially viable, the upkeep of the church and meeting mortgage payments, and the physical and spiritual needs of the congregation. Though the major concerns of the average pastor tend to be church-centered, he soon finds that the perils of the city--drugs, alcohol, crime, poverty, joblessness, corruption, lack of affordable housing, teen-age pregnancies, inferior public education and resulting despair--adversely affect not only his members but the lives of hundreds of other people in the neighborhood of his own church. Many pastors and their congregations have faced up to these perils by launching a number of programs to benefit the members and the surrounding communities. Such programs include Alcoholics Anonymous, Narcotics Anonymous, after-school tutoring and recreation, counselling for teen-age mothers and troubled families, neighborhood crime-watch programs, day-care centers, church-sponsored rehabilitation and housing construction projects. To support such commendable undertakings, some churches have sought financial support from City Hall, corporations and foundations.

Thankful for such outside assistance, many pastors and church members of these assisted churches are often reluctant to add their support to any advocacy cause which takes issue with City Hall or the corporate powers.

Amidst the perils of the city and the existing racial, ethnic, class and denominational differences, and based on my own personal experiences in the city during the last ten years, I have concluded that the clergy and their lay leaders will never be able to bring fundamental changes for the better in Newark unless (1) they agree upon a list of major issues of concern requiring their cooperative efforts; (2) they unite in a common strategy to confront unjust principalities and powers; (3) they establish some type of church-supported community organization in the Alinsky tradition similar to those organizations already existing in Brooklyn and Jersey City and assisted by the Industrial Areas Foundation; and (4) they find the means of creating a higher level of mutual trust among churches, which will lay the foundation for greater inter-church cooperation, and enable clergy and lay leaders of the City to speak with one voice and to develop together more programs of service and advocacy.

Aware of this need for greater unity among the churches, several Newark clergy in early 1987 formed an organization named the Newark Church Consultation for the initial purpose of holding an All-Church Assembly of Remembrance, Repentance and Recommitment some twenty years after the racial rebellion of 1967. An All-Church Choir of 125 voices was formed, and in June of 1988 the Consultation held a Baccalaureate Service at the Sacred Heart Cathedral to honor all high school graduates. Troubled by the lack of broad church support for the Consultation and by the inability of members of the Consultation's Planning Committee to agree upon a list of issues needing immediate inter-church action, the Committee members concluded that the greatest barrier to inter-church unity was the prevailing "lack of trust" among both clergy and laity.   To speak to this problem, the Consultation invited the Rev. Dr. Wyatt Walker, present pastor of the Canaan Baptist Church in Harlem and for many years a co-worker with Dr. Martin Luther King in the civil rights struggle in both the North and the South, to address a luncheon in Newark sponsored by the Consultation.

In the meantime, the cause of greater inter-church unity is being served by four existing organizations. The Newark-North Jersey Committee of Black Churchmen, which meets at St. James AME Church each Wednesday noon, is a loose federation of more than 300 predominantly black churches of several denominations.   The Committee sponsors a youth employment program, is an agent for the distribution of Federal surplus foods, takes a stand on certain public issues and occasionally supports candidates running for public office.   There are two Baptist Conference meetings each Monday, one at noon and the other at night. Members, who are mostly clergy, come from Newark and other cities of northern New Jersey, and have much in common with the larger Committee of Black Churchmen.

The fourth inter-church organization is the Metropolitan Ecumenical Ministry (MEM), which was formed in the wake of the 1967 racial rebellion. Supported initially by the local judicatory bodies of five major Protestant denominations--American Baptist, Presbyterian, United Methodist, Episcopal and United Church of Christ--the organization, during its first six years, enjoyed the direct financial backing of the national headquarters of some of these churches in the form of assigned full-time clergy. These clergy were skilled in community organizing and shared concerns about housing, crime, drugs and public education. This group ministry was terminated in the mid-1970s when some national church agencies ended their support of MEM as interest in the problems of poor urban neighborhoods waned in their respective denominations. In 1975 the Rev. Arthur Thomas, who had been active in the civil rights campaign in the South and was later employed by the New Jersey Department of Education, became the new MEM Executive Director. With generous federal and state financial support, he established three distinct service programs: Project Read, to help illiterate adults to read and to write with the aid of volunteers trained in the Frank Laubach method of instruction; Project Go, which was a city-wide transport program for senior citizens who were ill and isolated; and Project Schools, to help parents take a more active part in the public education of their children. VISTA Volunteers were recruited and paid by federal funds to work in Project Read and Project Schools. All the costs for Project Go were covered by state funds. Having established these programs, the able Art Thomas died in late 1980 at the age of 49. For the next three years, MEM went through a period of troubled transformation: from a service-centered, government-aided and church-supported agency to an agency with both service and advocacy programs, receiving less assistance from government and more from churches, judicatory bodies, national denominations and private foundations. In the early 1980s the leaders of the Catholic Archdiocese of Newark (with jurisdiction in four counties), the Newark Classis of the Reformed Church in America, the Newark-North Jersey Committee of Black Churchmen and the Essex County Chapter of Church Women United were persuaded to affiliate their respective agencies with MEM and to name two representatives to the MEM Board of Directors. They joined a Board made up of two representatives from each of the founding judicatory church agencies and five at-large members.

From 1984, when I was appointed as the new Executive Director of MEM, and up to the present day, our inter-church agency has enlarged

Project Read and Project Schools, has started the MEM Housing Task Force, the MEM Toxic Waste Task Force, and the Youth Employment Referral Network (Project YERN), has begun publication of the newspaper Voices of Hope, and has helped to launch Project SHARE--a massive food supplement program benefiting thousands of families in northern New Jersey. The following is a summary of MEM's inter-church programs and associated programs:

Project Read, which became separately incorporated in 1987, has recruited and trained more than 150 tutors, and has helped thousands of adults to read and write in recent years.

Project Schools, which is the largest and best MEM support program, is directed by a 100-parent Schools Senate; is working to improve school management at 15 of the City's 87 public schools; has joined with the local chapters of the NAACP and the Urban League, the Newark Coalition for Neighborhoods and other community organizations to form the Newark Council on Education Priorities, which has set forth a broad program of education reform in the city, and has been influential in the formation of an organization of urban educators advocating greater funds for city schools from the State Board of Education and the General Assembly.

MEM's Housing Task Force, made up of twenty local tenants and four community organizers, has formed the Newark Coalition for Low-Income Housing, which recently filed a class action lawsuit to stop the Newark Housing Authority from destroying public housing units; the Task Force has also organized tenants living in the public and privately-managed housing projects, and has been one of the charter members of the state-wide Right to Housing Coalition, which champions the cause of the homeless and the ill-housed in many parts of New Jersey.

<u>MEM's Toxic Waste Task Force</u> has fought against the building and operation of huge garbage-burning and dioxin-creating plants in Newark and in other parts of the State, and has become a charter member of the state-wide Grass Roots Environmental Organization (GREO). Today, in the state with the largest number of toxic waste sites, 80 local community groups have joined GREO.

<u>Project YERN</u> (Youth Employment Referral Network), sponsored by MEM, recruits each month six to eight jobless, drop-out and at-risk youths between the ages of 16 and 21, teaches them pre-employment skills, and finds employment for them with the help of adult advisors from church and community groups.

<u>Project SHARE</u> (Self Help and Resource Exchange), patterned after a food supplement program which began in San Diego five years ago and is now established in thirteen other U.S. cities, was started in Newark in 1985. Supported today by more than 150 churches and community organizations and housed at the MEM office during its first year, SHARE obtains $12 from each member family in the form of cash or food stamps at the beginning of each month. After such families contribute two hours or more in voluntary community service during the respective month, each family will obtain near the end of the month a 40 pound package--worth $30 to $35 in the store--which contains fresh meat, poultry, fruit, fresh vegetables and staples such as beans, rice or pasta together with vitamins and a monthly SHARE newspaper having menus and nutrition information. In Newark the Project is located in a large warehouse, brings supplementary food to over 12,000 families each month and also distributes surplus U.S. Government foods to 15,000 families. Project SHARE in Newark is headed by a Catholic nun and relies heavily on many hours of voluntary labor from its recipient families. It is separately incorporated.

With the exception of Project SHARE and Project READ, which have their own sources of support, the above listed MEM programs are made possible by grants from foundations, a few corporations, national denominational headquarters, local judicatory bodies and urban and suburban churches in the Greater Newark area. MEM's full-time staff consists of one white and four blacks and its part-time staff is made up of three other persons. Project READ employs three persons and Project SHARE has a larger full-time staff.

Though by conventional standards of ecumenical success our Metropolitan Ecumenical Ministry may get high marks, I am far from sanguine about the future of the organization. During the last ten years of my labors in Newark, I have learned some painful lessons and yet have a greater enthusiasm and a deepened faith in the value of inter-church agencies. At a time when the leaders of many national denominations have not placed a high priority on support for inter-church agencies and instead have emphasized the importance of membership growth of their affiliated churches in both urban and suburban areas, I have come to the following conclusions about our ecumenical efforts in urban areas:

(1)   The current barriers to inter-church cooperation have resulted in the shutting down of some city church councils and the weakening of other church councils. Other barriers to effective cooperation include rivalries among clergy for power and congregational growth; existing racial and class differences among congregations and within congregations; national denominational pressure on affiliated churches to channel outreach funds into denominational programs at home and abroad; the already over-crowded schedules of some of the best clergy; the opposition of secular powers to clergy and churches which question the status quo and work for basic social changes; efforts of these same powers to influence clergy and local

congregations through corporate gifts or City Hall favors; a low "trust level" among clergy; and lack of consensus about ways and means to combat the evils of the city.

(2)   For an urban inter-city agency to overcome the above listed barriers and to grow and prosper, (a) the agency's leaders must have a clear and accurate assessment of the power structure within the city in question; (b) these leaders must place a top priority upon establishing a broad basis of both participation and support of many congregations; (c) under the guidance of a representative board of directors these leaders must meet with many clergy and with members of ruling boards and mission committees, and preach from pulpits and at other church gatherings; and (d) based on a broad understanding of the needs of local congregation members and the needs of the city in question, the agency must gradually start well defined service and advocacy programs in which clergy and church members participate and which churches eventually support with regular annual contributions.

(3)   Beyond support from local churches, the agency leaders must seek funds from local church judicatory bodies, national denominational agencies, foundations and corporations. No large contribution must be allowed to shape the agency. No contribution should be solicited from any outside organization which might compromise the agency. Because potential contributions from the above listed sources are so unpredictable and subject to the whims of officials of these organizations, it is also important that the leaders of the inter-church agency make every effort to seek participation and support from a large network of local churches including Catholic, Protestant, Pentecostal and even storefront congregations. A broad base of support from many individual local churches often insures the longevity and continued effectiveness of any urban inter-church agency.

(4)   The inter-church agency should hold workshops and conferences on church grounds to which clergy and lay persons are invited and topics of mutual interest--such as crime, homelessness, hunger, poverty, unemployment, toxic waste, public education, threats to the environment and inter-church cooperation--are discussed. To increase participation in such workshops and conferences, it is essential that the agency's leaders reach out to local community organizations. We have found that leaders of these organizations are often more informed about local problems than are average clergy and church members. Staff members of these community agencies now head two of MEM's programs, and they have been most helpful in reaching top government officials, newspaper reporters and the very poor our agency seeks to assist.

(5)   "Beware when all men (or women) speak well of you" is a timely warning to any pastor or lay person who seeks through the work of an inter-church agency to gain personal popularity and public favor, particularly in support of controversial programs of advocacy helping the poor, the hungry, the homeless and other unwilling victims of the ruling principalities and powers. Prophets of the past were scorned, imprisoned and sometimes killed. Present day prophets of the Lord could suffer the same fate. If some clear-headed clergy and lay persons of a prophetic bent of mind are willing, with God's grace, to break down the walls dividing the races and classes and churches, we have reason to believe that their words and actions will lay the foundation for wider and stronger inter-church cooperation in obedience to the Gospel and in the name of our Master Jesus Christ.

(6)   We must remember that as enemies of injustice and champions of justice we labor not <u>for</u> the poor and forgotten but <u>with</u> the poor and forgotten. We work with them for their eventual liberation not as do-gooders but as brothers and sisters at their side. This realization lessens our

sense of self-importance and frees us to join hands with the victims of injustice.

For those who choose to deal with urban blight and hopelessness daily, it is easy, like the Irish poet William Butler Yeats, to become a prophet of doom. In the words of his poem, "The Second Coming," we lament that

> Things fall apart; the center cannot hold.
> Mere anarchy is loosed upon the world,
> The blood-dimmed tide is loosed, and everywhere
> The ceremony of innocence is drowned;
> The best lack conviction, while the worst
> Are full of passionate intensity.

Do we, the advocates of greater inter-church cooperation as a means of seeking greater justice, lack conviction? Do we carry within our hearts and daily lives the passionate intensity of those who have been called and healed by Jesus Christ and who have experienced the peace of God passing all human understanding?

The Work of the YMCA with College Students
1935 to the Present
An Autobiographical Reminiscence
Edward L. Nestingen

This account of the work of the YMCA with college and university students and faculty members in the U.S.A. will be largely autobiographical. I have been deeply involved in this highly important work from my undergraduate days at the University of Wisconsin. My entire professional life has been devoted to the college and university outreach of the YMCA.

I arrived at the University of Wisconsin, located in Madison, in the fall of 1935 from a small town in southwest Wisconsin. My parents and the principal of the high school in that little town of Sparta, Wisconsin, had decided that their respective sons would be well taken care of and soundly counseled by the U. of W. YMCA.

And so, Bob, the principal's son, and I were roommates in the YMCA. This was a residence for about 100 men in the heart of the campus community. C.V. Hibbard, the director, was a genial and wise man with whom we felt very much at home. We sensed immediately his warmth and his interest in us and we perceived that he would help us to move into that exhilarating university environment with a sense both of support and of freedom to discover our strengths and talents--and, also, our limits--on our own.

The U. of W. YMCA had some sound basic program structures. There were excellent Sunday evening forums in a major university auditorium which drew student and faculty participants from the campus community. There were discussions in the large "Y" lounge with many exciting members of the faculty which I yet vividly remember. There was an annual "before registration" Freshman Camp. These four days in an off-campus setting provided an excellent way for freshmen to get really acquainted with upper class students and fuaculty members.

All in all, the University of Wisconsin "Y" provided an interesting and stimulating context for the formal studies of the classroom.

Within this university YMCA context and stimulated by the issues swirling all through the campus community, a new and exciting concept of Christianity began to emerge for this "small town fellow." My parents and the high school principal had not suspected the spirit-opening power that the University of Wisconsin YMCA tapped into.

This larger, strong-moving reality was the many-dimensioned, purposeful, international student Christian movement.

My Growing Awareness of a National Student Christian Movement

I began to perceive a tiny part of this movement as I would listen to C.V. Hibbard tell of his many years as a YMCA leader in China and why he had so dedicated his life. I began to feel the challenge of how the way he had lived might relate to my own life. What he had to say differed from my hometown church missionary exposures. There was an absence of denominationalism in his approach. From him I gained a sense of the larger political reality of China and a respect for its autonomy and its people. He introduced me to a Christianity that was "participant" and not blindly proselytizing. And I found it attractive.

The U. of W. YMCA was my path to the student Christian movement. I vividly remember my first YMCA Geneva Region Conference. It was one week in length at Lake Geneva in Wisconsin with about 200 undergraduate men from an eight state area. It was there that I first met Claude ("Buck") Shotts who was then the director of the Northwestern University YMCA. His soft Southern drawl really impressed my Wisconsin-conditioned ears. He told us about racial injustices and insensitivities in the U.S.A. He particularly impressed me because of his Alabama background and his intercollegiate football prowess. He introduced me to the concepts of pacifism and to the co-operative movement. I was strongly moved by the way Christianity might directly relate to the dynamics of our society.

Six months later, in Indianapolis, I was a U. of W. delegate to the quadrennial Student Volunteer Movement conference. Two highly influential persons gave daily addresses. One was the very British William Temple, Archbishop of Canterbury. His world-wide grasp of the challenges Christianity must face was impressive. The other was Toyohiko Kagawa, the Japanese Christian leader who freely gave up a life of comfort as an intellectual and political leader in order to live with the poor and sick and rejected in the slums of Japan's cities. He told how people who were desperately poor were learning to help themselves by forming economic cooperatives and how the way in which they cooperated with each other was a sound societal concept and in fundamental harmony with Jesus' teachings about the kingdom of God. His deep conviction that pacifism must gradually replace military power politics opened me more strongly than ever to the crucial importance of relating the Kingdom of God to our everyday world. Through both of these men, Christian love became an inescapable demand as the basic norm of political and economic action.

My "small town" mentality was really being stretched by these insistent demands that Christianity become practical and everyday. And my global awareness was also growing rapidly.

I could continue this story of powerfully stimulating experiences by telling of the thrill of hearing and talking with Kirby Page, Sherwood Eddy and John R. Mott. They were all in the late years of their influence when I met them in the '30's and the early '40's. They saw the approaching cataclysm of World War II and made clear that it was not a simplistic conflict between good and evil. They were quite specific that radical behavior changes must be made by the democracies as well as the totalitarian nations.

Many more spirit-opening insights came to me--the terrible blindnesses that I, as well as most Americans, had to shake free of in race relations--the ethnic openness we need to attain unto--the economic injustices within the U.S.A. that needed to be faced squarely--and the all too fast use of police and military power in solving conflicts "our" way. I was helped to see the creative changes which the Kingdom of God opens for all persons.

As I participated in the annual Lake Geneva (Wisconsin) conferences, I got increasingly well acquainted with Hal Colvin, the YMCA staff person for the Geneva Region and always at the heart of those well planned and exciting conferences. In addition to his keen societal insights, he was a wise and patient counselor whose guidance and understanding has been an exceedingly important part of my professional life with the YMCA.

YMCA and YWCA

It was during the late '30's that I participated in the first Student YMCA and YWCA Conference at Lake Geneva. This was not the first joint YMCA-YWCA college and university conference in the U.S., but it was a major landmark in what became for 40 years a strong joint movement to the mutual benefit and enlightenment of both partners.

The Geneva Region guided the work of college and university YMCA's and YWCA's in nine north mid-west states. There were eight vigorous regional structures covering the 48 states, each very well organized and directed by full time staff members who carried out a systematic program of campus visits designed to strengthen campus Christian Associations. Most important were the annual, one week long conferences at the close of each academic year. These were, almost without exception, carefully planned, inspirational, Biblically grounded and action impelling.

Participating in a World Student Christian Movement

Up to this time, I had thought basically in terms of a world outreach emanating from a gradually Christianized U.S.A. Then came an experience that battered that "mission" image.

That experience was the First World Conference of Christian Youth held in Amsterdam in 1939.

Students from about seventy countries to the number of nearly two thousand assembled for a week. Powerful Christian leadership from every part of the globe were present.

Inescapable were the crying challenges of the poverty and neglect of human respect which the industrial and rich countries left in their wake. Impressive were the yearnings for working together, surmounting the national and ethnic barriers between vast populations. And, of course, over-riding all this was the horrendous and terrifying reality of German Nazi imperialism which one sensed to be ready and eager to crush all who stood in the way of "Nordic superiority".

To these matters and to the basic Christian faith which empowers one to face creatively such great and monstrous evils, we heard truly great and courageous persons speak, many of them persons whose lives were on the line.

About midway through the conference, several of us were sipping coffee one evening at a sidewalk cafe on a busy Amsterdam avenue. Hal Colvin, our American YMCA delegation leader, was with us. I heard him say, "Good evening, Reinie! Won't you join us?"

I looked up and saw a tall angular man wearing a beret. He looked at each of us and I felt the power of that intense glance. He greeted Hal and said, "Thank you, but I'm on my evening walk and so I won't stop."

Hal asked, "What are you going to say in your address to the conference tomorrow morning?"

Reinie's response was, "I don't have any idea what I will say." He bade us farewell and strolled down the street.

The next morning the entire conference was electrified by Niebuhr's address "Christ at the Edge of History," bringing to bear on the tragic and terrifying dynamics of world history both the judgment of Christ <u>and</u> the power of His love to work toward justice.

For me, he brought to a white heat focus the ideas and challenges which W.A. Visser 't Hooft, M.M. Thomas of India, Philippe Maury and many others had been presenting.

A Vocation

My university work was by now transformed. Well along on a graduate degree in public finance, it was now clear that my life must be guided by this great movement.

After two years on the staff of the U. of W. YMCA, I enrolled in Union Theological Seminary where much of what I had become opened to was explored carefully and demandingly. My objective was to gain the Biblical and theological understanding to open the hearts and minds of students and faculty members to the transforming power of the Bible.

After three positions as director of college Christian Associations in New York City and in St. Louis, I was asked to serve as staff person for program development in the headquarters office of the National Student YMCA. These were exhilarating and challenging years. Following that national assignment, I have been on the staff of the University of Illinois YMCA. These have been life fulfilling years for which I am profoundly grateful.

The Waning of a Dynamic Movement

At its height in the 1930's, '40's and early '50's, there were YMCA's, YWCA's and joint Christian Associations on over 400 campuses. These associations were active in large state universities, in private colleges, in teachers' colleges and in many church colleges.

Some were guided by full time "Y" staff persons. Many had their own buildings. However, the large majority of these Christian associations were guided and nurtured by faculty advisors and their quarters were in college buildings. Through the years, thousands of faculty members gave long and devoted and inspired leadership to these associations and to the student Christian movement in its larger dimensions.

Unfortunately, this movement almost completely disappeared during the late '50's and the '60's. The reasons for the waning of this magnificent student Christian movement are complex. Partly this resulted from a lessening of the prophetic fervor of the '30's and '40's. Partly this resulted from a gradual withdrawal of funds from the two parent movements. Partly this grew out of difficulties in keeping campus units soundly financed and vigorous. A national movement which once included over 400 campus associations now numbers less than 50.

What is Needed Now

Higher education is becoming more and more specialized. This is an inevitable trend as the "knowledge explosion" develops apace and as the "computer revolution" continues its awesome momentum. What is increasingly left out of the educational experience are basic questions of "What is human life about?" and "What will be the meaning of my life?"

There is little coherent and sustained inquiry into the dynamics of individual and societal political and economic behavior from a Christian perspective. It is crucial that a constant and carefully planned dialogue be sustained between the "life of the mind" and "the life of faith."

What is largely absent from higher education today, among students and faculty members alike, is a transcending sense of life purpose. This is the central task of a college Christian association. This work is needed today more urgently than it ever has been.

Building From Where We Are Now[1]

Those student associations which still exist, a truly scattered remnant, are like embers in the ashes of the historical student movement. With a breath of inspiration they could be rekindled; the spark is till there but there is little to fuel a fire. To grow beyond its present status as a resource for student volunteerism which also provides experiences in leadership roles, or as an open forum in which issues can be raised and examined without much threat of action, two things would need to happen. There would need to be a renewal within the student movement, and there would need to be encouragement and commitment from the broader YMCA movement for student work.

Over the past eight years staff and student leadership of the National Association of Student YMCA's, with a growing membership approaching 40 campuses, has met regularly for fellowship, skill development, and inspiration (in that order). But there is no solid core of Biblically grounded, theologically rich disciples of social justice within the student movement. (This may be as true for mainline Protestant campus ministry, and the national YMCA movement, as it is for the YMCA). And there is little impetus to ecumenicalism; there is no enmity, but there is also little energy committed to interfaith dialogue. Most student YMCAs exist with no awareness of the student Christian movement, either its history or its present incarnations.

---

1. These concluding paragraphs have been contributed by Mark C. Johnson, Executive Director of the University YMCA at the University of Illinois, where he continues to serve as Director of the University YMCA's Fred S. Bailey Scholarship Program.

There are probably a proverbial dozen staff in student YMCA work whose underlying motivations are grounded in probing spiritual issues and whose commitment is to peace and social justice, but the network is weak and unbolstered. And the competition for the attention of students is fierce, especially from the quarters of materialism and specialization, but also from the salvationist theologies which inspire no strong commitment to the needs of the powerless.

There are signs of hope, however. There is today a loose coalition of more than 400 campuses where students are committed to <u>community service</u>. From such a base may grow a renewed interest in <u>community development</u>. This coalition is coordinating work on illiteracy, homelessness, hunger, and the environment as its chosen fronts. And national interdenominational student conferences are being discussed for the first time in 25 years. Here and there a voice calls out in inspiration: Parker Palmer, Sharon Parks...Student YMCAs are not at the center of these activities but they are in communication with them. Perhaps the day will come again when acts are integrated with examined beliefs, when the call to witness is answered through service to community needs, and when the student YMCA is central to this enterprise.

Those student associations which have survived have done so, in most cases, because of their historical autonomy. Where they are branches of metropolitan associations they are not at the center of association life, but they have grudging and continued respect. What is needed today is an initiative for campus work by local YMCAs and particularly by metropolitan associations. With incentives and support from the YMCA of the USA such initiatives could emerge and succeed as quickly as any other initiative.

The YMCA today, by and large, abandons its youth members precisely at that point where they are ready to open themselves to questions of life purpose, at that point when they leave home and community to go to college. Many do not return until they are integrated into an unquestioned materialistic economy and individualistic society, starting families of their own. Many probably never return at all. How ironic that a Movement founded on the critical need for spiritual support and direction in young adults, that grew most effectively through the work of this age group in urban and collegiate America and around the world, should find this area of mission so in need of attention. But how wonderful to have such a clear and present opportunity!

Ecumenism on Main Street:
Reality in a Southern Indiana City
Edward F. Ouellette

The fifty years since Amsterdam 1939 correspond almost exactly with the fifty year history of the Evansville (now Evansville area) Council of Churches. The story of its search for identity, its failures, its "enemies," reveals itself as a parable of the Council Movement as a whole, indeed, of the Church in the World. We departed Amsterdam as the world divided into bloody conflict. Each of us went to some one place. After fifteen years the present writer came to Evansville, Indiana, to assist one church in its participation in an ecumenical program of data gathering and self-study. Evansville was a city of 120,000 on the Ohio River, neither southern nor northern, strongly Germanic, with declining industry and many churches. Many attempts at cooperation and a crusade remembered as "successful" had preceded this venture into a city-wide religious census as a basis for further "ecumenism in Evansville."

The laymen and some ministers from a loosely organized Evansville Ministers' Association who had met in 1937 to consider what the churches might do together (like increase church attendance) may have heard of Oxford and Edinburgh. More likely some were aware of Church Federations in Indianapolis and Chicago. But this was Evansville, recovering from near total flooding which had taxed the resources of all civic agencies, with churches hardly mentioned in that history.

Some rumors of the gathering storm on the world scene were scantily reported in Evansville in 1937, even if the relevant agenda of the Oxford Conference on Life and Work was not. These ministers and laymen certainly had some awareness of what Dr. Michael Kinnamon summarized in a paper presented in India in 1987 to the Bangalore Theological Forum.

> "When the history of the Twentieth Century is finally complete, 1937-1938 will not stand out as a banner year. The Spanish Civil War, a dress rehearsal for WWII, was in full swing. In Germany, Hitler was increasing the attacks on Jews and other perceived enemies of the Nazi State--including the Confessing Church. Stalinist Russia was the scene of massive purges and of new techniques for religious persecution. Japan had invaded China, causing enormous human suffering. Italian Fascists were dropping gas on Ethiopia, a sign that the curse of colonialism was not at an end. And throughout the west, economics lay snared in a depression that left millions without employment or adequate nutrition."

In this world climate the wind and fire of the Pentecost experience was faintly felt in flood-ravaged Evansville.

Plans were made for a meeting at the Y.M.C.A. in January 1938; "Church Council to be Dinner Topic," read the headline. They turned to the Indianapolis Church Federation (1912) for their speaker, Dr. Ernest Evans, Executive Secretary since 1925. A clergyman would preside, the president of the Evansville Ministers' Association, an intimation that a Council is itself a ministry.

On January 13, 1938, 80 laymen, 17 ministers, from 24 local churches gathered to confirm that an Evansville Council of Churches was "in process of formation," as the world flood of ominous events was touching Evansville with depression, employment, hunger. From his experience, from his awareness of the Council Movement, Dr. Evans caused them to ask the questions: Can we work on this in Christ's name more faithfully together than separately? What forms will a Council of Churches take? If Paul were to write letters, not to the church in Corinth but to the church in Evansville, where would they be delivered? Can we together BE the church in Evansville?

The vision of ecumenism had been glimpsed, even though "seen through a glass darkly," a hint of the Christus Victor banner which was to confront us daily in the Concertgebouw in Amsterdam. A planning committee was established, the parallels to the post-Conference strategies following Oxford and Edinburgh 1937 were emerging on Main Street. Plans for a Council were submitted to the executive bodies of all Protestant churches (about 200) in the city, discussed in many individual churches, and ignored or dismissed in the majority. Five months of consideration led to the awareness and inclusion of three groups already cooperating across denominational lines: the Evansville Council of Church Women, the Evansville Ministers' Association, the Vanderburgh County Council of Religious Education. The umbrella character of a Council program was coming into view. In Geneva and in Evansville the process involved persons freed in some measure from the constraints of a fragmented church in the world, the "scandal of Christianity."

While Amsterdam 1939 was in preparation on Rue de Fernay in Geneva, ecumenism in Evansville began its decade of groping for the shape and work, the organization and program, of "Church in Evansville," all in each place one. The steering committee made appointments for constitution and finance. Among the first official acts was pledge of cooperation with an already existing Laymen's Missionary Assembly which staged an annual Men and Missions event in December. Assembly and Council called upon the same leadership, appealed to the same constituency. Question: should this not be Council sponsored? Already the ecumenical focus was blurring. The two groups confused the headlines until after WWII.

With the first of many part-time executive secretaries, a "church loyalty month," October, was agreed upon, emphasizing that "no unified progam" was to be urged upon any participating church. Already there was the misperception that Christian unity meant Christian uniformity. Thirty civic organizations, civic clubs, labor organizations, the public schools, colleges, indicated cooperation. Churches not Council members "are invited to cooperate," the press noted, placing these churches in the category of other organizations. (Christianity clubs?) The Proclamation by the mayor hinted at a difference between church and world, making one the arena of "the threat of war and social and moral degradation" and the other "the repository of spiritual insight and social morale" proclaiming a message which "holds life steady at all times." Here was secular notice of an "outward and visible sign" (a common Protestant enterprise) of an "inward and spiritual truth" (the Church IS one). Even if only a few of many churches acknowledged it, ecumenism became visible.

Beginning with "Go to church Sunday" October 7, churches did their own thing, but the titles of the sermons, the special collections for others, even the emphasis given to communion, let it be known that churches were acting in concert, ecumenically. World Wide Communion Sunday was yet in the future.

How could the annual pledge drives of the various churches be done in a co-ordinated fashion? Something which later came to be known as the United Church Canvass produced this early headline: "Church Council Offers Advice on Charity Giving." A united approach, individual benefit, increased funds--to support competitiveness? With help from the National Council of Churches, in due time Evansville became a regional model for the United Church Canvass.

It was discovered that the new thing called radio was available as a "public service" to a Council of Churches, free. Various approaches to this access to the air waves continued under Council auspices till total eclipse by the highly funded programs of radio preachers and televangelists. Five ministers in five days with ecumenical messages was an early offering. The titles foreshadowed an agenda for the new Evansville Council of Churches. Later the Council sponsored a weekly Saturday noon spot, "The Good News," which for many years began with the line, "When the things most generally believed among us come alive in people, that's good news."

An experiment with a mass meeting gave the city one more outward and visible sign of the Council's presence. A former governor of Ohio chose to speak on "Some Problems of the Day." Against the background of immanent strife abroad as Hitler threatened Europe and present strife at hand between capital and labor he asked: Will we have better government or undergo a revolution? The church has a Word for the world. "The spirit of Protestantism has too long been a spirit of competitiveness." The church is growing weak because of its unwillingness to cooperate; it is falling short of "its real purpose."

1939 saw the establishment of community Holy Week services in a downtown theater with a bishop from Chicago as speaker, local choirs and a broad list of ministers identified in the five programs. The concerns of the Council which had thus far commended themselves emerged that year as Committees: Evangelism, Publicity and Radio, Missions (China Relief), Women's Work, Finance, Christian Education (including unreached children). This is hardly the agenda of Oxford and Edinburgh, much less Amsterdam 1939. As far as Ecumenism in Evansville is concerned, gathering unreached children proved to be the most enduring "outward and visible sign." With the experimental program of "released time" in Chicago and Fort Wayne as models, the program became known in Evansville as "Weekday." Weekday Religious Education came to comprise more than half the budget, reached children in far more than Council churches, was accepted by the community at large, was recognized by the roving trailers parked near nearly every school on a weekly schedule. "But some doubted." A later study discovered negative attitudes in school administration and on the part of certain teachers at both ends of the religious spectrum. Nevertheless, "Weekday" persisted, a ministry of the Council, reaching one to three thousand children, a high percentage "unchurched," with mutually acceptable curriculum, a staff of dedicated teachers, devoting too much energy to financing itself because the Council member churches failed to meet the Council budget. Member churches needed to support their own program of Christian Education.

Weekday started, it might be said, when one of the laymen, "touched by the fire," gathered children off the streets at the Y.M.C.A. in the name of the Council, that they might have some Christian Education. This during the year of Amsterdam. Thus, perhaps, ecumenism really came to Evansville, reaching toward "the last and the lost and the least" with the good news of Jesus Christ.

Coincident with this, denominationalism raised itself to visibility when one of the large member churches, through its United Church Councils (an organization of the governing entities of the many Evangelical and Reformed Churches) invited the members of the fledgling Evansville Council of Churches to its annual meeting. The invitation was generous, reflecting the stance of the "large" church. The speaker was "their" denominational representative at the 1938 Madras meeting of the International Missionary Council (IMC). Thus the world perspective came first hand to Evansville in 1939.

The speaker helped focus the perception of ecumenism on the faithful word of the post-Oxford-Edinburgh report: not a plan for interdenominational cooperation, but "we intend to stay together." The speaker celebrated that intent: the unity of the Christian Church is manifested because foreign mission has done, is doing, a "tremendous job," responding to such of Christ's words as "go heal the sick, cleanse the leper, raise the dead, drive out devils, preach the gospel." We are "engaged in the greatest enterprise the world has ever seen"...a family group...with "still greater unity possible." His address to the church women was entitled: "The Church in a World Christian Community." The women would have much to do with keeping ecumenism in focus.

In far away Amsterdam, R.H. Edwin Espy's two years of preparation looked for near 2000 young people from 72 countries. German young people could get no exit visas. The delegates from the mission fields were far more one than the delegates from the sending nations of the west. The 400 young people from the divided churches of the U.S.A. had had access to a preparatory study outline entitled "Ten Authorities Other than God"[1], a reprise of the agendas of Oxford and Edinburgh: Nation, State, Race, Science, dogmas of Faith and Order, were identified as "idols," false gods, as the young people came to assemble each day under the huge banner: Christus Victor. The post-Amsterdam study guide was entitled: "Can You Say Christus Victor?" Before many of the delegates and leaders had reached home, Germany had invaded Poland. National<u>ism</u> had declared itself God. Commun<u>ism</u> was yet to come, denominational<u>ism</u> was the order of the day, ecumen<u>ism</u> was entertained as an idea, recognized as beckoning: come, your oneness is <u>given</u>, you <u>are</u> one in Christ.

For its public statement "in this tense and trying time," the Evansville Council of Churches turned to the World Council (in process of formation). What is the task of the church in time of war? The Provisional Committee of the WCC spoke thus: First and foremost, let preaching and prayer be truly Christian--no Holy Crusade. Next, hold to relations of churches between nations. Then, work for a just peace, counteract the spirit of vengeance,[2] the lust for power, and resist insidious and uninvestigated propaganda. Also, minister to prisoners, discourage reprisals, and face refugee problems. Comfort the victims. Confess our own sins, then maintain fellowship with conscientious objectors. ("Thou shalt not kill").

In this do we hear the Council of Churches trying to speak the word of God with one voice? Will the churches also act out their common faith together? In subsequent years we find many of these prophetic words as program items, with the executive director supported by a faithful few.

----

1. Authored by the present writer, to whom Evansville was as yet unknown, but who had been deeply involved at Oxford before attending the sessions at Edinburgh.

2. For a Biblical correction of the common understanding of "vengeance," see the Interpreter's Bible Dictionary. Not "revenge" but "wholeness."

In the midst of this world view imposed by events, local concerns received attention. There were mailings to couples applying for marriage licenses: Christian Ideals. An overture was made to the city concerning "Church Night": let public scheduling keep Wednesday open. China Relief: a city-wide concern. The annual "Men and Missions" event in December took notice: "The World Situation Confronts Christianity and Democracy." A year later, Council members helped turn this broader non-Council event around: "The Church Faces the World Crisis." In between the Council members held their first annual meeting with a sharpened awareness of what their business was about: "No Hitler Can Crush the True Church." 130 persons were in attendance from the fewer than 30 churches of 9 denominations. The assistant superintendent of schools was elected president of the Council for its second year.

Council efforts seemed to be energized by the encroaching and engulfing world conflict. If Hitler cannot engulf the true church (this began to seem possible), what about the "yellow horde"? The remaining years of WWII brought high employment in building planes and boats in converted industries and a nagging question: does the Council have a ministry to war workers? 20,000 of them? A "Mission" was the response, its ecumenicity evident in its leadership: a prominent Methodist preacher from Chicago, a representative of the International Council of Religious Education, a speaker from the Federal Council of Churches. The Council stance regarding war itself had been set forth (with help from the W.C.C.) earlier. During these years, a series of clergy served as Secretary of the Council. Most were busy ministers. One or two of the founding laymen filled in till a clergyman became the first full-time Director near the end of the Council's first decade.

In the meantime, the Council did undertake a ministry to conscientious objectors, acting out the faith at some risk. Effort and funds were directed toward the expanding Weekday program reaching three elementary grades. (Later, two). The school superintendent took a favorable view of this "Wedge in American Culture," a place where the church consistently and visibly entered one of the systems of the world, the school system. All the problems of Church and State are still with us, but the Council was committed--is still committed--to that "wedge."

Another stand was taken during these war years involving a widening of ecumenism, an overture to the Roman Catholics, the Lutherans, the Jews. The religious bodies outside the Council membership could join in a common resistance to "encroaching secularism," a witness wider than the plea for the city to recognize a "Church Day." Is Christ Lord of All?

Participation by the local College in Council affairs gave solid grounding to a major educational effort during these war years: teacher training, a School for Christian Leadership. Teachers from all levels of the church school program came together annually, meeting for six weeks with an ecumenical and qualified staff to improve what went on in the Sunday schools of the churches. American culture's faith in education was given a visible religious emphasis. Numbers rose to over 300 from participating churches. There are those who 40 years later refer to that early Council offering as important in their lives. This educational effort persisted in various mutations: training for ministers in counseling and management; seminars for laymen; family life studies; surviving in the present Christian Educators Support Group which each month provides excellent material for planning ahead to ten or twelve professionals and volunteers from half a dozen churches.

After Pearl Harbor, the lead of the Federal Council of Churches and the London-based World Evangelical Alliance was followed by the Council in promoting the Week of Prayer, a global fellowship "to bind the churches together in this time of tragedy." Could the churches of Evansville become aware that they belong to this "world-wide, unbroken, unbreakable Christian fellowship"? In subsequent years, down to the present, women of the churches observe a World Wide Week of Christian Unity, with materials emanating from the World Council of Churches and the National Council of Churches.

As the war moved toward Hiroshima and Nagasaki, the Council of Church Women, which preceded 1938 and was a part of the Evansville council of Churches from its beginning, promoted an ecumenical service, with massed choirs, in connection with the Council's 7th Annual Meeting. The emphasis for this was to be "a working understanding between the denominations." The featured speaker was to appeal to the wider participation of all invited Protestant communions: "the whole household of faith." This was to be a visible evidence of the world wide movement for Christian unity. Dr. Wilhelm Pauck, who came via Chicago from the Confessing Church in Germany, which alone had stood against Hitler, went beyond the notion of denominations working together when he declared, "there is no Christianity without the Church," (a fact which distinguishes Christianity from all other religions) and further, the Church is more than a social institution, it is "an inspirational reality...not yet realized, speaking...who knows how many languages." (This was Pentecost Sunday).

The annual inter-denominational "Men and Missions" event, its focus on China, signified the durability of an institution still "competing" with the Council for support and leadership, but during the next year the Council could share sponsorship with a strong member denomination of an

Ecumenical Conference celebrating the publication of the New Testament portion of the Revised Standard Version of the Bible, as authorized by representatives from the International Council of Religious Education. Evansville people heard the difference between the United Nations, just formed, and the ecumenicity represented by their Council of Churches. The former asks each nation to give up some sovereignty. The latter is a different institution altogether, calling on each to place sovereignty elsewhere, each to give allegiance to Jesus Christ. In Evansville, a strong denominational church let the Council co-sponsor the event. Within two weeks, Christian Endeavor, an interdenominational youth enterprise, put on a rally with a well-known song leader. The focus was blurred again.

The impetus of 1937-1939, the excitement of exploratory ecumenical ventures, the stimulation of the war years were giving way to "what now?" The Council churches persuaded one of their clergy to become a full-time Director. Someone was needed to take charge and pull the enterprise together. His term lasted till his denomination transferred him to Indianapolis.

In the months of his administration some of the fears concerning uniformity were overcome by the hope and strength that come from unity. The acceptance and expansion of Weekday undergirded that strength. A Council appeal to developers asked for their cooperation with a Comity Committee. (Another "wedge" in a system?) The rather larger 10th Annual Meeting brought more than 200 persons to hear a speaker asking them together "to confront the enemy with our adventure in Christian fellowship." The enemy? The advancing wave of totalitarianism and the rise of secularism: both had been energized by the same war years that had brought the Council to its present clarity of purpose and program.

A third possible "enemy" had gone unnamed. Early in the next year the strong parallel denominational organization, the United Church Councils of the Evangelical and Reformed Church, invited a prominent Judge as the speaker for their meeting. This commanded as much newspaper coverage as any Council event. But soon after, the churches of Evansville had the Council proposal that the United Church Canvass would include in each church's budget a proportion undergirding the Council. The concurrent Annual Meeting called as its speaker one who had been present at the now realized World Council of Churches, no longer "in process of formation." Once again, Evansville had a chance to hear that the movement of the churches is toward unity, not uniformity. He spoke of the "Effect of World Ecumenism on Grassroots Christianity." This essay is an account of the actuality of that effect in one place. At that point Evansville appeared to be one of the grassier places. An institution called RIAL, Religion in American Life, took notice of Evansville and the second United Church Canvass was part of a nation-wide November campaign. Twenty-one religious bodies acting together to further the budgets of each: is this the outward and visible sign of the one church of Jesus Christ? Ecumenism? The future would tell.

The future came quickly. The first full-time Executive Secretary was transferred by his denomination. The search committee took its cue from recent experience and called the first of two long-term Directors whose tenure spanned 33 years. Twelve years of high-profile Council programs were followed by 21 years of faithful efforts to carry on and innovate, burdened always by increasing pressures to administer in a more "business-like" manner. The ecumenical vision became clouded by a lack of "results." The figures finally indicated, if not failure, then certainly the need for "new leadership."

The first long tenure announced itself with an area Evangelistic Campaign proclaiming "Christ is the Answer." The N.C.C. provided the speaker who had been "successful" in Washington, D.C. A follow-up event at Pentecost drew the crowds to a football stadium to hear of a remarkable mission in West Africa: "Christ's Answer to World Communism." The missionary was a Negro. Joining with the NAACP, the Council was already calling attention to what is now called "racism" and the segregation of the Evansville schools. The N.C.C. leader was recalled in July to an outdoor amphitheater where 10,000 sang hymns and heard of their "Brothers in Christ Throughout the World." "Anyone who lets his local church separate him from his brothers (and sisters) in Christ is no true Christian." The events had high visibility attesting the new Council Director's experience in newspaper publishing and radio beyond ordination.

Continuing the momentum, Council churches were soon involved in a complete religious survey and census. "One of the greatest stories this paper has carried in many, many years," declared the Evansville Press of this "second chapter" of "Christ is the Answer."[3] Both Weekday and the School for Christian Leadership felt the energy of the highly visible events. The 200 page report, An Evansville Profile, was a first.

The city responded within a year or two with an outside consultant who produced an elaborate "Fantus Report." This professional product generated Council criticism for its neglect of the role of the churches. The Director pointed out that the churches together have a concern for the future of Evansville. The Council works to promote a better understanding

---

3 The present writer came first to Evansville as the Invited Leader in one of the churches as it undertook its week-long directed self-study and participated in gathering the census data. Some three quarters of the population of Evansville was reached. Religion in American Life (RIAL) named Evansville as an "outstanding city."

among Christians, to determine the religious needs of the community, to work toward solving common problems. The city responded the next year with a Foundation for Evansville's Future incorporating Council-civic-industry joint approaches to "common problems" and "the future." Riding this wave, a caravan of 500 traveled the 300 miles to Chicago to be present at the opening event in Soldiers Field of the 1954 Evanston Assembly of the W.C.C. Likewise, the United Church Canvass took hold till it reached 250 churches in a "Sector Project" which commended itself to RIAL (Religion in American Life) and the sponsoring N.C.C.

The high visibility and ecumenical awareness were pressed over four summers by the presence of a dozen notable persons. The first was a third visit of Charles Templeton, the National Council of Churches speaker who had drawn thousands to hear him proclaim that "Christ is the Amswer." There followed such world figures as E. Stanley Jones, Muriel Lester, Martin Niemoeller, Toyohiko Kagawa, Rosa Page Welch, Otto Dibelius, and Frank Laubach (twice). Finally Alan Walker came from Australia with his "Mission to the Nation." He declared that "the future depends on Christian Laymen...prepared to meet the new age with conciliation, negotiation, patience, understanding."

Two from Evansville with help from the Council attended the 1956 Kirchentag in Germany. Could we learn something from this unity, this oneness, this expression of ecumenicity? The mass event (600,000) did not translate; the year long discipline of Bible study on a common theme, "Let Us Be Reconciled In Christ," was a precondition. However, the Council could call for discipline: a small group undertook a year long study of one revelation of the Profile--Family Life had been revealed at that early date to be headed for what we know call "breakdown." The consequent "Family Life Clinic" for which the NCC supplied leadership notably called for greater participation by youth in the life of the churches. It recalled the press for Youth Sections at Oxford and Edinburgh and the Youth Assembly in 1939. The substance of the continuing School for Christian Leadership was enhanced as well as the relevance of the radio and TV programming. The Bauman Bible Study Series involved as many as 700 T.V. viewers from 18 churches over 14 weeks.

The Profile had also revealed Urban Renewal (the displacing of the poor) and the Aged as in need of disciplined study and attention. Another year-long study by 16 persons from four Council churches, including an ex-chief of police, resulted in the calling of an Associate Director with primary responsibility for Youth. He devised a program of weight lifting in an unused coal-bin renovated by young men taken off the streets. Another team effort enlisted special sponsorship from the churches for first offenders caught in the Juvenile Court system. Alongside this the Council developed and coordinated a ministry in homes for the Aged. The Director himself gave attention to the displaced poor by becoming head of the Family and Child Care Division of the Welfare Council of the city. He had put forth a "new approach to welfare" by bringing to the attention of the churches the 6000 persons in a well-defined area the Profile had revealed as dependent on the system. (The churches were not much interested in the possibility of a ministry together). The Council clergy were not neglected. The Director guided refresher courses for ministers in collaboration with a major hospital and industry and civic leaders: Counseling, in hospital and otherwise, and "Work Simplification," a seven-week course in which "experts" from business and industry outlined their methods to already too-busy pastors. The WCC drew upon his experience at an Oberlin conference on "the Nature of the Unity We Seek."

It was apparent that this unity was still eluding the Council in Evansville at the end of 20 years. Another year-long study led by a staff person from the Church Federation of Greater Indianapolis revealed that in spite of all the events and surveys and reports and programs the attitude of the city toward the churches was to look elsewhere for guidance and leadership in the affairs of the total community. The "new spirit" headlined in the Council 20-year brochure had not become significant in the body politic. At this juncture the Director resigned and the first long tenure came to an end.

The Associate was soon moved "up" to Director of the Council. With the change in leadership there followed a shift in form if not the elusive substance of "Ecumenism in Evansville." High visibility diminished; "out of sight, out of mind." Over the next twenty years, the astonishing number of "fluid" responses to perceived need was interrupted by no more than two or three ecumenical "events" comparable to those now history, still remembered by many with nostalgia. The succession of small ministries which the churches were called upon to do together ("unto the least of these") asked for imagination and effort and did not fit established categories easily grasped by members of the congregations of Council member churches.

The story of these ministries to need as ascertained by the Director is accompanied by a growing sentiment that ecumenism needs to be what is now called "cost effective." This led in ten years to a revised structure of the Council including as an equal to other departments more obviously ecumenical (the Life and Work, Faith and Order of churches), a Department of Evaluation. The first well-founded, well-crafted and sympathetic report came from three prominent business and professional members of supportive Council churches and one clergyman. It contained "What's Right," "What's Wrong," and "Recommendations" sections for each aspect of the Council operation. It revealed a common element in what was "wrong" (overworked Staff, too few volunteers, underfunding) and a certain vagueness after 35 years of experience as to the nature of ecumenism, what Christus Victor signified at Amsterdam. Something like "success" seemed to be a criterion in the evaluation process. One visible outcome was that the Director became Administrator, with increases in paperwork, emphasis on communications, reports, budgets, lists of personnel in various functions. Guidelines, a monthly publication, expanded, including TV recommendations requiring considerable research time. Most of this paperwork fell to the Administrator and the office secretary, with "Did You Know" items in the widely distributed news-letter not as inspiring as would have been time spent telling the story of a perceived need and a new mission in some setting in a member church. At successive Annual Meetings, the Administrator's Report listing ventures not fully realized was heavily overshadowed by pages oriented toward structure and budget and names of persons. Members were together in one place, the fire was present touching a few, the wind was not mighty. After another ten years some members of a new Board of Operations were restless for "new leadership" and a weary Administrator resigned.

A recounting of some of the innovative and "pioneering" responses to perceived need, the difficulties in finding broad-based support among busy member churches, the transfer of some ministries to jobs with acronyms in the city and county bureaucracy, comprises this segment of the reality of ecumenism in Evansville.

Weekday enrollment fell from 3000 to a low of 800 during this period. The Department of Evaluation noted diminished school promotion, the opening of "Christian" schools. The Director was occupied with administration and innovation. The 400 unchurched children were not celebrated as Council ministry with adequate support, but required energy for special Weekday funding efforts by cooperating churches. Awareness of Weekday was increased, but Council support stood at sixty-nine cents per church member per year.

Nevertheless Project Awareness and Project Commitment addressed emerging school integration with visits in the homes of children in Negro Weekday classes and public forums regarding impending busing. Members of Council churches revealed an "us" and "them" spirit: "What do 'they' want in 'our' schools?" In addition the Director launched a Summer Employment Program for hard-to-employ young people; he was also responsible for what is now Big Brothers/Big Sisters; the Council was called upon for large input for what became the city's Youth Services. Out of Weekday came an accepted High School course where students could explore the religious significance of other subjects as well as become acquainted with the Bible as literature. The original Viking Athletic Club reaching as many as 60 was absorbed into Youth Services, complete with a Crisis Line. The Council's team approach with the juvenile was approved by Roman Catholics and then absorbed by the Probation Department of the Court system. (It was hard to get church member volunteers). A UNICEF alternative to "Trick or Treat" caught on and then faltered. Again, volunteers were needed to administer the program, and one heard the UNICEF canard, "communistic." A CROP walk in connection with Church World Service continues, captures media attention, besides directing participants' efforts toward "others", including the hungry. Hunger was emerging as a Council issue.

The 25th year, 1972, offered an occasion for the NCC to recognize the "greatness" of local ecumenicity in Evansville. The Administrator's response struck the appropriate note: "We hope we are participating in the life and work of the Kingdom of our Lord." He told of that life and work on Main Street and from this base the story continues. "We've discovered that we are obviously capable of doing a great deal more together. Our experiences together serve as a spring-board for even more imaginative, powerful services in the name of Christ."

Hunger was clearly an issue. A Council "Hunger Project" that collected 7000 pounds of food and $700 grew into a Food Pantry system starting with a Council church location, a Roman Catholic location, and later adding a Y.W.C.A. location. A truckload of food was gathered and sent to the Delta Ministries, seven communities of the poor in the bootheel of Missouri. Along the way the Council coordinated Garden Patch, an innovative inner-city church and agency plan to gather surpluses from church members' (suburban) gardens and sell the produce for 25 cents a bag. Seven pantries are now coordinated by a civic referral agency and supplied in large part by the Food Bank. The extension into the national Food Bank source started in the Council offices with a staff person assigned part-time. The local Food Bank now serves 33 counties in three states from a warehouse location but is still "related" to the Council.

The Radio and TV Ministry (Mass Media Ministries) was enlarged to meet its opportunity, including non-Council clergy, and adding a Roman Catholic priest to administer the logistics within the Council structure. In cooperation with Catholic Charities the Council launched a Refugee Resettlement Program for Vietnamese and others from S.E. Asia to help "the stranger within our gates." This later evolved into a Literacy Program in cooperation with the School Board with a Council-published newsletter. The Council Administrator devised an opportunity for concerned Christians to "meet your legislators" and chaired the forum on Saturday mornings in the City Council chambers. The Council coordinated the continuing ministries to as many as 14 nursing homes and launched a jail ministry which still continues with some non-Council clergy participating. (Pentecostals). With a new advocacy group in the inner city, the Council offered a Seminar for Clergy: Counseling with Abusive Families. This venture was too far ahead of its time. And the Council sponsored the introduction into Evansville of the Family Cluster Program, a new intergenerational approach to Christian Education. At the same Roman Catholic Retreat Center, the Council gathered 80 persons for a two-day seminar on Religion and Aging, finding the special abilities and gifts of the elders mostly ignored by the churches. The Administrator noted in an Annual Meeting that "the actual services rendered (to the community) and the further potential (of the Council) are mind-bending, exhausting."

In the midst of all these services rendered, the Council responded to two events of major import and bore the extra burden of administering locally a national crusade called "Key 73," whose stated purpose was to "confront the people of North America with the gospel of Christ." (After it was over the Council received an overture from the Jewish community and heard a frank talk from the rabbi of the Jewish Temple; and subsequently initiated a continuing dialogue). Twenty-five organizations joined the more than 200 churches enlisted to do similar things at the same time and attend mass meetings, even if only 60 churches could work together as a Council. The Council was the clearing house for information. The Council coordinated all radio and TV announcements. The Council Administrator acted as Secretary-Treasurer. A Council representative commented that the "lack of emphasis on ecumenism might be a plus. When we try a program like this, people are just turned off." The next year the Council welcomed a major Roman Catholic church as a member and heard a Jesuit from the National Council of Churches lift up ecumenicity in these words: "Our incorporation into the Body of Christ is the single most important fact uniting denominations." Convergence on the same path is not "one union." "Organized ecumenical units are not the only or even the most important expression of Christian unity."

The major event disturbing and dividing the community was a Rock Festival bringing 250,000 people to an unready site nearby. The Council (Administrator) spearheaded an area church response, some to the actual physical and medical needs of the young people. There were other reactions (many negative) and responses by various agencies. All agreed when it was over that "all together the churches had barely nicked the surface of the need." But Christ was "present" in the facility serviced "in the midst" in the name of the Area Council of Churches. A consequence was the withdrawal of some support from the Council: one heard the word "communism."

The other event united the community in grief following the airplane crash at the local airport which killed the entire roster of the college basketball team, the coaches, the press. Out of the sorrow and confusion came the realization that there was no structure in place to cope with disaster. The "task forces" in the churches, the inventory made earlier of spare hospital equipment provided a place to start. A memorial plaza on the college campus is all that remains.

Toward the end of this period the Council dealt with "Faith and Order" matters at the invitation of the World Council of Churches. Under the leadership of the Administrator a widely representative group met regularly for more than a year to consider "Women in Ministry." The results from five continents became input for the publication "Baptism, Eucharist and Ministry." We who participated felt once again the scope of the Pentecost vision "that they all might be one." There was little general interest among the churches or clergy during the study or after publication. At the subsequent Annual Meeting the Council made a presentation of a first Peace and Justice award to celebrate a lifetime of faithful effort of one local person. The Administrator had urged the authorization of the award as in keeping with the Council's initial purpose 45 years ago.

At this point a Board of Operations was formed to oversee the Council ministry. Some on this Board felt strongly that "new leadership" was needed to inspire ecumenicity in Evansville. Member support was diminished or was withheld. The weary administrator resigned. Nevertheless, one venture of the Board of Operations was the launching of Habitat of Evansville, which, in 1988, has become a familiar and independent program on the Evansville scene. The task was laid on the Council during this period to explain again the difference between the local area organization and the maligned NCC and WCC. Once more that word "communism."

An interim Director occupied the office while the search committee concluded its work, and new leadership arrived in the midst of the 10th Mayfair in support of the continuing Weekday ecumenical ministry. He was soon answering questions for the newspapers, because, as was revealed years before in the study of attitudes, people looked not to the church, but elsewhere for answers where religion touches life: the hungry, the homeless, the hurting, those in prison, "the last and least." Yet early in this short period, the Council acted to acquire and furnish shelter for the family homeless. The Food Bank and the Food Pantry system, now reaching 12,000 families, were administered from a cubicle in the Council offices. A "Christmas Care Line" was put in place for people who "fell through the cracks" of the annual Christmas Basket efforts of separate agencies. Weekday reached 1600 children with many unchurched. The year of the 50th Anniversary of the Council was appropriately opened with a service in a large Roman Catholic sanctuary. And the Director brought to Evansville his firsthand account of two well-prepared visits to the Soviet Union under the auspices of the National Council of Churches. For those who had ears to hear, some truths were told of the 1000 year history of the Orthodox Church in Russia and of Jews and Christians living under persecution.

At this point, midway in the 50th year, the "new leadership" accepted the call of the Church Federation of Greater Indianapolis to become its Director. A woman, acting as interim Director, followed through to a well-prepared celebration of the life and work of the Council, complete with a published 50 year "History": "Like Wind, Like Fire." The Council at present writing has called "new leadership," well-qualified, ecumenically-minded, eager to be "pastor to pastors," and work with the rabbi newly come to Evansville. The wonder is that the 50 year reality on Main Street in all its manifestations still disclosed a spirit and a potential which attracted this "ecumenically-minded" couple to accept the call. As of this writing, the Evansville Area Council of Churches is poised to begin its second 50 years.

Responding at the time that "cost effectiveness" (results) emerged as the criterion for ecumenism in Evansville, the Council president gave perspective to the perennial task of furthering ecumenical understanding and cooperation.

> "Councils of Churches these days," he observed, "like parish churches and individual Christians, are struggling to identify the nature of the struggle and the proper tools to do battle with the Lord for the redeeming of the world. We now realize that we ought to be doing together all but what we must do separately, whereas ten years ago it was we ought to do together what we can't quite manage separately. Your Area Council of Churches, not always popular, often the brunt of criticism, some just and some unjust, continues to bring strong and effective witness for Christ and humanity in this larger community. The mileage we get out of the staff dollars is absolutely phenomenal."

Here are echoes of the Letter to the Ephesians (6:12), plausibly written about fifty years after the first Pentecost.

> "For we are not contending against flesh and blood, but against the principalities and powers, against the world rulers of this present darkness, against the spiritual hosts of wickedness in heavenly places."

In the midst of the world of business practice, of competition, of nationalism (parochialism), communism and denominationalism, the Council "takes the form of a servant" (Phil. 2:1-11).

This Council story of the reality of ecumenism on Main Street is a story of contending; contending against "Authorities Other Than God," and asking of the churches, some cooperating, asking of the member denominations the Amsterdam question, "In this that you are doing, in this that together we are doing, 'can you say Christus Victor?'"

Making The Circles Larger
Franklin H. Littell

In remembrance of the summer of 1939, especially of the First World Conference of Christian Youth, I want to direct this pilgrimage report to the theme of religious dialogue. The Europe which we visited, especially the Third Reich that some of us entered, was dominated by shrill monologue. The atmosphere was not, contrary to much misunderstanding and misinterpretation, "secular." The false creeds and ideologies (Ersatzreligionen) of our time have commanded vast spiritual strength, and they have directed demonic energies far greater than that evident in most of our politically or socially assimilated church establishments.

The talker who believes that "secularity" or "secularization" or "secular humanism" is the problem of the age hasn't been where the action is. The problem of the age is deafening monologue, mounted on brutal, ruthless, primal vitality. One of its medicines is open-faced, sensitive, caring dialogue.

Dialogue--A Way of Working

In a recent article, Diana Eck, Moderator of the Working Group on Dialogue with People of Living Faiths of the World Council of Churches, has explained the way in which her group has expanded the scope and meaning of "dialogue."[1] Dealing with the role of women in the churches, her paper mentions that her sub-unit joined with the sub-unit on Women in Church and Society to sponsor a conference of Women in Interfaith Dialogue in Toronto in June 1988. She speaks of dialogue as "a way of addressing issues, a way of working..."

Over fifty years, we have seen the Spirit working to break down barriers, often in unexpected ways and locations. When we met in Amsterdam, the boundaries between peoples were soon to become fighting lines. Yet Amsterdam demonstrated a great widening of the circles: Edinburgh:1910 had been overwhelmingly European and North American and white, but Amsterdam was more representative of the Church Universal in composition. The colonial and color barriers still lingered, but within a decade they were to be permanently shattered in both politics and religion.

The way of dialogue, which began generations ago in some Protestant circles[2], led to a widening of perspectives in many directions. After World War II, in good part as a result of lessons in ecumenism learned in the Church Struggle[3] and in the concentration camps, the circles expanded to

---

1. Eck, Diana L, "Moderator's Report," in Current Dialogue (World Council of Churches, 1989), vol 16, pp 9-21.

2. One of the most brilliant and succinct statments of the connections between democratic religious thought and democratic political development was initially presented at Swarthmore College by A.D. Lindsay: The Essentials of Democracy (Philadelphia: University of Pennsylvania Press, 1929).

3. Cf. my article, "Die Bedeutung des Kirchenkampfes fuer die Oekumene," XX Evangelische Theologie (1960) 1:1-21.

include Roman Catholic official participants. Later, the Eastern Orthodox came in.

Just as dramatic, in a way, was the expansion of dialogue that brought together participants from the Protestant established churches and Protestant Free Churches within European Christendom. In the first decades, many of the great leaders of the pre-World War II ecumenical movement were quite willing to dialogue with churchmen from other lands, while they totally ignored the "sects" (read "Free Churches") within their own lands.

Post-War Germany

After the war, spontaneous movements--often, like the <u>Deutscher Evangelischer Kirchentag</u>, led by laymen--broke the barriers between established churches and Free Churches, barriers that went back for centuries[4]. As a specialist in German religious history, I was called to post-war Germany to assist in the American occupation's relations with churches, theological faculties and other religious institutions. We conducted ourselves as fraternal workers, even though there was an element of control in the connection with de-Nazification. And we brought to the scene a view of lay participation that strengthened those who were in revolt against the familiar <u>Pastorenkirche</u>.

Our resources were considerable, and our work was extensive in outreach. In 1950, to mention an example of the ecumenical work I was directly involved in, we facilitated the founding of a <u>Landeskirchliche-Freikirchliche Arbeitsgemeinschaft</u> for Wuerttemberg-Baden. Delegates met annually at Bad Boll <u>Evangelische Akademie</u> under the chairmanship of the

---

4. See my paper, "Church and Sect (with special reference to Germany)," VI <u>The Ecumenical Review</u> (1954) 3:262-76.

former Basel Mission statesman, Prelate Karl Hartenstein. This work, fraternally associated with the <u>Arbeitsgemeinschaft der christlichen Kirchen</u> in Frankfurt/Main, provided the first official dialogue between Baptists, Methodists, Evangelical Association people and other Free Church men, and the <u>Landeskirchen</u>.

In 1953, before the Hamburg <u>Kirchentag</u> of that year, with the encouragement of the great lay leader Reinold von Thadden-Trieglaff I pulled together an Ecumenical Committee consisting of state-church and Free Church members from Germany and abroad. When I returned home five years later, I was succeeded as committee chairman by Mark Gibbs, a British layman, author, and Iona Community member. Ever since 1953 the Committee has shepherded the several hundred participants in the <u>Kirchentag</u> who come each time from abroad.

In the <u>Kirchentag</u> and the Evangelical Academies, the opening afforded by the dialogue method was applied to lay life and work, to the reconstruction of a society shattered by dictatorship and war. The laymen were questioning the received authoritarian structures of both politics and religion. Thadden-Trieglaff, who had been an officer in the World's Student Christian Federation before the war, once commented in an informal meeting of <u>Kirchentag</u> activists: "The way the theologians answer the laymen's questions is to take the question, re-shape it to something familiar, and give back to the laymen answers to questions they never asked!" The usual cry of the professionals is that the laymen won't listen: the <u>Kirchentag</u> and the Academies turned the charge around and directed it from the laymen to the ecclesiastics.

The General Secretary of the <u>Kirchentag</u> was Hans Hermann Walz, who had been the director of lay work for the World Council of Churches and associated with Hendrik Kraemer and Suzanne de Dietrich at Bossey.

Besides working with Walz in many programs, I co-edited with him an ecumenical manual only recently superseded by David Barrett's superb World Christian Encyclopedia. Our thick volume, which held its own for nearly three decades, was called Weltkirchenlexikon: Handbuch der Oekumene.

Joining with Eberhard Mueller in the launching of the Academies movement after the war was Hanns Lilje, another old-timer from the Student Christian Movement between the world wars.

Thus in the Western zones, where the churches were able to operate freely and to maintain close international contacts, the reconstruction of a shattered German society was substantially assisted by the flowering of initiatives already rooted in and fed by the spiritual energies of the WSCF and WCC and their constituent bodies. And, in contrast with the long inter-church alienation that followed World War I, after World War II the fraternal relations between the Western churches and the churches of West Germany were restored almost immediately.

A Restored International Christian Dialogue

The way for this reconciliation was greatly helped by the Stuttgart Declaration of Guilt which was issued by leaders of the active (Confessing Church) and passive ("Intact Churches") resistances to Nazism, after a consultation held October 18-19, 1945[5]. I had occasion to work with all of the German signatories, and some of them became warm friends. Among the fraternal visitors present on this occasion was Willem Visser't Hooft, who as General Secretary of the WSCF had worked with several of the German church leaders before the war. He had maintained underground contact with

---

5. Translated in Appendix C of my The German Church Phoenix (New York, Doubleday& Co., 1960).

the Christian resistances during the war. He was already slated for the key post of General Secretary of the World Council of Churches, an appointment confirmed at the General Assembly in Amsterdam (1948).

In the United States, Reinhold Niebuhr had been one of the few churchmen who sensed and powerfully expressed the significance of the rise of Nazism for Christianity and for the Jewish people. He and James Luther Adams were my chief theological advisors and mentors in the USA during the decade 1948-58. Although a native-born American, Niebuhr used the German language and followed closely the struggle for the German people's soul. Through him I had met Dietrich Bonhoeffer before the war, as a student at Union Theological Seminary. And also through him I was introduced to the new beginnings in the post-war German church, especially in raising modest moneys to help Bad Boll--the original Academy--get started in October of 1945.

Eberhard Mueller, founder of Bad Boll and patriarch of the Academies movement, was one of the giants of the post-war scene in Germany. In 1957, in a message to his colleagues in the "Europaeischer Leiterkreis der Evangelischen Akademien und Laieninstitute," which I co-founded with him in October of 1955 (on the 10th anniversary of Bad Boll), Mueller gave his spoken testimony to the power of dialogue to work the unexpected. His Kunst der Gespraechsfuehrung[6] was already a manual used in dozens of vocational, professional and topical conferences where the art of dialogue came to be discussed. In that year, at the annual conference of the leaders of the Dutch Vormingszentren, the German Evangelische Akademien, the Swiss Heimatstaette and other centers, he commented that

---

6. Mueller, Eberhard, Die Kunst der Gespraechsfuehrung (Hamburg: Furche-Verlag, 1954), passim; see also his Widerstand und Verstaendigung: Fuenfzig Jahre Erfahrungen in Kirche und Gesellschaft 1933-1983 (Stuttgart: Calwer-Verlag, 1987), p.68.

as a Lutheran he had been trained to believe that the two marks of the Christian church were the Word and the Sacraments (Wort und Sakrament). He had now been brought to understand that there was a third mark of the true church: Dialogue (Gespraech).

Wort and Sakrament for centuries had served to build walls and tend fences between churches and communities. Gespraech opened a path for the surprising, the unexpected.

To the media, the "German miracle" was the economic recovery, accompanied by the political stability of the Bonn republic. To some of us, the real German miracle was the fact that the highly specialized vocations and professions on which a technically advanced society rests, Berufe that had been disgraced and dishonored by the behavior of their representatives during the Third Reich, were rehabilitated within a decade after the end of the war.

To this rehabilitation, especially in the restoration of a baseline of Berufsethik to policemen, surgeons, elementary school teachers, plant managers, etc., dialogue fostered by the Evangelical Academies made a massive contribution. Nor were lay vocations alone the issue, for had not a world-rank German theologian signalized the capitulation of many to idolatry and monologue in the summer of 1933 in his response to Hitler's inaugural address?

> "No other Volk in the world has a leading statesman such as ours, who takes Christianity so seriously. On 1 May when Adolf Hitler closed his great speech with a prayer, the whole world could sense the wonderful sincerity in that."[7]

---

7. Quoted in Ericsen, Robert P, Theologians Under Hitler (New Haven: Yale University Press, 1985), p. 145.

Emanuel Hirsch never abandoned the blend of nationalism, liberal theology and Teutonic <u>Volkstum</u> that he then expressed, but after the war the <u>Kirchliche Hochschulen</u> and <u>Kirchentag</u> and <u>Akademien</u> brought the churches' professionals as well as lay people back into the front line of the ecumenical dialogue--in the German Federal Republik, in a society which remarkably and quickly recovered from the ravages of Nazi ideology and practices.

The End of "Christendom"

At first, in the years between Edinburgh:1910 and Oxford:1937, the dialogue was confined to small working groups within the great established churches. The American Free Churches were regarded as an anamoly, cult-influenced if not cult-inspired, and the Free Churches of the missionary areas of the colonial empires were kept on a tight leash.

The two World Wars destroyed any illusions the Younger Churches of Asia and Africa may have had about the "Christian nations" of Europe. Nor was the disillusionment limited to Asians and Africans. At Amsterdam, Europeans too were keenly aware of Martin Niemoeller's imprisonment in one of Hitler's concentration camps, and they were beginning to reflect on the way the famous Pastor's witness cut through the historic pretensions of "Christendom." After the war even some of the most conservative of European ecclesiastics were prepared to distinguish between the duty owed the magistrate of Romans 13 and the resistance due the regime of Revelation 13.

In my function as a fraternal worker, albeit an officer in the occupation, I was able to help German colleagues re-think matters such as Religious Liberty, respect for integrity of conscience, the duty of resistance to illegitimate authority. When German rearmament was impending, I brought together German cabinet members with leaders of the American peace churches in a consultation at Arnoldshain, where we worked out the first terms of reference for German conscientious objectors. I also assisted the calling of a major conference at Tutzing Evangelical Academy, where Protestant and Roman Catholic theologians and statesmen discussed the right and/or duty of resistance at specific times and places. The report was published as a small book: Widerstandsrecht und Grenzen der Staatsgewalt (Berlin, 1956).

The ecumenical leaders who led the European and North American churches after World War II had as young men and women been inspired by D T Niles and Hendrik Kraemer and Reinhold Niebuhr at Amsterdam:1939. They had heard and understood the message of Willem Visser't Hooft's "None Other Gods" (1937). Facing boldly the central sin of the age, epitomized in the Nazi Third Reich, Visser't Hooft had put the issue sharply:

> "The real tragedy of our time is that we have on the one hand an incoherent mass of individual Christians and on the other hand powerful impulses towards new forms of community, but no Christian Community. Christians today do not form a true community, and the communities which shape the new world are not Christian."[8]

The young men and women of Amsterdam were ready to help shatter the identification of Christianity with white, male, Western national leadership cadres. Many of us also accepted the challenge to form new communities, new channels of disciplined Christian witness.

---

8. Visser 't Hooft, Willem A, None Other Gods (New York: Harper & Bros, 1937), p. 70.

But only later would we learn the terrible cost to "Christian nations" and to the Jewish people which the sin of idolatry (<u>Fuehrerprinzip</u>, Thousand Years' Reich) would let loose upon the world. When we met, a half century ago, Martin Niemoeller had already been in concentration camp for three years, and the first martyrs in the Christian testimony against an idolatrous Nazism had already fallen. We knew this. But only much later would scholars and religious leaders begin to explore the bonding between the <u>Kirchenkampf</u> (Church Struggle) and the <u>Shoah</u>. On the map of the world church, the circles were not yet large enough to include the Jewish people.

After the war, too, the Americans and Younger Churchmen were accepted into the inner councils of ecumenical discourse, even though their ecclesiastical polities did not satisfy the requirements of the Peace of Augsburg (1555) and the Treaty of Westphalia (1648), still considered normative in most established church circles.[9] With fraternal workers from the States, for example, some of the staid territorial churches even experimented with house-to-house visitation in the parishes and personal evangelism, assisted by fraternal workers from North America. But the map of the restoration of German Protestant <u>Landeskirchen</u> after 1948 was an almost perfect overlay to the church map that was drawn following the Congress of Vienna (1815), and the laws of gravity of the restoration soon expunged most lessons parish learned from American mass evangelism.

There were two large sections of today's inter-religious dialogue that yet remained outside the ecumenical circle. Missing were participants from

---

9. Cf. Littell, Franklin H., "Church and Sect (with special reference to Germany," VI <u>The Ecumenical Review</u> (1954) 3:262-76.

the Roman Catholic Church and the Jewish community.[10] In reference to those two sectors the Americans were to make major contributions to the whole Ecumene, post-Amsterdam.

American Contributions

In his essay on "Pluralism--Temptation or Opportunity," Visser't Hooft treated with his customary vigor the illusions of those who hoped to return to a pre-war "Christendom" and embraced the possibilities when all are "willing to enter into dialogue with all," a dialogue in which "all must be willing to give an account of their convictions and allow their own convictions to be challenged by the conviction of others."[11] Visser't Hooft was here expressing an ecumenical openness that reached circles outside the developing inter- and intra-denominational dialogue.

After Vatican II it became possible for Roman Catholics to cooperate in inter-religious affairs. (Two decades before, it had taken me two years of work at Michigan to get the director of the Newman Club to sit down once a month with the rabbi at Hillel and the chairman of the Protestant student chaplains!) To this expanded participation two great 1965 Declarations of the Council contributed: Dignitatis Humanae, the Declaration on Religious Freedom, and Nostra Aetate, the Declaration on the Relationship of the Church to Non-Christian Religions.

Dignitatis Humanae was often called "the American declaration," because of the part John Courtney Murray and other Americans played in

---

10. Cf Littell, Franklin H., "Amsterdam and its Absentees," XVI Journal of Ecumenical Studies (1979) 1:109-12.

11. Visser 't Hooft, Willem A, "Pluralism--Temptation or Opportunity?" in Bea, Augustin Cardinal and Visser 't Hooft, Willem A, Peace Among Christians (New York: Association Press/Herder & Herder, 1967), p. 230.

getting it accepted by the church fathers. But not only a broadened view of toleration came out of the Council because of American influence: after a dozen years of shrill monologue in Hitler's <u>Festung Europa</u>, ideas and agencies demonstrating the contribution of the dialogue method to public discussion of public policies were also welcomed.

Inter-religious Dialogue in America

In America, too, the dialogue was considerably enlarged and the circles involved grew steadily larger. From colonial America to the present era, there has been a steady shift from Protestant state-churches through Protestant cultural and religious dominance to open ethnic and religious pluralism.[12]

At the time of the first census (1790), there were c3.8 million Americans counted, of whom all but c20,000 Roman Catholics and c6,000 Jews were at least formally Protestant. Two hundred years later, the Roman Catholic Church is the largest "free church," with c53 millions adherents. There are 17 large Protestant denominations with a total of c60 million adult members, plus as many again numbered in small denominations and constituencies. The American Jewish community is twice the size of any other in the world, including the State of Israel.

The reality of religious pluralism was given institutional expression in America quite early, especially in ecumenical beginnings such as the Evangelical Alliance during the 19th century. In America, inter-Protestant cooperation has from the beginning years of the republic been expressed in social concerns -in voluntary crusades for the protection of children and

---

12. See my <u>From State Church to Pluralism</u> (New York: Macmillan Co., 1971), second edition PB.

women and animals, in anti-slavery and temperance crusades, in a host of other worthy purposes sometimes bracketed under "Kingdom-building." The Social Creed of the Churches, adopted by the Federal Council of Churches in 1912, was but the culmination of generations of active formation of individuals and social forces by joint Protestant effort.

During the 1920s, the circles were widened to include Roman Catholics and Jews where it could be managed. The first break-throughs came on the campuses, encouraged by the National Council on Religion in Higher Education founded by Charles Foster Kent of Yale. At the State University of Iowa, a School of Religion established by Willard Lampe brought together instructors from all three major faith communities in a joint curricular program. In Ithaca, Cornell United Religious Work--founded by Richard Henry Edwards--was the first official structuring of inter-religious extra-curricular cooperation on a university campus. At Lisle, New York near Ithaca, the Lisle Fellowship was founded in the middle 1930s by DeWitt and Edna Baldwin--the first student volunteer summer program stressing interreligious and international dialogue and service.

By 1959, the emphasis upon campus interfaith dialogue and cooperation had reached a sufficient number of schools to justify the founding of an association of professional campus interfaith workers: ACURA. After my return home from a decade in Germany, I served for 25 years as Consultant on Religion and Higher Education to the staff of the NCCJ, and from that base of operations brought together the group that launched ACURA. (Before going to Germany I had been Director of Religious Affairs at the University of Michigan, after Cornell University the second inter-faith campus program financed by tax-payers in the USA.)

In 1963, with Chief Justice Clark's obiter dicta in the Abington Township Case, the barriers (chiefly psychological) against the study of

Religion in state universities were broken. The Chief Justice said that although religious exercises were unconstitutional in tax-supported schools, of course the non-sectarian study of religion was part of an educated person's inventory. Dozens of Departments of Religion and offices of interreligious coordination sprang up across the country and were established and financed by tax moneys.

No Department moved further from the seminary and divinity school model than the one at Temple University, to which I moved in 1969 after years of seminary teaching. Temple brought together professors from all the major living religions and after 25 years of growth counts at any given time over 200 graduate students, over half from abroad. At Temple I set up the first Ph.D. major in Holocaust Studies, and its first graduate went on to head one of the divisions at Yad Vashem in Jerusalem.

1963 was a crucial year in expanding the circles of inter-religious dialogue. Also in 1963, the National Association of Biblical Instructors (NABI) was transformed into the American Academy of Religion; attendance at its annual meetings jumped from c75 to over 4000, and it became a staging ground for the most diverse of scholarly studies and dialogues. In the same year, 1963, Journal of Ecumenical Studies--a quarterly review--was founded. Leonard Swidler, my Temple colleague and JES Editor, has published a "Dialogue Decalogue" that is a fine summation of the guidelines and spirit of true intellectual and spiritual encounter.[13]

---

13. Swidler, Leonard, "The Dialogue Decalogue," Journal of Ecumenical Studies (September, 1984 revision), vol. XX, No. 1.

Public Expression of American Religious Pluralism

Off campus, the National Council of Churches had been for years the chief center of ecumenical discourse--once the circle widened beyond denominational events. In American interfaith cooperation, the key event had been the founding of the National Conference of Christians and Jews.

Following the upsurge of Protestant Nativism in the 1928 presidential election, Everett Clinchy--a product of Union and Yale--took the lead to bring together Christians and Jews in a cooperative offensive for tolerance. He led the NCCJ through the Depression and war years and after the war assisted in the founding of Christian/Jewish dialogue in West Germany and other countries after the war. His first four successors at the head of the NCCJ--Lewis Webster Jones, Sterling Brown and David Hyatt--continued to emphasize Christian/Jewish interaction and cooperative interfaith community service.

In speaking of the remarkable public acceptance of the tri-faith approach to public liturgical events, as well as in more substantive matters such as the civil rights movement, the interfaith experience during the war should not be minimized.   The contribution of the American military chaplains, with their lessons in "cooperation without compromise," carried over into civilian life. The sacrifice of the Four Chaplains of the Dorchester, who represented all three major traditions and who gave up their life belts to save men who had none, men whose religious affiliations (or lack of them) were never asked, became a major public symbol of American civic religion. The Chapel of the Four Chaplains long occupied a central place in the Temple University campus.

Also, after the war the Office of Military Government (US) and its successor, the U S High Commission in Germany, maintained a substantial inter-faith staff. The impact on post-war German public affairs was both direct and indirect, and the after-effect was large in America as well. Through Religious Affairs, major programs of education in tolerance and interreligious cooperation were financed and otherwise assisted. Overseas, the American commitment to interfaith dialogue matched the emphasis upon ecumenical dialogue at home.

As the British, French and American Zones were merged in administrative planning, the American emphasis upon interreligious discussion and cooperation spread throughout West Germany and into Berlin. In 1949 a conference was called at Wiesbaden on Christian/Jewish cooperation. President Heuss delivered a famous and often-cited message, "Mut zur Liebe."[14]   C Arild Olsen, who later served significantly in the National Council of Churches and in the NCCJ, was our Religious Affairs Chief at the time, and much of the immediate staff work was done by Knud C Knudsen--a young German whose story I told in motive magazine.[15]

As the German Coordinating Council of Societies for Christian/ Jewish Cooperation celebrates in 1989 their 40th anniversary, they can count over 50 societies led and financed and programmed in as many cities. The anniversary meets under the honorary chairmanship of President Richard von Weizsaecker, who before he became the highly respected head of the Bonn Republic was President of the laymen's movement, the Deutscher Evangelischer Kirchentag.

When the Religious Affairs Staff members came home to the States, a number of them had shared dramatic experiences in working with the

---

14. Heuss, Theodor, "Mut zur Liebe," an address at Wiesbaden, 7 December 1949; pamphlet published by Knud Knudsen; see also the book of essays edited by Knudsen as text for the starting Societies: Welt ohne Hass (Berlin: Christian-Verlag, 1950).

15. Cf. my presentation of the work of Knud C. Knudsen, in XI motive (October, 1950) 1:24-27.

Germans who had faced honestly the issues raised by their nation's record of genocide, a record accompanied by leadership betrayal and mass apostasy in the churches. Arild Olsen, James Egan, John Riedl, Sterling Brown and Dumont Kenny were among those from the Religious Affairs Staff who took key posts in the NCCJ and helped it to move the dialogue beyond purely humanitarian and civic issues to fundamental theological questions.

Germans and Jews

Along parallel lines, with the end of the occupation the German colleagues moved ahead on their own. In 1961, at the Berlin <u>Kirchentag</u>, some 26,000 crowded a great building at the fair grounds to discuss the topic, "What Do We Christians Owe the Jews?" The opening message was given by the Chief Rabbi of Germany, and among the panel members was Professor Helmut Gollwitzer--a famous theologians who during the Church Struggle had been an assistant in Martin Niemoeller's parish in Berlin-Dahlem. One of the practical results was the constitution of Working Group VI as a permanent instrument of inter-religious dialogue, its work and concerns later substantially strengthened by co-sponsorship by the Evangelical Academies. Of the Academies, Arnoldshain--the church conference center in the Taunus hills of Hesse--became especially important for Christian/Jewish dialogue.

In Germany, although there were only a few thousand Jews left where a great culture had onetime flourished, some churchmen came out of the Church Struggle with an utterly different theological understanding of the relationship of Christians and Jews.

In 1958 Lothar Kreyssig, one of the men of the church resistance, founded a volunteer work of reconstruction and peace -<u>Aktion Suehnezeichen</u>. Its young volunteers bear important reconciling witness among those peoples their country wronged during the Third Reich, notably in Israel and at Auschwitz.

In early June of 1971 the Kirchentag and the Katholikentag held a joint ecumenical meeting in Augsburg, in which they declared that "ecumenical encounters without Jewish participation are incomplete" and also that a "concrete consequence of ecumenical cooperation between Jews and Christians is expressed also in strategic solidarity with the state of Israel and its people..."[16] In June of 1975 the first German conference on the Holocaust and the Church Struggle was held at Haus Rissen in Hamburg, under the joint sponsorship of the NCCJ and the German Gesellschaften fuer christlich-juedische Zusammenarbeit. I served as Co-chairman of this conference with Claire Huchet Bishop.

In 1978 a large delegation from Germany was among the overseas national groups that participated in the International Theological Symposium on the Holocaust held in Philadelphia. Members of the delegation returned to the homeland to strengthen educational programs in the German Protestant parishes, which i. a. resulted first in the famous Declaration of the Rheinland Synod on reconstituting the relations of Christians and Jews after the Holocaust. The Declaration, adopted in January of 1980, took strong stands in opposition to traditional Hebrew Christian missions, in opposition to antisemitism, in support of Christian/Jewish dialogue and cooperation, and in affirmation of Christian support of the State of Israel.[17] Among the key leaders in this development was Eberhard Bethge, the friend, biographer and editor of Bonhoeffer. Bethge is one of the colleagues with whom I have

---

16. CCI Notebook (Philadelphia: 10/71), No. 4, p. 1.

17. Translation printed in XVII Journal of Ecumenical Studies (Winter, 1980) 1:211-12.

worked most congenially over four decades, in bringing concern for the Holocaust and concern for the Church Struggle together in the thinking of scholars and religious leaders.

The International Theological Symposium was one of many events and conferences organized and financed by the National Institute on the Holocaust, which I founded and chaired. I am now Founder and Honorary Chairman of its successor organization, the Anne Frank Institute of Philadelphia, from which my wife Marcia has recently retired after serving eight years as Executive Director.

From this quick survey it becomes evident that, quite apart from admirable theological work, the German colleagues have tackled forthrightly the two most important issues affecting Christian/ Jewish dialogue: the Holocaust and a restored Israel.   Unhappily, these are difficult issues which are still sedulously avoided by some "dialogue" agencies in America, including the leadership of the popular National Workshops on Christian/Jewish Relations.   But true dialogue requires true frankness as well as true sensitivity.

American Developments Showing Progress

In Germany, many of the changes that have occurred take on the color of official developments, whereas in the Free Church and pluralistic American situation most of the pioneer work has been done by strictly voluntary societies--semi-permanent minorities within their denominational communities. Nevertheless there have been important public developments that have profoundly affected the inter-action of Christians and Jews.

On the ledger of smaller interest groups, we should mention three organizations that went public within a few weeks of each other in 1970. All three grew out of the concern of a Christian minority that during the massive

Arab League assault on Israel called "the Six Day War" the establishments
again had shown themselves indifferent to the survival of Jews.

These three organizations are the Scholars' Conference on the Church
Struggle and the Holocaust (founded 1970 at Wayne State University, in
Detroit)--now approaching its 20th Anniversary Conference (4-7 March 1990,
at Vanderbilt University in Nashville); the Israel Study Group--now called
"the Christian Study Group on Israel and the Jewish People;" and
"Christians Concerned for Israel"--now, after a merger in 1978, called "the
National Christian Leadership Conference for Israel."

The Annual Scholars' Conferences

The host of the first Scholars' Conference, which for the first time in
discussion and published reports brought the Church Struggle and the
Holocaust into joint focus, was an Afro-American sociologist: Hubert G
Locke. Among others on the Conference Committee, which I chaired for
several years, were C Arild Olsen, Bernhard Olson of the NCCJ (author of
the authoritative study Faith and Prejudice), Arthur Cochrane (author of the
important study of the Confessing Church and the Barmen Declaration: The
Church's Confession Under Hitler), and John S Conway (author of the basic
text The Nazi Persecution of the Churches).

While in Germany I had started correspondence and a Newsletter
on the Nazi persecution of the Christian resistance and genocide of the Jews,
and I have carried this on from different locations in the States. With Dr
Locke's assistance I was able to regularize and expand the circulation of the
Newsletter on the Church Struggle and the Holocaust. Across the years we
have built a major microfilm archives, held many seminars and conferences,
and produced a number of books separately and in collaboration. After Dr
Locke moved to the faculty of the University of Washington in Seattle, we

worked together in staging a major conference on the 40th anniversary of Kristallnacht (1978) and also the North American 50th anniversary conference on the Barmen Synod (1984). Both conferences resulted in significant volumes.[18]

My most recent official American responsibility in this area has been as Chairman of the Church Relations Committee of the U S Holocaust Memorial Council, a Federal agency to which the President recently named me for a third five-year term. In the work of the Council I have made trips to a number of countries, three of them in deputations headed by Elie Wiesel, the wellknown Nobel laureate, author and activist. I have also served, by Israel government appointment, as a member of the Council of Yad Vashem--the International Holocaust Heroes' and Martyrs' Memorial in Jerusalem. For some years I was the only non-Jewish member.

Jerusalem, a Second Home

For more than a decade and a half I have been an adjunct faculty member of the Institute of Contemporary Jewry, Hebrew University. I travel there frequently for courses, seminars, examinations and consultations.

One of the most significant activities in which I have been involved there has been the America-Holy Land research and publication project, launched by Moshe Davis (then of Jewish Theological Seminary) and Robert Handy (Union Theological Seminary) more than three decades ago. Another is the research and teaching which among other things recently

---

18. On the 1978 Kristallnacht conference, see Legters, Lyman H., ed., Western Society After the Holocaust (Boulder CO: Westview Press, 1983); on the Barmen 50th anniversary, see Locke, Hubert G., ed., The Church Confronts the Nazis: Barmen Then and Now (New York & Toronto: Edwin Mellen Press, 1984), and by the same editor: The Barmen Confession: Papers from the Seattle Assembly (Lewiston/Queenston: Edwin Mellen Press, 1986).

resulted in the establishment of the international scientific quarterly Holocaust and Genocide Studies.

This latter activity brought me into executive leadership in the international conference "Remembering for the Future: Christian/ Jewish Relations During and After the Holocaust," which was held at Oxford and London in July of 1988. We had 650 educators from 25 countries, and the conference papers were published in three volumes totalling 3200 pages! On that occasion I presented the findings of some three decades of research and graduate instruction, in a paper called "Early Warning System--Detecting Early and Dealing Effectively with Potentially Genocidal Movements."[19]

Also in cooperation with the editor of the journal, Professor Yehuda Bauer, I have helped in projects of Hebrew University's Vidal Sassoon International Center for the Study of Antisemitism, and published a study of my own: American Protestantism and Antisemitism (1985). I am also a member of the Center's executive committee.

I have been able to help to bring in German participation in these different efforts. I believe that there are both religious and political reasons for holding Germany and Israel and America together in many joint undertakings at many levels. For instance, in the study of Israel's religious impact on churches and cultures, parallel to "America and the Holy Land" we now have a component "Deutschland und das heilige Land." The chairman of the German committee is a former student of mine at Marburg.

---

19. Littell, Franklin H., "Essay: Early Warning," III Holocaust and Genocide Studies (1988) 4:483-90.

A Theology of Jewish Survival

The red thread that ties together the Holocaust and a restored Israel is clearly seen when Christians ask themselves, "How do you stand to the question of the survival of the Jewish people?" My mentor Reinhold Niebuhr was the first American theologian to broach publicly a closely related question, when in 1966 he challenged the evangelization of individual Jews.[20]

To re-think and re-work Christian preaching and teaching after Auschwitz, a second major initiative was taken under the auspices of the National Council of Churches and U S Catholic Bishops' Conference. I was the group's chairman for several years. Originally called "the Israel Study Group," it consisted of ten Protestant theologians and ten Catholic theologians, brought together over two decades to study the theological issues involved in curing Christian preaching and teaching of its endemic antisemitism, and defining a relationship to the Jewish people different from that which has cursed them (and us) for at least a millenium and a half. This work, which has resulted in many articles and books,is now called "the Christian Study Group on Israel and the Jewish People" and functions under the hospitality of the Baltimore Institute on Christian/Jewish Relations.

Christian Action for Israel

The third organization was "Christians Concerned for Israel." I had, with the assistance of my wife Harriet (who headed our American Methodist delegation to Amsterdam), written 754 personal letters in the years 1968-70

---

20. A recent German student places Niebuhr's opposition to Hebrew Christian Missions much earlier, having found in the Library of Congress a 10 January 1926 sermon at Bethel Church in Detroit in which RN denied Judaism as a mission field and proposed cooperation in an entente cordiale. RN Papers, Container XIV:1, Folder 15.

to churchmen I thought concerned for Christian/Jewish relations. I expressed my concern at the indifference of organized Christianity to the planned destruction of Israel by the Arab League, a plan which had now resulted in three military assaults. Many replied that they had other priorities. A few wrote stunningly antisemitic diatribes. 230 said they shared my concern and would serve as sponsors. It was significant to me what a large proportion of those who agreed to be sponsors of CCI were former students of Reinhold Niebuhr.

The Yom Kippur rattlesnake attack came soon after we started CCI and was the occasion for considerable public activity and several declarations by Concerned Christians which I helped mobilize.

In 1978 CCI merged in a federation with more than 30 other Christian organizations supportive of Israel, and since then has united liberal Protestants, liberal Roman Catholics and conservative Protestants in joint action for Israel's survival and well-being. I served as the first President of the federation and am now listed as "Past President." Our present Executive Director is a gifted woman theologian, Sister Rose Thering of Seton Hall University.

My wife Marcia, whom I married after Harriet's death, shares my love of Israel, and together we have published an interfaith Pilgrim's Guide to the Holy Land. I am now National President of American Professors for Peace in the Middle East, an interfaith organization of c35,000 academics which also publishes the Middle East Review.

Ecumenical, Interfaith and Interreligious

In creating the conditions for a vigorous affirmation of faith, my twin foci of concern, going back before Amsterdam itself, have been Religious Liberty and persecution. Through this scale of tension, this historical dialectic, I have been led back and forth between such seemingly disparate subjects as the Left Wing of the Protestant Reformation--and lay formation and initiative, the Armenian massacres at the opening of the Age of Genocide--and the Holocaust. My research, writing and teaching on the one hand, and my practical organizational work on the other have often met somewhere on this line of concern for the dignity, liberty and integrity of the human person.

I have served for many years on the Editorial Council of The Mennonite Quarterly Review and Journal of Church and State, where the origins and present prospects of Religious Liberty come often to discussion, and likewise for decades on the Editorial Council of Journal of Ecumenical Studies--the premier journal of the ecumenical, interfaith and interreligious dialogues.

The expanding circles of dialogue have brought me in the last few years to a growing concern with the edge of bigotry and monolithic thinking that in America still produces persecution of off-beat religious societies and associations such as the Unification Church, Scientology, the Church Universal and Triumphant, Krishna-Consciousness, the Worldwide Church of God, and others. The bitter spiritual blindness that led a century and a half ago to the lynching of Joseph Smith Jr in Carthage, Illinois, and the subsequent flight of his people out of the then United States into western territories, seems now to infect some Jews and Roman Catholics as well as old-line Protestant nativists.   Kidnappings, de-programmings and other faith-breaking activities--as well as the misuse of courts and other instruments of government to crush those of religious opinions we think absurd--have recently provided in some circles the basis for a kind of spiritual underworld of "interfaith cooperation" between Catholics, Protestants and Jews.

I still prefer to take my stand with Menno Simons, John Milton, Roger Williams, William Penn, Thomas Jefferson and James Madison--to mention but a few of the saints I collected before I came to admire Dietrich Bonhoeffer and Alfred Delp and Mordecai Anielewicz and Willem Visser't Hooft and others who gave witness in death or in life against the demonic substitute-religions of our age, with their fervent service to idols and contempt for the unfettered conscience.

Fifty years ago, coming out of a pacifist and isolationist midwestern Kulturreligion, a lesson I had to learn was how to draw the line against demonic creeds and systems and to fight them both passively and actively. Today my comparable problem is to understand how to be unabashed in professing the faith I received as a gift, while being open to the yearnings, questions and urgent concerns of persons of quite different systems of belief.

In Conclusion (for the Time Being)

At the present time, blessed with good health in "retirement," I am chairman of the board of the William O Douglas Institute (Seattle) and chairman of the board of the American Conference on Religious Movements (based at Catholic University, Washington DC). There are other things, but I mention these two at the end of this report on my pilgrimage because they bracket in a way my scholarly and public concerns. Both have held international conferences and published for Religious Liberty. Both have championed the unpopular religious and ethnic groups--whether Jews or off-beat Protestants or Asian imports--that now compel us to re-think the role of religion in American life and the rights of Americans who don't fit the patterns of behavior most of us have taken for granted all our lives.

In opening my discussion of expanding circles of dialogue, I cited a paper on the status of women in the churches by the present Chairman of the World Council of Churches' relevant working committee. Diana Eck belongs to the post-war generation, and has also given significant attention to the status of new religious movements in the inter-religious dialogue.[21] I think it not too much to say that she not only holds a post in the WCC which is in the "apostolic succession" of Amsterdam:1939, but that her willingness to face the challenge of living with other religions and conquering the vertigo which sometimes arises from watching expanding circles of dialogue is born of the same Spirit that inspired our generation then.

I do not doubt that in each generation God will bring forth young idealists who will struggle, as we have, to fight the good fight--and who too will be blessed from time to time to hear, above the clash of arms, the harmony of the spheres. In the end, our dividedness and brokenness shall be blessed with Shalom.

---

21. See Diana Eck's address at the Amsterdam Consultation, 1987, published in Brockway, Alan R. and Rajashekar, J.P., eds., New Religious Movements and the Churches (Geneva: World Council of Churches, 1987).

Contributors' Notes

Robert S. Bilheimer has been engaged chiefly in national and international ecumenical work since 1945, before his retirement as head of the Ecumenical Institute at Collegeville, MD. He is the author of Breakthrough - The Emergence of the Ecumenical Tradition.

David S. Burgess is a graduate of Oberlin College and Union Theological Seminary. He has worked as a CIO labor organizer in the South, a U.S. Foreign Service Officer, a UNICEF Officer, and is a pastoral minister.

Olle Dahlen is a Swedish politician and diplomat. He has held numerous positions, including Member of Parliament, representative at the United Nations and to the Committee of Disarmament; ambassador at large; moderator of CCIA of WCC, 1971-1983.

R.H. Edwin Espy was the organizing secretary of the Amsterdam Youth Conference, and the general secretary of the Student Volunteer Movement, the National Student YMCA, and the National Council of Churches, U.S.A.

Stewart Herman is a Lutheran minister (ELCA). He has worked with the American Church in Berlin, 1936-41; the World Council of Churches, Geneva, 1945-47; and the Lutheran World Federation, Geneva and New York, 1948-63. He was president of the Lutheran School of Theology at Chicago, 1964-71.

Francis House was the travelling secretary of the WSCF in S.E. Europe 1938-40, and served on the General Secretariat of the WCC 1955-62. He is the author of The Millenium of Faith, the story of Russian Christians 988-1988 A.D. (also published in England under the title The Russian Phoenix).

Blahoslav Hruby is a Czech-born Presbyterian minister, before World War II international secretary of the World Student Association for Peace, Freedom and Progress and pastor of the Czechoslovak Protestant Mission in Paris. At present he is executive director, Research Center for Religion and Human Rights in Closed Societies, and editor of its quarterly RCDA - Religion in Communist Dominated Areas.

Gerald M. Hutchinson was ordained to Ministry in the United Church of Canada in 1943; he has been National Secretary of the Student Christian Movement of Canada and Executive Secretary of the Alberta Conference of the United Church of Canada.

Chester A. Kirkendoll is Retired Bishop of the Christian Methodist Episcopal Church and former President of Lane College, Jackson, Tennessee.

Thomas J. Liggett was born in Tennessee, and is a member of the Christian Church (Disciples of Christ). He has been a pastor, seminary professor in Argentina, seminary president (Puerto Rico and Indiana), and mission board executive.

Virginia Liggett, nee Moore, was born in Kentucky; a member of the Christian Church (Disciples of Christ), she has been a seminary professor in Argentina, seminary librarian in Puerto Rico and Indiana, and mission board executive.

Franklin H. Littell is Emeritus Professor of Religion, Temple University; he has been a campus interfaith worker, seminary professor, and college president. From 1958-1983 he was Consultant on Religion and Higher Education to the NCCJ.

Phillips P. Moulton, a post-doctoral scholar at the University of Michigan, is studying military history and foreign policy. His latest book, Ammunition for Peacemakers: Answers for Activists, won the Pilgrim Press Award as the outstanding volume providing ethical perspectives on social issues.

Edward L. Nestingen graduated from Union Theological Seminary in 1945. He has been a YMCA director at several leading universities, retiring from that work at the University of Illinois. During 1952-59 he was Program Director of the National Student YMCA.

Luis Odell is leader in the youth, conciliar, and "Church and Society" ecumenical movements in Latin America; he is formerly lay president of the Uruguayan Methodist Church.

Edward F. Ouellette, retired U.C.C. minister, served on the preparation and administration staff of the Oxford conference, 1937. College and University teaching accompanied four pastorates until 1971. He is co-author of the 1986 biography of Henry Smith Leiper, "What Kind of a Man?"

David S. Russell was formerly General Secretary and President of the Baptist Union of Great Britain, Vice President of the British Council of Churches and a member of the WCC Central Committee (1968-82).

Oliver S. Tomkins was born of missionary parents in China. He has worked on the staff of the British SCM and the W.C.C. He was Warden of Lincoln Theological College from 1953-59, Bishop of Bristol 1959-75; Chairman of the Faith and Order Commission of the WCC 1959-67.

Raymond M. Veh was religious journalist and youth leader in the United Methodist Church. He served as editor for 41 years of the youth publication of the Evangelical United Brethren Church. He twice served as press representative to the assemblies of the World Council of Churches.

W.A. Visser 't Hooft was General Secretary of the World Council of Churches, formerly of the staff of the World's Committee of YMCA's, General Secretary of World's Student Christian Federation, and General Chair of the First World Conference of Christian Youth.

Herman Will is the author of A Will for Peace, 1984; he has contributed chapters to Peace and Powers, 1959, and to Freedom and Unfreedom in the Americas, 1971. He was an executive of the World Peace Commission and Board of Christian Social Concerns of the Methodist Church.

TORONTO STUDIES IN THEOLOGY

22. Manfred Hoffmann (ed.), **Martin Luther and the Modern Mind: Freedom, Conscience, Toleration , Rights**

23. Eric Voegelin, **Political Religions**, T. J. DiNapoli and E. S. Easterly III (trans.)

24. Rolf Ahlers, **The Barmen Theological Declaration of 1934: The Archeology of a Confessional Text**

25. Kenneth Cauthen, **Systematic Theology: A Modern Protestant Approach**

26. Hubert G. Locke (ed.), **The Barmen Confession: Papers from the Seattle Assembly**

27. Barry Cooper, **The Political Theory of Eric Voegelin**

28. M. Darrol Bryant and Hans Huessy (eds.), **Eugene Rosenstock-Huessy: Studies in His Life and Thought**

29. John Courtney Murray, **Matthias Scheeben on Faith: The Doctoral Dissertation of John Courtney Murray**, D. Thomas Hughson (ed.),

30. William J. Peck (ed.), **New Studies in Bonhoeffer's** *Ethics*

31. Robert B. Sheard, **Interreligious Dialogue in the Catholic Church Since Vatican II: An Historical and Theological Study**

32. Paul Merkley, **The Greek and Hebrew Origins of Our Idea of History**

33. F. Burton Nelson (ed.), **The Holocaust and the German Church Struggle: A Search for New Directions**

34. Joyce A. Little, **Toward a Thomist Methodology**

35. Dan Cohn-Sherbok, **Jewish Petitionary Prayer: A Theological Exploration**

36. C. Don Keyes, **Foundations For an Ethic of Dignity: A Study in the Degradation of the Good**

37. Paul Tillich, **The Encounter of Religions and Quasi-Religions: A Dialogue and Lectures**, Terrence Thomas (ed.)

38. Arnold van Ruler, **Calvinist Trinitarianism and Theocentric Politics: Essays Toward a Public Theology**, John Bolt (trans.)

39. Julian Casserley, **Evil and Evolutionary Eschatology: Two Essays**, C. Don Keyes (ed.)

40. John Quinn and J.M.B. Crawford, **Christian Foundations of Criminal Responsibility: Historical and Philosophical Analyses of the Common Law**

41. William C. Marceau, **Optimism in the Works of St. Francis De Sales**

42. A.J. Reimer, **The Emanuel Hirsch and Paul Tillich Debate: A Study in the Political Ramifications of Theology**

43. George Grant, *et al.*, *Two Theological Languages* **by George Grant and Other Essays in Honor of His Work**, Wayne Whillier (ed.)

44. William C. Marceau, **Stoicism and St. Francis De Sales**

45. Lise van der Molen, **A Complete Bibliography of the Writings of Eugene**

Rosenstock-Huessy

46. Franklin H. Littell (ed.), **A Half Century of Religious Dialogue, 1939-1989: Making the Circles Larger**

47. Daniel M. Davies, **The Life and Thought of Henry Gerhard Appenzeller (1858-1902): Missionary to Korea**

48. John Tiemstra, **Reforming Economics: Calvinist Studies on Methods and Institutions**

49. Max Meyers, **Studies in the Theological Ethics of Ernst Troeltsch**

50. Franz Feige, **Varieties of Protestantism in Nazi Germany: Five Theopolitical Positions**